Latin Primer: A First Book of Latin for Boys and Girls

Joseph Henry Allen

LATIN PRIMER:

A

FIRST BOOK OF LATIN

FOR

BOYS AND GIRLS.

BY

JOSEPH H. ALLEN.

BOSTON:
GINN AND HEATH.
1880.

597651

UNIVERSITY PRESS: JOHN WILSON & SON.
CAMBRIDGE.

NOTE.

THIS book is designed for a class of learners too young to use the "Grammar" or "Lessons" to advantage, including those who have not yet studied English grammar. While the inevitable drill-book had better be left till they are some years older, I do not see why intelligent children of ten or twelve — as the way was, forty or fifty years ago — should not learn to know Latin and enjoy it in some of its simpler forms; which, indeed, seems to me the best possible introduction to a systematic school-course. But, to serve this end, it must be taught, first of all, *as a living and flexible tongue*, not in the abstract principles and method of its grammar; and, in the second place, by familiar use *in actual narrative and dialogue*, not by committing to memory disjointed examples and dry forms. If we consent to regard it as a dead language merely, or study it as if it had no other than an antiquarian or a scientific interest, we cannot long uphold the general study of it at all. An easy and familiar reading knowledge of a language is worth incomparably more, to most students of it, than any supposed advantage in the study of its grammatical theory. These lessons aim to give as much of the grammar as is essential for this, and no more.

The selections which follow have a vocabulary of considerable variety and range; and the learner who has mastered them all will be prepared either for the severer method of a classical course, or (if old enough) for entering directly on a line of reading in the masterpieces of classical antiquity.

CAMBRIDGE, March 26, 1870.

INDEX OF TOPICS.

CONTENTS.

DIRECTIONS TO TEACHERS.

THE words and sentences at the head of each Lesson should be thoroughly learned by the scholar, being carefully explained, when necessary, by the teacher. All the examples should be *well learned by heart*. REVIEW OFTEN.

The Reading Exercises that follow (from *Historiæ Sacræ*) are not designed to be studied as task-work by the pupil; only to afford practice in easy reading at sight. They should, therefore, be neither parsed nor analyzed, except so far as to make sure that the pupil understands properly what he is reading. If an hour a day should be given to the lessons, they will probably not be found too long; or, if they should, they may be abridged at the discretion of the teacher.

The Dialogues (selected from Corderius and Erasmus), which follow in parallel columns, should be studied beforehand, so that the pupil can recite the Latin from the English, or the English from the Latin, without the book, explaining the words or phrases by the Notes, or by the Lessons that have been previously learned.

The Reading Lessons, consisting of short fables and familiar pieces, are to be learned by the pupil by aid of the Vocabulary, which is designed to include also the words that have been explained in the Lessons.

The Tables of Inflection (taken from the "Manual Latin Grammar") may be used, at the discretion of the teacher, for practice on the declensions and conjugations, after they have been learned from the Lessons.

If a scholar has not studied English Grammar, he must learn the following Definitions:—

Definitions.

1. A NOUN is the name of any thing; as *man, ship, George.*

If a noun is the name of a Person, or of any thing spoken of by its own name, as if it were a person, it is a Proper Noun; if not, it is a Common Noun. In the sentence "Boston is a large city," *Boston* is a proper noun, and *city* a common noun.

If a noun means only one, it is Singular; if it means more than one, it is Plural: *boy* is singular; *boys* is plural. This is called NUMBER.

If a noun means a male person or creature, it is Masculine; if it means a female, it is Feminine; if it means a thing, it is Neuter: *boy* is masculine; *girl* is feminine; *stone* is neuter. This is called GENDER.

2. An ADJECTIVE is a word used to describe a noun: if I say, "a tall man rode a white horse," the words *tall* and *white* are adjectives.

The Comparative of an adjective means *more*, and the Superlative, *most*: if I say, "he is taller than I; this is the fastest horse," the word *taller* is comparative, and *fastest* superlative.

3. A PRONOUN is a word used instead of a noun: as, *he runs*, instead of *that boy runs.*

I and *we* are the pronouns of the First Person; *you* is the pronoun of the Second Person; *he, she, it, they,* are pronouns of the Third Person. These are the PERSONAL PRONOUNS.

The words *this, that, these, those,* are called DEMONSTRATIVE PRONOUNS; *who* and *which* are RELATIVE PRONOUNS; *who, which, what,* used to ask a question, are INTERROGATIVE PRONOUNS.

4. A VERB is a word which tells of any thing that is done or happens. In the sentence "we ran together, and I fell," *ran* and *fell* are verbs.

The SUBJECT of a verb is the person or thing it tells of: if I say, "the horse runs," *horse* is the subject of *runs.*

The OBJECT of a verb is the person or thing that any thing is done to: if I say, "he wrote a letter," *he* is the subject, and *letter* the object of *wrote.*

If a verb tells that one *does* any thing, it is in the ACTIVE VOICE; if it tells that any thing *is done*, it is in the PASSIVE VOICE. If I say, "he threw a ball," *threw* is active; if I say, "the ball was thrown," *was-thrown* is passive.

LATIN PRIMER.

Lesson 1.

et, *and.*　　　sed, *but.*　　　nōn, *not.*
ē, ex, *out of.*　in, *into,* or *in.*
fēcit, *made.*　　diēs, *day,* or *days.*

1. There is no word in Latin for *a* or *the*. The word **dies** may mean *a day,* or *the day;* **prīmō diē** means *on the first day.* The words *a, an, the,* are called ARTICLES.

2. There is no word in Latin for *he, she,* or *it.* The word **fēcit** may mean *he made,* or, *she made.* Sometimes we may use, for *he, she, it,* a Demonstrative Pronoun: as,

hīc, hæc, hōc, *this one;* or, is, ea, id, *that one.*

3. The third person of a verb in the Active Voice ends in **t**; the third person plural in **nt**.

i. *The Creation.*

DEUS creāvit cælum et terram intrā sex diēs.
GOD　　created　heaven　　earth　　within　six
Prīmō diē fēcit lūcem. Secúndō diē fēcit firmā-
　　　　　　　light.　　Second　　　　　firma-
méntum, quod vocāvit cælum. Tertiō diē coēgit
ment,　which　he-called　　　　　Third　　gathered
aquās in ūnum locum, et ēdūxit ē terrā plantās et
waters　one　place,　　led-out　　　　plants
árborēs. Quārtō diē fēcit sōlem, et lūnam, et stellās.
trees.　Fourth　　　　sun,　　moon,　　stars.
Quīntō diē fēcit avēs quæ vólitant in āëre, et piscēs
Fifth　　birds which　fly　　air,　　fishes
quī natant in aquīs. Sextō diē fēcit omnia animántia,
which swim　　　　Sixth　　　all　live-creatures,
postrēmō, hóminem; et quiēvit diē séptimō.
lastly,　　man　　　rested　　seventh.

Lesson 2.

inter, *between* or *among.*   qui, quæ, quod, *who* or *which* (nom.).
nam, *for.*   quem, quam, quod, *whom, which* (acc.).
si, *if.*   est, *is,* erat, *was;* erant, *were.*
ut, *that.*   eum, *him;* eam, *her* (acc.).
cur, *why.*   dixit, *said.*   ibi, *there.*

> pater vocat filium, *the father calls* [his] *son.*
> filius audit patrem, *the son hears* [his] *father.*
> hæc puella amat sororem, *this girl loves* [her] *sister.*

4. In these examples, **pater, filius, puella,** are in the Nominative Case; and **patrem, filium, sororem,** in the Accusative.

5. The Nominative is the Subject of the sentence, and the Accusative the Object.

6. The nominative singular of almost all masculine nouns, and many feminine nouns, ends in **o, r,** or **s;** and their accusative always ends in **m.** Very many feminine nouns end in **a.**

7. Many names of Things are masculine or feminine in Latin.

ii. *The Garden of Eden.*

Deus pósuit Adāmum et Evam in hortŏ amœ-
níssimŏ, quī solet appellāri Paradīsus terréstris.
Ingēns flúvius irrigābat hortum. Erănt ibi omnēs
árborēs jūcundæ aspectū, et frūctūs gustū suāvēs;
inter eās arbor scientiæ bonī et malī. Deus dixit
hominī: "Ūtere fructibus omnium árborum paradīsi,
præter fructum árboris scientiæ boni et malī; nam
si cómedās illum fructum, moriēris."

Serpēns, quī erat callidissimum omnium animan-
The-serpent,   most-cunning
tium, dixit mulierī: "Cur nōn cómedis frūctum
                    to-the-woman:
istíus árboris?" Mulier respondit: "Deus id prō-
of-that   replied: for-
híbuit. Sī tetigérimus illum, moriēmur." "Mínimē,"
bade.   we-touch   that   we-shall-die.   Not-at-all
inquit serpēns; "nōn-moriēminī; sed éritis símilēs
said   you-shall-not-die;   shall-be   like
Deō, scientēs bonum et malum." Mulier, decepta
      knowing   deceived
hīs verbīs, dēcerpsit fructum, et comēdit; deinde
by-these words,   gathered   ate   then
óbtulit virō, quī páriter comēdit.
offered-it to-the-man,   also

Tum Deus ējēcit Adāmum et Evam ex hortō, ut
Then   cast-out
cóleret terram; et collocāvit ángelum, quī præferē-
he-might-till   stationed   an-angel   held-
bat manū ígneum gladium, ut custōdíret áditum
out in-his-hand fiery   sword   might-guard   entrance
paradīsī.
of-

Lesson 3.

ego, *I.*	ad, *to.*
me, *me.*	autem, *but.*
meus, mea, meum, *my.*	cur, *why.*
tu, te, *you* (singular).	quid, *what.*
tuus, tua, tuum, *your.*	quidem, *indeed.*
ii, eæ, ea, *they.*	quum (or cum), *when.*
eos, eas, ea, *them.*	sin, *but if.*
ille, illa, illud, *that.*	ubi, *where* or *when.*

PRESENT TENSE OF THE VERB esse, *to be.*

	SINGULAR.	PLURAL.
FIRST PERSON.	sum, *I am.*	sumus, *we are.*
SECOND PERSON.	es, *you are,* or *thou art.*	estis, *you* or *ye are.*
THIRD PERSON.	est, *he, she,* or *it is.*	sunt, *they are.*

8. The nominative plural of most masculine and feminine nouns ends in **i**, **æ**, or **es**, and the accusative in **as**, **es**, or **os**; most of those in **i**, **os**, are masculine, and in **æ**, **as**, feminine.

9. In neuter nouns, the nominative and accusative are always alike: in the plural, they end in **a**.

10. The pronouns **ego**, *I*, **nos**, *we*, **tu**, **vos**, *you*, are not used in Latin, except sometimes for the sake of emphasis: **bonus es**, means *you are good*; **tu es bonus**, *it is you that are good.*

11. In English we say *you are*, whether we mean one person or more than one. In Latin, we say **es** if we mean one person; and **estis** if we mean more than one.

12. The word **num** is used in asking a question when the answer would be *No.*

III. *Cain and Abel.*

Adámus hábuit multos líberos, inter quos Caïnus
had   many   children,   whom

et Abel numerantur: hic erat pastor, ille agricola.
are-reckoned: shepherd   farmer

Utérque óbtulit dona Dómino: Caïnus quidem
each   offered gifts to-the-Lord:

fructus terræ; Abel autem oves egrégias. Dona
fruits   of-   sheep[2] excellent.[1]

Abélis placuérunt Deo, non autem dona Caïni;
of-   pleased

quod Caïnus ægrè tulit. Dóminus dixit Caïno:
hardly[2] bore.[1]

Cur ínvides fratri? si rectè fácies, recípies mer-
do-you-envy brother.   rightly[2] you-do[1] you-shall-receive re-

cédem; sin autem malé, lues pœnam peccáti.
ward   badly will-suffer punishment of-sin.

Caïnus non páruit Deo: dissímulans iram, dixit
obeyed   hiding   anger,

fratri-suo: "Age eámus deambulátum." Itaque
to-his-brother Come, let-us-go to-walk.   therefore

unà ambo abiérunt foras: et quum essent in agro,
together both went   abroad   they-were   field,

Caïnus írruit in Abélem, et interfécit eum. Deus
sprang upon   killed   him.

dixit Caïno: "Ubi est tuus frater?" Caïnus respondit: "Néscio; num ego sum custos fratris mei?"
<small>I-know-not; keeper of-</small>
  Deus dixit Caïno: "Caïne, quid fecisti? sanguis
<small>have-you-done blood</small>
fratris tui, quem ipse fudísti manu-tuâ clamat ad
<small>of- yourself have-shed with-your-hand cries</small>
me. Infésta tibi erit terra, quæ bibit sánguinem
<small>hostile to-you shall-be drank</small>
Abélis: quum colúeris eam longo et duro labore,
<small>you-cultivate it with-long hard labor,</small>
feret nullos fructus: eris vagus in orbe-terrárum.
<small>it-shall-bear no you-shall-be wanderer the-whole earth.</small>
Caïnus, despérans véniam, fugit.
<small>despairing pardon, fled.</small>

Lesson 4.

cum, *with.*	se, *himself, herself, themselves.*
per, *through.*	suus, sua, suum, *his, hers, theirs*
-que, *and.*	tum, *then.*
ita, *so.*	postquam, *when, after.*
simul, *at the same time.*	deinde, *then, afterwards.*
tandem, *at length.*	totĭdem, *as many.*

TENSES OF THE VERB esse, *to be.* I.

PRESENT, *I am.*		IMPERFECT, *was.*		FUTURE, *will be.*	
SING.	PLUR.	SING.	PLUR.	SING.	PLUR.
sum	sumus	eram	erāmus	ero	erĭmus
es	estis	eras	erātis	eris	erĭtis
est	sunt	erat	erant	erit	erunt

13. If a word has only two syllables, always give the Accent on the first syllable.

14. If a word has more than two syllables, accent the syllable before the last when it is marked *long*, like erā′mus; if it is marked *short*, like erĭmus, accent the one before it.

15. After the verb esse, *to be*, the nominative is used, not the accusative: as, **pater meus est agricŏla,** *my father is a farmer.* This is called the predicate-nominative. (See 111)

16. When **est** or **erat** comes at the beginning of a sentence, we generally say, *it is, it was, there is,* or *there was:* **erant arbŏres in horto,** means *there-were trees in the-garden.*

17. A few short words, like **-que,** *and,* are written as if they were part of another word. They are called Enclitics.

iv. *The Flood.*

Postquam Noëmus ingressus-est arcam cum
       Noah   had-entered   ark

cónjuge, tribus filiis, et tótidem núribus, aquæ
his-wife,   three   daughters-in-law,

maris et ómnium fóntium erupérunt. Simul
of-the-sea   fountains   broke-forth

plúvia ingens cécidit per quadraginta dies, et tóti-
rain   great   fell   forty

dem noctes. Aqua opéruit universam terram, ita ut
    nights.   covered   the-whole   so

superáret quíndecim cúbitis altíssimos montes.
it-overtopped   by-fifteen   cubits   the-highest   mountains.

Omnia absumpta-sunt dilúvio: arca autem, suble-
things   were-swept-away   by-the-flood: lifted

vata aquis, fluitábat in alto.
    by-   floated   on the-deep.

Deus immísit ventum veheméntem, et sensim
     sent   wind   violent   slowly

aquæ imminútæ-sunt. Tandem undécimo mense,
    were-lessened.   eleventh   month,

postquam dilúvium cœperat, Noëmus apéruit
              began   opened

fenéstram arcæ, et emísit corvum, qui non est-
window   of-   sent-out   raven,

reversus. Deínde emísit colúmbam: quum ea non
returned.   dove:

invenisset locum ubi póneret pedem, reversa-est
had-found   place   to-set   foot,

ad Noëmum, qui extendit manum, et íntulit eam
           held-out   *his*-hand,   brought

in arcam. Columba, rursum emíssa, áttulit in
              again   sent-out,   brought

ore suo ramum virentis olívæ, quo finis diluvii
mouth   branch   of-green   olive,   by-which end   of-

significabátur.
was-shown.

Noëmus egressus-est ex arcâ, postquam ibi inclú-
        went-out   shut-up

sus fúerat per annum totum, ipse et familia ejus :
   had-been   year²   whole¹   himself   family   his :

eduxit secum aves cétera-que animántia. Tum
 led-out   with him birds   other

erexit altáre, et óbtulit sacrificium Dómino. Deus
 built   altar   sacrifice   to-

dixit illi : "Non delébo posthac genus hóminum ;
   to-   will-destroy hereafter race   of-men ;

ponam arcum meum in núbibus ; et erit¹⁶ signum
 will-put bow   clouds ;   sign

fœderis quod facio vobis-cum. Quum obdúxero
of-the-covenant   make   with-you.   bring-on

nubes cælo, arcus meus apparébit, et recordábor
 clouds   to-   will-appear,   will-remember

fœderis mei, nec unquam dilúvium erit, ad perden-
        nor   ever   destroy

dum orbem terrárum.

Lesson 5.

TENSES OF THE VERB esse, *to be*. II.

PERFECT, *was.*		PLUPERFECT, *had been.*		FUT. PERF., *will have been.*	
SING.	PLUR.	SING.	PLUR.	SING.	PLUR.
fui	fuĭmus	fuĕram	fuerāmus	fuĕro	fuerĭmus
fuisti	fuistis	fuĕras	fuerātis	fuĕris	fuerĭtis
fuit	fuĕrunt (ēre)	fuĕrat	fuĕrant	fuĕrit	fuĕrint

18. In a Latin verb there are six Tenses, in two groups or sets : Present, Imperfect, Future ; Perfect, Pluperfect, Future-Perfect. The first set are called tenses of the Present Stem ; the second set, tenses of the Perfect Stem.

19. A Tense shows the Time when any thing was done or happened ; whether it is Present, Past, or Future.

20. There are two past tenses in a Latin verb, the Perfect and the Imperfect : in English, the same tense serves for both. In the verb esse, *to be*, fui and eram both mean *I was.*

21. The Perfect, in Latin, is used to tell *that any thing happened at a particular time ;* the Imperfect, to describe *how any thing was at that time :* so we should say,

heri fuit in horto, ubi erant aliquot flores, *yesterday he was in the garden, where there were a few flowers.*

22. The Perfect tense (**fui**) is often translated *have been;* and the Imperfect (**eram**), *used to be.* The Perfect, **fecit,** is *he made;* the Imperfect, **faciebat,** *he was making.*

23. In the Active Voice of all verbs, and in all the tenses except the Perfect, the First Person singular ends in **o** or **m;** the Second in **s,** and the Third in **t;** in the plural, the endings are **mus, tis, nt.** These endings stand instead of the Pronouns, which we must use in English.

24. When the meaning is given by a change in the ending of a word, it is called INFLECTION. Latin is a language of many inflections; and English, of very few inflections.

25. In all verbs, the Perfect, Pluperfect, and Future-Perfect are inflected like **fui, fueram, fuero.** Thus from

    amo, *I love;* **amāvi, amavĕram, amavĕro.**
    facio, *I make;* **feci, fecĕram, fecĕro.**
    cado, *I fall;* **cecĭdi, cecidĕram, cecidĕro.**
    fero, *I bear;* **tuli, tulĕram, tulĕro.**

The perfect ending **ēre** is often circumflexed: as, **fuêre.**

Lesson 6.

TENSES OF THE VERB **esse,** *to be.* III.

SUBJUNCTIVE MOOD.

	PRESENT.	IMPERFECT.	PERFECT.	PLUPERFECT.
SING.	sim	essem (forem)	fuĕrim	fuissem
	sis	esses	fuĕris	fuisses
	sit	esset	fuĕrit	fuisset
PLUR.	simus	essēmus	fuerĭmus	fuissēmus
	sitis	essētis	fuerĭtis	fuissētis
	sint	essent	fuĕrint	fuissent

IMPERATIVE MOOD.

PRES.	**es,** *be thou.*	**este,** *be ye.*
FUT.	**esto,** *thou shalt be;*	or, **estōte,** *ye shall be.*
	he shall be.	**sunto,** *they shall be.*

INFINITIVE MOOD.

PRES. **esse**, *to be.*   PERF. **fuisse**, *to have been.*
FUT. **fore** (or **futurus esse**), *will* or *would be.*
FUTURE PARTICIPLE. **futurus, a, um,** *going to be.*

MOODS.

26. The tenses given before were all in the Indicative Mood. The Indicative Mood is used *to tell of any thing.*

27. The Subjunctive Mood is often used after such words as *if, when, though, so that, I wish,* and in many other ways. It is generally translated in English by the Indicative; sometimes with the words *may, might, would,* or *should* (called Potential), and is sometimes used for the Imperative.

We use the Subjunctive Mood in English, when we say, "if it *be* so," "I wish he *were* here," "it *were* better not to do it;" where it is more common to say *is, was,* or *would-be.*

28. The Imperative Mood is used in giving Orders, Directions, or Laws: **es** (or **sis**) **memor** means, *be mindful;* **ita esto,** *be-it so,* or *it-must-be so.*

29. The Infinitive Mood is generally used after other verbs: as,

> **volo esse cum fratre,** *I-wish to-be with* [my] *brother.*
> **vidētur fuisse lætus,** *he-seems to-have-been glad.*
> **putāvi ita fore,** *I-thought it-would-be so.*

30. A Participle is a word that belongs to a noun, like an Adjective, but has partly the meaning of a Verb. It is sometimes used to make the tenses of a verb; as we say, *he was coming,* instead of *he came.*

For example, there is nò Future Subjunctive in Latin; but we may use the Future Participle with the Present Subjunctive **sim:** thus, —

futurus sim	**futuri simus**
futurus sis	**futuri sitis**
futurus sit	**futuri sint**

This is sometimes called the Future Subjunctive.

Lesson 7.

vos, *you* (plural).

vester, vestra, vestrum, *your.*

mi fili, *my son.*

inquit, *said he* (or *she*).

ligna, *sticks-of-wood.*

ac, *and.*

de, *from, down-from.*

ecce, *look! behold!*

ignis, *fire.*

super, *on.*

VOCATIVE CASE.

31. In this list, the words **mi fili** are in the Vocative Case. When we speak to a person, his name is in the Vocative.

32. The Vocative is the same as the Nominative, except in the singular of some masculine nouns that end in **us**: the vocative of **Carŏlus**, *Charles*, is **Carŏle**; the vocative of **Georgius**, *George*, is **Georgi.**

33. Words which are used only as exclamations, like **ecce**, *behold!* are called INTERJECTIONS.

v. *Abraham and Isaac.*

NOTE. — The Figures refer to the Sections in the foregoing Lessons.

Deus fecit fœdus cum Abrahámo his verbis :
covenant in-these words

" Exi [28] e domo paternâ, désere patriam, et pete
Go-out house your-father's forsake native-land seek

regionem quam datúrus [30] sum pósteris tuis : nam
country going-to-give to-your descendants

eris pater multárum gentium, ac per te omnes
of-many nations

orbis nationes erunt bonis cumulátæ. [30] Adspice
of the-world nations with-good-things heaped behold

cælum; dinúmera stellas, si potes : tua progénies
count stars you-can posterity

eas æquábit número."
them shall-equal in-number.

Filius natus-est Abrahamo, qui vocávit eum
son was-born to- called

Isaácum. Postquam Isaacus adolévit, Deus, ten-
was-grown try-

tans [30] fidem Abrahami, dixit ei : " Abrahame, tolle
ing faith of- to-him take

filium tuum únicum, quem amas, et ímmola eum
only whom you-love sacrifice him

mihi in monte quem osténtam tibi." Abrahámus
to-me   mountain   I-will-show   to-you

non dubitávit parére [29] Deo : impósuit ligna Isaaco ;
hesitated   to-obey   he-put   upon-

ipse verò portábat ignem [6] et gladium. Dum iter
himself[2] but[1]   carried   sword.   While   way

faciébant simul, Isaacus dixit patri : "Mi pater, ecce [33]
they-made   together   to-his-

ligna et ignis ; sed úbinam est hostia immolanda ? '[30]
             where   victim   to-be-killed

Cui Abrahamus : "Deus" inquit "sibi providébit
to-whom   for-himself will-provide

hostiam, fili mi.".

Ubi pervenérunt ambo in locum designátum,
   they-came   both   place   appointed

Abrahámus exstruxit aram, dispósuit ligna, alligá-
        built   altar   arranged   bound

vit Isaacum super struem lignorum, deinde arrípuit
           pile   of-   caught-up

gladium. Tum ángelus clamávit de cælo, "Abra-
         angel   cried

hame, cóntine [28] manum tuam, ne nóceas [27] púero :
     hold-back   haud   lest   hurt   boy

remunerábor spléndidè fidem tuam." Abrahamus
I-will-reward   nobly   faith

respexit, et vidit árietem hærentem [30] córnibus inter
looked-back   saw   ram   sticking   by-his-horns

vepres, quem immolávit loco filii.
brambles   he-slew   in-   of-

Lesson 8.

cui, *to-whom.*

mihi, *to-me.*

tibi, *for-you.*

sibi, *to him* or *herself.*

filio suo, *for his son.*

camélis, *to the camels.*

mater, *mother.*

matri suæ, *to her mother.*

postea, *afterwards.*

ait, *said.*

domi, *at-home;* domum, *home.*

foris, *out-of-doors.*

inde, *thence, from-there.*

statim, *immediately.*

tunc, tum, *then.*

dein, *then.*

etiam, *also, even.*

prope, *near.*

DATIVE CASE.

34. In this list, the words **cui, mihi, tibi, sibi, matrī, suæ, filio, camēlis,** are in the Dative Case. The Dative is generally translated with the word *to* or *for :* it is called the case of the Indirect Object.

When we say, in English, " give me the book," *me* and *book* are both the Object of *give ;* in Latin, *book* will be accusative, and *me* dative : as, **da mihi librum,** *give the-book to-me.*

35. Such words as *to, for, in, by,* are called PREPOSITIONS. This means that they are *put before* the noun.

36. The Dative is used as the object of many words in Latin which have a direct object in English : as, **nocet mihi,** *it injures me.* Especially, verbs which are compounded with prepositions : as, —

    obstĭtit mihi, *he opposed me (stood-in-the-way to-me.)*

37. The Dative singular, in Latin, generally ends in **æ, i,** or **o :** when it ends in **æ** it is generally feminine ; in **o,** masculine or neuter. In the plural it ends in **is** or **bus.**

VI. *Rebecca at the Well.*

Posteà Abrahámus misit servum Eliezérem ad
                sent   servant
cognátos suos qui erant in Mesopotámiâ, ut inde
  relations
addúceret uxórem filio [34] suo.   Qui ubi pervénit in
he-might-bring wife   arrived
Mesopotámiam, cónstitit cum camélis prope púteum
              stood   well
aquæ ad vésperum, quo-témpore múlieres solébant [21]
of-   evening   at the time that   women   were-used
conveníre ad hauriendam aquam.   Et ecce, statim
  to-gather   draw
Rebecca, virgo eximiâ pulchritúdine, pródiit, gerens
      maiden of-remarkable   beauty   came-out carrying
urnam húmero, quæ descendit ad púteum, et implé-
pitcher on-*her*-shoulder   went-down   filled
vit urnam.   Tunc Eliézer, progréssus óbviam
                     going-forward   to-meet

puellæ,[36] "Da," inquit "potum mihi." Cui Rebecca
girl   *give*   *to-drink*

"Bibe" ait "dómine [32] mi;" et simul demísit urnam;
drink   *master*   *let-down*

et quum ille bibisset, óbtulit etiam aquam camélis.[34]
            had   *offered*   *to-*

Eliezer prótulit inaures aúreas et armillas, quas dedit
       brought-out ear-rings   *of-gold*   *bracelets*   *gave*

Rebeccæ; tum interrogávit cujus esset [27] filia.   Cui
           asked   *whose she-was daughter*

respondit: "Ego sum filia Bathuélis; avus meus est
                                 grandfather

frater Abrahami; est [16] domi locus ad commorandum
                      room   *stay*

amplíssimus; est etiam plúrimum fœni et paleárum
abundant   *very-much*   *hay*   *straw*

ad usum camelorum."
   use   *of-*

Tum Rebecca properavit domum, et narravit
              hastened   *told*

matri suæ ea-quæ sibi contígerant. Labánus,
mother   *what*   *to-her*   *had-happened.*

frater Rebeccæ, quum audivisset sororem narrantem,
                 had-heard   *telling*

adivit hóminem, qui stabat ad fontem cum camélis,
went-to   *the-man*   *stood*   *spring*

et compellans eum, "Ingrédere" [28] inquit, dómine
addressing   *come-in*

mi; cur stas foris? paravi hospitium tibi,[34] et locum
       stand out-of-doors have prepared lodging

camelis." Dein deduxit eum domum, ei-que cibum
for-   *led*   *him*   *food*

appósuit.
set-before

Lesson 9.

an, *whether.*	**continuo,** *at once.*
ergo, *therefore.*	**en,** *here! behold!*
forte, *by chance.*	**ejus,** *his, hers, its.*
postridie, *the next day.*	**filii,** *the son's or of the son.*
propter, *on-account-of.*	**itinĕris,** *of the journey.*
matris, *the mother's,* or *of the mother.*	

GENITIVE CASE.

38. In this list, the words **ejus, filii, matris, itinĕris,** are in the Genitive Case. This is generally translated with the preposition *of*, or by the Possessive Case, in English; as when we say, —

video matris tuæ vultum, *I see your mother's face;* or, *the face of your mother.*

The words *my, your, his, her, son's, mother's,* are Possessive.

39. The Genitive is used as the object of several verbs, in Latin, especially those of memory and feeling; as, —

memento officii, *remember* [your] *duty.*
miserētur tui, *he pities you.*
pudet me pigritiæ meæ, *I am ashamed of my laziness.*

40. The Genitive singular, in Latin, generally ends in **æ, i,** or **is**; and in the plural it always ends in **um,** often in **ārum, ērum, ōrum**: those ending in **æ, arum, erum,** are mostly feminine; those in **i, orum,** masculine or neuter.

VII. *Betrothal of Rebecca.*

Continuò Eliezer expósuit paréntibus[34] Rebeccæ
(explained) (parents)
causam itíneris,[38] rogávit-que ut annúerent postula-
(reason) (asked) (would-consent) (demand)
tioni suæ.[34] Qui respondérunt: "Non póssumus
(answered) (we-can)
Deo[36] obsístere. En[38] Rebecca: proficiscátur
(resist) (let-her-go)
te-cum, nuptúra[30] Isaaco." Tum Eliezer deprompsit
(to-marry) (took-out)
vasa aúrea et argéntea, vestes-que pretiósas, quas
(vessels) (of-gold) (silver) (garments²) (precious¹)
dedit Rebeccæ; óbtulit etiam múnera matri ejus
(gave) (offered) (gifts)
et fratri; et iniérunt convívium.
(entered) (banquet.)
Postridié Eliezer, surgens mané, dixit parentibus
(rising) (early)
Rebeccæ, "Herus meus me exspectat; dimíttite-me,
(master) (expects) (let-me-go)

ut redeam [27] ad eum." Qui respondérunt, "Vocé-
may-return   let-us-call

mus [27] puellam, et percontémur ejus sententiam."
                          ask   her   opinion

Quum Rebecca venisset,[27] sciscitati-sunt an vellet [29]
             had-come   they-asked   whether she wished

discédere [29] cum hómine. "Volo," inquit ea.
to-go-away   I-will

Dimisérunt ergo Rebeccam et nutrícem ejus, pre-
                                   nurse   praying

cantes [30] ei omnia prospera.
for-her   prosperous.

Isaacus forte tunc deambulabat [22] in agris, et
                         was walking   fields

vidit [22] camélos venientes.[30] Simul Rebecca, con-
saw   coming   see-

spicata virum deambulantem, desíluit e camelo, et
ing   man   leaped-down

interrogavit, "Quis est ille vir?" Eliezer respondit,
asked   that

"Est [16] herus meus." Ea statim opéruit se pallio.
                                covered herself with-a-mantle

Eliezer narravit Isaaco omnia quæ fécerat. Et
          told   had-done.

Isaacus introduxit Rebeccam in tabernáculum
          brought   tent

matris [38] suæ, et facta est ejus uxor; et lenítus est
                she-became   wife   was-comforted [2]

dolor quem senserat propter mortem matris.
grief [1]   had-felt   death

Lesson 10.

a, ab, *by* or *from.*   quis, quæ, quid, *who? which?*

ante .. quam, *before.*   quo, quā, quo, *with whom or which.*

igĭtur, *therefore, then.*   multo, *by much.*

ităque, *therefore, and so.*   irā, *with anger.*

jam, *now, already.*   lamentis, *with laments.*

modo, *only, just now.*   a matre, *by* [his] *mother.*

rursum or rursus, *again.* a venatione, *from hunting.*

tanquam (tamquam), *as if.* de venatione, [some] *of the game.*

valde, *very, very-much.*   venātum, *to hunt, a-hunting.*

ABLATIVE CASE.

41. In this list, the words **quo, multo, irā, lamentis, matre, venatione,** are in the Ablative Case. This is generally translated in English with the prepositions *by, from, in,* or *with.*

42. The Ablative is used after many of the Latin prepositions, as the object of several verbs, after a few adjectives (as **dignus,** *worthy*), and to tell the time *when.* After the Comparative degree, it generally means *than.*

43. The Ablative singular ends in one of the five vowels, **a, e, i, o, u** : most ablatives ending in **a** are feminine, and those ending in **o, u,** masculine or neuter. In the plural, it ends in **is** or **bus,** like the Dative.

It is common to mark a of the ablative with a circumflex; as, **e terrâ,** *out-of the-earth.*

44. The word **venatum** is called the Supine of the verb **venor,** *I hunt.* It is used only after verbs of motion; and means what one is *going to do.*

VIII. *Jacob and Esau.*

Quum Isaácus jam senuísset, et factus-esset
               had grown old   had become

cæcus,[15] vocávit Esaüm filium suum majorem:
blind   elder

"Súmito"[28] inquit "pháretram, arcum et sagíttas;
take   quiver   arrows

affer mihi, et para pulmentum, ut cómedam[27] et
bring   prepare broth (or pottage)   may-eat

benedícam tibi[36] ántequam moriar." Esáus itaque
bless   die

profectus-est venátum.
went-away

Rebecca audíerat Isaacum loquentem:[30] vocavit
        had heard   talking

Jacóbum, et "Afferto" inquit "mihi duos hædos
              bring   two   kids

opímos; conficiam pulmentum, quo pater tuus valdè
fat   will-make

delectátur; appónes ei [36] cibum, et bene precábitur
is-pleased shall-set to-him food he-will-pray

tibi." Itaque Jacobus ábiit, et áttulit matri duos
for- went-away brought

hædos; illa paravit seni [34] cibum quem nóverat
old-man she-knew

suavem esse paláto ejus. Deinde Jacobus áttulit
sweet taste

patri suo escam paratam a matre. Esaus autem
dish prepared now

pilósus erat, sed Jacobus lenis: mater ígitur indúerat
hairy smooth had-put

ei [36] vestes fratris; et aptáverat pellem hædi máni-
clothes had-fitted skin hands

bus [34] ejus et collo. Cui Isaacus dixit: "Quisnam es
neck who

tu?" Jacobus respondit: "Ego sum Esáus,
primogénitus tuus: surge, et cómede de venatione
first-born rise

meâ." [11] Isaacus rursum: "Tu-ne es Esaus, [15] primogénitus meus? accéde propiùs, ut attrectem te." Ille
come nearer may-touch

accessit ad patrem, qui dixit, "Vox quidem est
came voice

Jacobi; [38] sed manus sunt Esái." Tum Isaacus
amplexátus-est Jacóbum, et antepósuit-eum fratri, [36]
embraced set-him-before

et tríbuit ei omnia bona primogéniti.
gave-up good-things

Non multo post, Esaus rédiit a venatióne, et ipse
returned

óbtulit patri pulmentum quod paráverat. Cui
had

Isaácus mirans dixit: "Quis est ergo ille qui modó
wondering

áttulit mihi cibum, et cui benedixi, tamquam primo-
blessed

génito?" Quod aúdiens Esaus édidit magnum
hearing uttered great

clamórem, et implévit domum lamentis; et, ardens
cry filled house blazing

irâ minabátur mortem Jacobo. [34]
threatened death

Lesson 11.

FIRST DECLENSION OF NOUNS.

	SINGULAR.	PLURAL.
NOMINATIVE.	puella, *girl.*	puellæ
GENITIVE.	puellæ	puellārum
DATIVE.	puellæ	puellis
ACCUSATIVE.	puellam	puellas
VOCATIVE.	puella	puellæ
ABLATIVE.	puellā	puellis

Decline in the same way, ala, *wing* (Table 1), ara, *altar,* stella, *star,* terra, *earth* or *land.*

45. There are five ways of inflecting Nouns in Latin. They are called Declensions; and are known by the ending of the genitive singular.

In the First Declension most of the nouns are Feminine, and end in **a**; the genitive singular, in **æ**.

46. There are six Cases, which have been already explained. They are generally arranged in this order: Nominative, Genitive, Dative, Accusative, Vocative, Ablative. They are used thus:—

NOM. puella saltat, *the girl dances;* puellæ saltant, *the girls dance.*

GEN. puellæ frater, *the girl's brother;* ludus puellarum, *the girls' game.*

DAT. da pomum puellæ, *give an apple to the girl.*

ACC. puellam or puellas vidi, *I saw a girl, or girls.*

VOC. da manum, parva puella, *give me your hand, little girl.*

ABL. mater ambulat cum filiābus suis et alterā puellā, *the mother is walking with her daughters and another girl.*

47. A few words, like filia, *daughter,* have **abus** in the dative and ablative plural; cum filiis suis would mean *with her sons.*

48. The Latin prepositions ad, *to,* ante, *before,* apud, *near,* circa, *around,* contra, *against,* inter, *among,* per, *through,* post, *after,* trans, *across,* with several others, are followed by the Accusative.

49. The prepositions a or ab, *from*, *by*, cum, *with*, e, ex, *out-of*, pro, *for*, sine, *without*, with several others, are followed by the Ablative.

50. The preposition in with the accusative means *into;* with the ablative, it means *in* or *among*.

Lesson 12.

SECOND DECLENSION OF NOUNS.

SINGULAR.

Nom.	puer, *boy*.	liber, *book*.	equus, *horse*.	donum, *gift*.
Gen.	puĕri	libri	equi	doni
Dat.	puĕro	libro	equo	dono
Acc.	puĕrum	librum	equum	donum
Voc.	puer	liber	eque	donum
Abl.	puero	libro	equo	dono

PLURAL.

Nom.	puĕri	libri	equi	dona
Gen.	puerōrum	librorum	equorum	donorum
Dat.	puĕris	libris	equis	donis
Acc.	puĕros	libros	equos	dona
Voc.	puĕri	libri	equi	dona
Abl.	puĕris	libris	equis	donis

51. Most nouns of the Second Declension, which end in er or us are Masculine (M.); those in um are Neuter (N.). The genitive singular ends in i.

The noun vir, *man*, is declined like puer. Most nouns ending in er are declined like liber.

52. All Latin nouns which end in um are neuter, and are declined like donum.

53. Nouns of the Second Declension ending in us are the only nouns in Latin that have a vocative different from the nominative. Almost all names of men are in this form.

Names which end in ius, like Horatius, *Horace*, have the vocative in i: as, Horati; also filius, *son*, and meus, *my* (31).

Lesson 13.

apud, *with, at, near.*
donec, *until.*
atque, ac, *and.*
ei, *to him.*
nec, *nor, and-not.*
itĕrum, *a second time.*
confestim, *at-once.*

tres, tria, *three.*
diu, *a long time.*
eo, *thither, there.*
unde, *whence, from where.*
ipse, ipsa, ipsum, *self* (himself, &c.).
sibi, *to him* (self), &c.
se, *himself,* &c.

54. There is no word in Latin for *yes* or *no.* Sometimes, instead of *yes,* we say **immo,** *nay indeed,* or **etiam,** *even so;* and for *no,* **minĭme,** *least-of-all,* or non, *not.* But generally, we answer a question by repeating the verb: as,

valet-ne? *is he well?* **valet,** *yes* (*he is well*).
erat-ne tecum? *was he with you?* non erat, *no* (*he was not*).

55. The syllable **-ne** (enclitic) is added to a word, when we ask a question to be answered *yes* or *no.* It is combined with **non,** *not,* and **nec,** *nor,* in such sentences as these :

nonne te vidi heri? *did not I see you yesterday?*
mater tua domi est, necne? *is your mother at home, or not?*

56. The word **ipse,** *self,* may agree with the subject or object of the verb in any person. Thus,

ipse ibi eram means *I myself* (or *I too*) *was there.*
ipse te nimium laudas, *you* (yourself) *praise yourself too much.*

57. The word **se** (or **sese**) *himself, herself, themselves,* is called a Reflective Pronoun. It means the same person as the subject of the sentence.

Thus, **audivit me sibi loquentem** *he heard me speak to him* (himself): if I had been speaking to some one else, it would be **ei,** or some other word. In the sentence **ipse se laudat,** *he is praising himself,* **ipse** is nominative, and **se** accusative.

There is no nominative to the reflective pronoun; the only cases are, genitive **sui,** dative **sibi,** accusative and ablative **se.**

58. Such words as *and, if, but, though, nor,* which connect words or sentences together, are called CONJUNCTIONS.

IX. *Jacob and Rachel.*

Rebecca, timens dilecto filio suo,[34] " Fuge " inquit
fearing *dear* *fly*

" fili mi;[31] abi ad Labánum avúnculum tuum, et
go *uncle*

commoráre apud eum, donec ira fratris tui defer-
stay *anger* *cools-*

véscat."[27] Itaque Jacobus profectus-est in Mesopo-
down *went-away*

támiam. Et in itínere, pervénit ad quemdam locum,
journey *came* *a-certain* *place*

ubí fessus de viâ pernoctavit; suppósuit-que lápidem
weary *of* *way* *passed-the-night* *put-under* *stone*

capiti[36] suo, et obdormivit. Et vidit in somnis
head *fell-asleep* *saw* *sleep*

scalam, innixam terræ,[34] quæ pertinébat ad cælum,
ladder *resting* *reached*

atque ángelos Dei ascendéntes[30] et descendéntes.
angels *ascending* *descending*

Et audívit Dominum dicentem sibi, " Ego sum
heard *the-Lord* *saying*

Deus patris tui: dabo tibi et pósteris tuis terram cui
I-will-give *posterity*

íncubas: noli timére;[29] ego favébo tibi; ero custos
lie-upon *do-not* *fear* *will-favor* *guard*

tuus, quòcumque perréxeris; et redúcam te in
wherever *you-go* *will-bring-back*

pátriam; ac per te omnes orbis nationes bonis
country *nations*

implebuntur." Tum Jacobus, expergefactus, adora-
shall-be-filled *waking* *worshipped*

vit Dominum.

Ubi Jacobus pervénit in Mesopotamiam, vidit
had-come

tres pécorum greges propter puteum cubántes,
of-cattle *flocks* *near* *well* *lying-down*

nam[58] ex eo puteo[49] greges solébant adaquári;[29]
were-wont *to-get-water*

et os putei clausum erat ingenti lápide.[41] Jacóbus
mouth *shut* *great* *stone*

accéssit eò, et dixit pastóribus,[34] " Fratres, unde
came *shepherd*

estis?" Qui respondérunt, "Ex urbe Haran."
town

Interrogávit íterum, "Nôstis-ne Labánum?" Dix-
asked   do-you-know

erunt, "Novimus." "Valet-ne?" "Valet," inquiunt;
we-know   is-he-well

"ecce, Rachel filia ejus venit cum grege suo."
daughter   comes

Dum Jacóbus ita lóquitur cum pastóribus, Rachel
speaks

filia Labani venit cum pécore paterno; nam ipsa [56]
father's

pascébat gregem. Confestim Jacóbus, videns
pastured   seeing

cognatam suam, amóvit lápidem ab ore pútei.
cousin   took-off   mouth

"Ego sum" inquit "filius Rebeccæ." Et osculatus-
he-kissed

est eam. Rachel, festínans, nuntiávit patri suo,
hastening   told

qui agnóvit filium soróris [38] suæ, dedit-que ei
knew   sister's   gave   him

Rachélem in matrimónium, cum sorore ejus Leâ.
marriage   her

Jacobus diu commorátus-est apud Labánum:
staid

intérea mirè auxit rem suam; et factus-est dives. [15]
meanwhile wonderfully increased property   became   rich

Longo post témpore, métuens invidiam Labani,
long   after   time   fearing   jealousy

rédiit in patriam suam, cum duabus uxoribus, et
returned   country   two   wives

filiis, et camelis, omnibúsque pecóribus.

Extimescébat autem iram fratris sui: et, ut placáret
dreaded   anger   might-appease

ánimum ejus, præmísit ad eum núntios, qui offérrent
mind   sent-forward   messengers   might-offer

ei múnera. Esaüs, mitigátus, occúrrit obviam Jacobo
gifts   made gentle   ran-up   to-meet

advenienti: insíluit in collum ejus, flens-que oscula-
coming   leaped upon neck   weeping

tus-est eum, nec quicquam ei [36] nocuit.
at-all   harmed

Lesson 14.

noster, nostra, nostrum, *our.* enim, *for.*
procul, *far-away.* potius, *rather.*
quomŏdo, *how.* præ, *before, by reason of.*
iste, ista, istud, *that* (yonder or yours). postea, *afterwards.*
quidam, quædam, quoddam, *a-certain.* an, *whether.*

ADVERBS.

59. In this list, the words **procul, postea, potius, quo-mŏdo,** are called ADVERBS. They are said to qualify the verb of the sentence where they belong; that is, they show how its meaning is to be taken.

If I say, procul **stabat,** sed postea **accessit,** *he stood a great way off, but afterwards he came up,* procul qualifies **stabat,** and postea qualifies **accessit.**

60. Such words as **nunc,** *now,* **tum,** *then,* **mox,** *presently,* are called adverbs of Time; **hic,** *here,* **ibi,** *there,* are adverbs of Place; **quomodo,** *how,* **sic** or **ita,** *so,* are adverbs of Manner; **cur,** *why,* **ubi,** *where,* are Relative or Interrogative adverbs.

61. Adverbs are very often made from Adjectives by a change in the ending: as, **bene,** *well,* **fortĭter,** *bravely,* from **bonus,** *good,* **fortis,** *brave.*

The accusative or ablative neuter of some adjectives is used as an adverb without any change: as, **multum,** *much;* **vero,** *truly,* or *but.*

It is common to distinguish Adverbs from other words of the same spelling by a grave accent: as, multùm, verò.

62. Adverbs sometimes qualify adjectives or other adverbs. If I say, "It is very true; he did it perfectly well," the adverb *very* qualifies *true; well* qualifies *did,* and *perfectly* qualifies *well.*

63. The Adverb, in Latin, is generally put directly before the word which it qualifies: as, non hic **erat,** *he was not here;* statim **venit,** *he came soon.*

x. *Joseph and his Brothers.*

Jacóbus habuit duódecim filios, inter quos erat
had   *t..elve*

Joséphus. Hunc pater amabat præ céteris,[44] et
him   *loved*   *before*   *the-rest*

dedit ei[34] togam textam[30] e filis varii colóris. Et
gave   *coat*   *woven*   *threads various*   *color*

Josephus narravit frátribus suis duplex somnium,
told   *double*   *dream*

quo[41] futura[30] ejus magnitúdo portendebatur.
future   *greatness*   *was-shown*

"Ligabámus" inquit "simul manípulos in agro: et
were-binding   *together* *sheaves*   *field*

ecce,[83] manípulus meus surrexit et stetit rectus;
       rose-up   *stood*   *upright*

vestri autem manípuli, circumstantes,[30] veneraban-
       standing-round   *reverenced*

tur meum. Postea vidi in somnis solem, lunam et
     saw   *sleep*   *sun,*   *moon*

úndecim stellas adorantes[30] me." Cui fratres
eleven   *stars*   *worshipping*

respondérunt, "Num[12] tu eris rex[15] noster? Num
             king

subjiciemur ditióni tuæ?" Fratres ígitur invidébant
shall-we-be-subject *rule*   *envied*

ei;[36] at pater rem tácitus considerábat.
       silent   *considered*

Quâdam die fratres Joséphi pascébant greges pro-
             were-feeding

cul, ipse autem remánserat domi. Jacóbus misit eum
   had-staid   *sent*

ad fratres, ut cognósceret[27] quómodo sese habérent.
     might-learn   *they-fared*

Qui, videntes eum venientem, consilium cepérunt
   seeing   *coming*   *counsel*   *took*

ejus occidendi: "Ecce" inquiunt "somniator
him   *of-killing*   *dreamer*

venit; occidámus[27] eum, et projiciámus in púteum:
    kill   *cast*   *well*

dicémus patri[34] fera devorávit Joséphum; tunc
will-say   *wild-beast has-devoured*

apparébit quid isti[36] prosint somnia."
will-appear   *him*   *profit*

Ruben, qui erat natu-maximus, detérruit fratres
oldest   deterred
a tanto scélere: "Nolíte" inquit "interfícere [29]
so-great crime   do-not   kill
púerum; est enim frater [15] noster; demíttite eum
let-down
potiùs in hanc fóveam." Erat [16] autem ei in ánimo,
pit   mind
liberare [29] Joséphum ex eorum mánibus, et ipsum
to-free   hands
extráhere e fóveâ, [49] atque ad patrem redúcere.
draw-out   lead-back
Ubi Joséphus pervénit ad fratres suos, detraxérunt
came   pulled-off
ei togam quâ indútus erat, et detrusérunt eum in [50]
clad   thrust
fóveam. Deinde, quum consedissent 'ad sumendum
had-sat-down   take
cibum, conspexérunt mercatóres, qui petébant
food   they-saw   traders   were-going-to
Ægyptum cum camélis portántibus [30] vária arómata.
carrying   various spices
Venit eis in mentem Josephum véndere illis merca-
mind   to-sell
tóribus: qui emérunt Josephum viginti nummis
bought   for-twenty coins
argénteis, eum-que deduxérunt in Ægyptum.
of-silver   brought
Tunc fratres Josephi tinxérunt togam ejus in
stained
sanguine hædi quem occíderant, et misérunt eam
blood   kid   had-killed   sent
ad patrem cum his verbis: "Invénimus hanc togam;
we-found
vide an toga filii tui sit." Quam quum agnovisset,
see   he-knew
pater exclamávit: "Toga filii [33] mei est: fera
cried-out   wild-beast
ferocíssima devoravit Josephum." Et Jacobus
most-fierce has-devoured
noluit accípere consolatiónem; dixit-que, "Ego
would-not receive comfort
descendam mærens cum filio meo in sepulcrum."
will-go-down mourning   tomb.

Lesson 15.

annus, i, M., *year.*
somnus, i, M., *sleep.*
gemma, æ, F., *bud.*
uva, æ, F., *grape.*
poculum, i, N., *cup.*
idem, eădem, idem, *the same.*
alter, altera, alterum, *the other.*

duo, duæ, duo, *two.*
ambo, ambæ, ambo, *both.*
bonus, bona, bonum, *good.*
pauci, paucæ, pauca, *few.*
pristĭnus, a, um, *former.*
oblītus, a, um, *forgetful.*
parātus, a, um, *ready, prepared.*

ADJECTIVES. I.

Decline **annus** and **somnus** like **equus**; **poculum** like **donum** (Lesson 12); **uva** and **gemma**, like **puella** (Lesson 11).

Learn the declension of **bonus, solus, miser, ater,** Table 3.

64. Almost all Adjectives, and all Participles, ending in us, are declined like **bonus.** These are called Adjectives of the First and Second Declension.

65. These six — **alius,** *other* (N. aliud), **nullus,** *no one,* **solus,** *only,* **totus,** *whole,* **ullus,** *any,* **unus,** *one* — have the genitive singular in **īus,** and the dative in **i,** in all the genders; also, **alter,** *other,* **uter,** *either,* **neuter,** *neither.*

66. An Adjective is put in the same Gender, Number, and Case as the noun it belongs to. This is called AGREEMENT.

XI. *Joseph in Prison.*

Paucos post annos, Joséphus, accusátus ab uxóre

accused   *wife*

Putípharis heri sui, conjectus-est in[50] cárcerem.

master   *was-cast*   *prison*

Erant in eodem carcere duo minístri regis Pharaónis :

servants   *king*

alter præerat pincérnis,[36] alter pistóribus. Utríque

one   *was-chief-of*   *butlers*   *other*   *bakers*   *to-each*

eâdem nocte obvénit somnium ; et ambo præ

night   *came*   *dream*

formídine mæsti erant. Quos quum Josephus mane[41]

fear   *sad*   *in-the-morning*

animadvertisset, interrogavıt, "Quænam est causa

had-noticed   *asked*   *what*   *reason*

mæstitiæ vestræ? narráte mıhı[34] somnıa vestra."

sadness   *tell*

Tum prior sic expósuit somnium : " Vidi in somno
first   set-forth   I-saw
vitem in quâ erant tres pálmites; paulátim [59]
viue   branches   by-degrees
prótulit gemmas; deinde flores erupérunt, ac postea
produced   then   flowers burst-out
uvæ maturuérunt; et expressi uvas in póculum
ripened   I-pressed   cup
Pharaonis, ei-que porrexi." " Bono sis animo " [41] in-
held-out   courage
quit Joséphus; " post tres dies Pharao te restítuet in
will-restore
gradum prístinum; rogo ut tunc memíneris mei."
rank   remember

Alter quoque narravit somnium : " Gestábam in
was-carrying   on
cápite tria canistra, in quibus erant liba, quália
head   baskets   cakes   such-as
pistóres solent confícere. [29] Ecce autem aves circum
are-wont to-make   birds   about [2]
volitábant, [21] et liba ista comedébant." Cui Jose-
flew [1]   ate
phus: " Hæc est interpretatio istíus somnii: tria
meaning
canistra sunt tres dies; quibus elapsis, Pharao te
being-spent
fériet secúri, [41] et aves carne [42] tuâ vescentur."
will-strike axe   flesh   will-feed
Die [42] tértio, qui dies natális Pharaonis erat,
birthday
spléndidum convívium parátum-est. Et rex remi-
splendid   feast   was-prepared   calls-
níscitur ministrórum [39] suorum qui erant in cárcere.
to-mind
Restítuit ígitur præfecto [34] pincernarum prístinum
restored   chief
munus; álterum verò [61] secúri percussit. Ita res
office   struck
sómnium comprobavit. Tamen præfectus pincer-
proved   yet
narum oblitus-est Josephi, [39] nec ejus in se mériti [39]
forgot   nor   service
postea recordatus-est.
remembered

Lésson 16.

septem, *seven*.   certe, *surely*.

idem, eădem, idem, *the same*.   enim, *for*.

eōdem eādem, eōdem (abl.).   quare, *wherefore*.

nemo, *no one*.   mox, *presently*.

uter, utra, utrum, *which* (of two).   collum, i, N., *neck*.

uterque (65), *each, both*.   cura, æ, F., *care*.

quisquam, quidquam, *any*.   vacca, æ, F., *cow*.

VERB FORMS.

Learn the Conjugation of amo (Table 7).

67. The endings of the Present, Imperfect, and Future, of the Active and Passive Voice, are these:—

	ACTIVE.		PASSIVE.	
	SINGULAR.	PLURAL.	SINGULAR.	PLURAL.
1st Person.	o or m	mus	r (ar, er, or)	mur
2d Person.	s (as, es, is)	tis	ris or re	mĭni
3d Person.	t (at, et, it)	nt	tur	ntur

The vowel before the ending is called the Connecting Vowel: it may be **a, e,** or **i**; but in the third person plural **i** is changed to **u.** These endings are seen in the following examples:—

amat patrem, *he loves his father*; amātur a patre, *he is loved by his father*.

urbem regit, *he rules the city*; urbs regĭtur, *the city is ruled*.

fruges sumunt, *they take the crops*; fruges sumuntur, *the crops are taken*.

68. For the Perfect, Pluperfect, and Future-Perfect, Passive, the tenses of **esse,** *to be,* are used, with a Participle ending in **tus** or **sus** (64); as,

amatus est, *he was loved*; jussi sunt, *they were ordered*.

amata erat, *she had been loved*; capti erĭmus, *we shall have been taken*; fixum est, *it was fixed* (x=cs).

69. Many verbs which are active in English have, in Latin, the form of passive verbs, and are called Deponents; as, sequĭtur, *he follows*; nascĭtur, *it grows*.

Several deponents have their object in the ablative; as, fungor officio, *I perform my duty*; vescĭtur carne, *he feeds on flesh*.

XII. *Pharaoh's Dreams.*

Post biennium, rex ipse[56] habuit sómnium.
  two-years   had

Videbatur sibi adstare Nilo[36] flúmini; et ecce[33]
seemed   stand-near   river

emergébant de flúmine septem vaccæ pingues,
came-forth   cows   fat

quæ pascebantur[69] in arvo. Deinde septem aliæ
   grazed   meadow

vaccæ macilentæ[66] exiérunt ex eodem flúmine,
      lean   went-out

quæ devorárunt prióres.
    devoured   former

Pharao, experrectus, rursum dormívit, et alterum
        being-roused   slept

habuit sómnium. Septem spicæ plenæ[66] enasce-
                       ears   full   grew

bantur[69] in uno culmo, aliæ-que tótidem exíles
                   stalk   thin

succrescébant, et spicas plenas consumpsérunt.
grew-near   consumed

Ubi illuxit, Pharao perturbátus convocavit omnes
    it-grew-light   troubled   called-together

intérpretes ac divínos, et narravit somnia; at nemo
interpreters prophets   told

ea interpretari[69] potuit. Deinde præfectus pincerná-
   interpret   could

rum dixit regi:[34] "Confiteor[69] peccátum meum;
                    I-confess   fault

quum ego et præfectus pistórum in cárcere essé-
mus, uterque somniavimus eâdem nocte.[42] Erat[16]
            dreamed

ibi puer Hebræus, qui nobis sapienter interpretatus-
                          wisely   interpreted

est somnia; res enim interpretationem comprobavıt."
                                        proved

Rex arcessívit Joséphum, ei-que narravit utrum-
    summoned

que somnium. Tum Josephus Pharaoni " Duplex "
                                          double

inquit "somnium unam et eamdem rem signíficat.
                                        signifies

Septem vaccæ pingues, et septem spicæ plenæ,

sunt septem anni ubertatis mox ventúræ; septem
                 of-plenty   to-come

verò vaccæ macilentæ et septem spicæ exíles sunt

tótidem anni famis, quæ ubertatem secutura-est.[80]
        of-famine   will-follow

Itaque, rex,[31] præfice[28] toti[65] Ægypto[36] virum
              appoint

sapientem et industrium, qui partem frugum
  wise   diligent   part   of-the-crops

recóndat in hórreis públicis, servet-que diligenter
may-lay-up   barns   public   may-keep   diligently

in subsidium famis secuturæ."[30]
for   help   that-will-follow

    Regi[36] placuit consilium: quare dixit Josépho:
        pleased   counsel

"Num[12] quisquam est in Ægypto te[42] sapientior?
                                      wiser

nemo certè fungétur[69] meliùs isto múnere.[42] En,[33]
        will-perform   better   office

tibi trado curam regni mei." Tum detraxit de
   I-give   kingdom   took-off

manu suâ ánnulum, et Joséphi digito[36] impósuit;
hand   ring   finger   placed

induit ei vestem byssinam; collo[36] torquem
put-on   robe   of-fine-cotton   chain

aúreum[66] circúmdedit; eum-que in curru suo
of-gold   put-around   chariot

secundum collocavit.
second   set

    Joséphus erat triginta annos natus,[a] quum summam
               thirty   chief

potestátem a rege[49] accépit.
power   received

---

a "*Joseph was thirty years old:*" literally, *had been born thirty years* (68, 69).

Lesson 17.

THIRD DECLENSION OF NOUNS.

SINGULAR.

honor, M.	*man*, C.	*city*, F.	*guide*, C.	*ship*, F.
N. honor	homo	urbs	dux	navis
G. honōris	homĭnis	urbis	ducis	navis
D. honōri	homĭni	urbi	duci	navi
Ac. honōrem	homĭnem	urbem	ducem	navem (im)
V. honor	homo	urbs	dux	navis
Ab. honōre	homĭne	urbe	duce	nave (i)

PLURAL.

N. honōres	homĭnes	urbes	duces	naves
G. honōrum	homĭnum	urbium	ducum	navĭum
D. honorĭbus	homĭnibus	urbĭbus	ducĭbus	navĭbus
Ac. honōres	homĭnes	urbes	duces	naves (is)
V. honōres	homĭnes	urbes	duces	naves
Ab. honorĭbus	homĭnibus	urbĭbus	ducĭbus	navĭbus

Practise the examples of the Third Declension in Table L

70. In the Third Declension, the genitive singular ends in **is**; the dative, **i**; accusative, **em**; ablative, **e**. These endings are added to the Stem. In the Plural, the nominative, accusative, and vocative are alike.

71. The Stem of most nouns of the Third Declension ends in a consonant; and in masculine or feminine nouns (except those in **l**, **n**, or **r**), the nominative is formed from it, as in **urbs**, by adding **s**.

In the word **honor**, the nominative is the same as the stem; in **dux**, the stem ends in **c**, which is joined to **s** in the nominative, making **x** (cs); in **ætas, ætatis**, it ends in **t**, which is dropped before **s**; in **navis**, it ends in **i**, which is dropped before **e** in some of the cases.

72. Nouns like **dux**, *guide*, and **homo** (which means *a human being*, either male or female), are said to be of Common Gender.

Lesson 18.

FOURTH AND FIFTH DECLENSIONS OF NOUNS.

SINGULAR.

fruit, M.	needle, F.	knee, N.	house, F.	thing, F.
N. fructus	acus	genu	domus	res
G. fructus	acus	genu (us)	domus (i)	rei
D. fructui	acui	genu	domui	rei
Ac. fructum	acum	genu	domum	rem
V. fructus	acus	genu	domus	res
Ab. fructu	acu	genu	domo	re

PLURAL.

N. fructus	acus	genua	domus	res
G. fructuum	acuum	genuum	domorum	rerum
D. fructĭbus	acŭbus	genĭbus	domĭbus	rebus
Ac. fructus	acus	genua	domos	res
V. fructus	acus	genua	domus	res
Ab. fructĭbus	acŭbus	genĭbus	domĭbus	rebus

73. In these examples, **fructus, acus, domus,** and **genu** are of the Fourth Declension. Most nouns of this declension are formed from verbs; and are rarely used except in the nominative, accusative, or ablative singular. The genitive ends in **us** (old form **uis**); dative in **ui** (old form **u**).

74. In the word **domus**, *house* or *home*, several of the cases are like the second declension: **domi** (genitive singular), *at home*, **domum**, *towards home*; **domo**, *from home*.

The word **domi** is sometimes said to be in the Locative form, which means *the place where*. In the singular of the Second Declension, this is the same as the Genitive; in the Plural and in the other Declensions, it is generally like the Dative: as, **Romæ**, *at Rome*; **Corinthi**, *at Corinth*; **Tiburi** (sometimes **Tibure**), *at Tibur*; **Athenis**, *at Athens*. The Locative form is used only with the names of towns or small islands, and a very few other words, as in **domi**, *at home*, **ruri**, *in the country*.

75. Most nouns of the Fifth Declension end in **ies**, and all but **dies** are feminine: only **dies** and **res** have the plural complete. The genitive singular ends in **ei**.

Lesson 19.

regio, ōnis, F., *country*.

obses, ĭdis, C., *hostage*.

os, oris, N., *mouth*.

frater, fratris, M., *brother*.

pater, patris, M., *father*.

superstes, *surviving* (*survivor*).

quoque, *also*.

parum, *not, not enough*.

huc, *hither*.

eōdem, *to the same place*.

praeter, *besides, except*.

omnis, omne, *all*.

Decline, in this list, the nouns of the Third Declension.

Decline the adjective **omnis** like **facĭlis** (Table 3); and **superstes** like **sospes** (Table 4).

76. Many adjectives are declined like nouns of the Third Declension. Thus **omnis** (M. and F.), *all*, is declined like **avis**; and **omne** (N.), like **rete** (Table 1, vowel-stems); and **superstes**, like **aetas** (Table 1, consonant-stems).

77. Adjectives in Latin are very often used as nouns. Thus **superstes** (*surviving*) means *a survivor*; **amīcus** (*friendly*) means *a friend*; **omnes** (pl.) means *all persons* or *everybody*; **omnia** (N. pl.) means *all things* or *every thing*.

78. If I say, "*Who is there?*" this is a Direct Question; and the sentence is called an Interrogative Sentence.

If I say, "I do not know *who is there*," the same words are called an Indirect Question; and that part of the sentence is called an Interrogative Clause. An Indirect Question is a clause which tells what was or might be asked.

The verb of an Indirect Question in Latin is in the Subjunctive Mood.

XIII. *Jacob's Sons in Egypt.*

Per septem annos ubertatis, Joséphus congessit
heaped-up

máximam fruménti cópiam; et ubi secúta-est inó-
very-great   plenty   scar-

pia septem annorum, apéruit horrea, et frumentum
.ity   opened   barns

vendebat. Ex aliis quoque regiónibus hómines
sold

conveniébant in Ægyptum, ad emendum cibum.
<small>thronged   buy</small>

Et inter eos eódem sunt-profecti decem fratres José-
<small>went   ten</small>

phi; sed pater retinuit domi mínimum-natu,
<small>kept   youngest</small>

Benjamínum. Et agnóvit eos Joséphus, nec ipse[56]
<small>knew</small>

ab iis est-cógnitus.[68]
<small>was-known</small>

Noluit autem indicáre statim quis esset,[78] sed
<small>would-not   declare</small>

interrogavit tamquam alienos:[77] "Unde venistis, et
<small>asked   as-if   strangers   come-you</small>

quo consílio?" Qui respondérunt, "Profecti-sumus
<small>design</small>

e regione Canaan, ut emamus frumentum." "Non

est ita" inquit Joséphus, "sed vultis explorare urbes
<small>you-wish   spy-out</small>

nostras, et loca Ægypti parum muníta." At illi
<small>places   fortified</small>

"Mínimè"[54] ínquiunt; "nihil mali meditamur;[69]
<small>evil   we-intend</small>

duódecim fratres sumus; mínimus retentus-est domi[74]
<small>twelve   kept-back</small>

a patre; alius verò non[63] súperest."
<small>survives</small>

Joséphum angébat quòd Benjamínus non áderat
<small>it-displeased</small>

cum céteris. Quare dixit: "Expériar[69] an verum
<small>others   will-try   truth</small>

dicátis;[78] máneat unus e vobis obses apud me, dum
<small>you-say   let-one-stay   till</small>

huc adducatur[27] frater vester mínimus: céteri abíte
<small>be-brought   go-away</small>

cum frumento." Tunc cœpérunt inter se dícere:
<small>began   among</small>

"Mérito hæc pátimur;[69] crudéles fúimus in fratrem
<small>deservedly   we-suffer   cruel   to</small>

nostrum; nunc pœnam istíus[65] scéleris lúimus."
<small>penalty   crime   pay</small>

Putábant hæc verba non intélligi a Josépho, quia
<small>thought   words   understood</small>

per interpretem cum eis locutus-erat. Ipse autem
_{had-spoken}

avertit se parumper, et flevit.
turned-away   a-little   wept

Josephus jussit fratrum saccos impleri tritico, et
ordered   bags   to-be-filled   with-wheat

pecuniam quam attúlerant repóni in ore saccorum;
money   had-brought   put back

áddidit ínsuper cibaria in viam.
added   besides   food   for   way

Deinde dimisit eos, præter Simeónem, quem
sent-away

retínuit óbsidem. Itaque profecti-sunt fratres Jose-
kept

phi, et quum veníssent ad patrem, narravérunt ei
had-come

omnia quæ sibi accíderant. Jacóbus, ut audívit
had-happened   heard

Benjamínum arcessi a præfecto Ægypti, cum
to-be-called

gémitu questus-est: "Simeon retentus-est [68] in
groan   complained

Ægypto; Benjamínum vultis abdúcere; hæc omnia
wish   take-away

mala in me recidérunt; Benjamínum non dimittam;
fall-back   will-let-go

nam, si quid ei adversi accíderit in viâ, non pótero
mischief   happen   can

ei supérstes vívere, sed dolóre oppressus móriar."
live   crushed   shall-die

Lesson 20.

munus, ŏris, N., *gift.*
senex, senis, M., *old-man.*
facies, ĕi, F., *face.*
fides, ĕi, F., *faith.*
mors, mortis, F., *death.*
prior, prius, *former.*
major, majus, *greater.*
salvus, a, um, *well,* in health.
sine, *without.*
tandem, *at length.*

quoniam, *since.*
ne, *lest, so-that-not.*
forte, *perhaps.*
adhuc, *yet, still.*
quia, *because.*
quam, *than.*
ínsuper, *besides.*
neodum, *and not yet.*
longe, *far.*
tute, *you yourself.*

COMPARISON.

Decline the nouns, in this list, of the Third and Fifth Declensions: also the Comparatives prior and major like altior, Table 4.

79. The Comparative of adjectives in Latin ends in **ior** (M., F.), and **ius** (N.); the Superlative ends in **ĭmus** (generally **issĭmus**). These endings are added to the Stem: as, in

carus, carior, carissĭmus, *dear, dearer, dearest;*
lĕvis, levior, levisĭmus, *light, lighter, lightest;*
potens, potentior, potentissĭmus, *powerful, more* and *most powerful.*

80. Other examples of comparison are:—

miser, miserior, miserrĭmus, *wretched, more* and *most wretched;*
facĭlis, facilior, facillĭmus, *easy, easier, easiest;*
bonus, melior, optĭmus, *good, better, best;*
malus, pejor, pessĭmus, *bad, worse, worst;*
magnus, major, maxĭmus, *great, greater, greatest;*
parvus, minor, minĭmus, *small, smaller, smallest.*

In the comparatives **major,** *greater,* and **pejor,** *worse,* the letter **j** is considered the same as **i.**

81. Adverbs are compared nearly like Adjectives: as, from

carus: care, *dearly,* carius, carissime;
miser: misere (or miserĭter), *wretchedly,* miserius, miserrime;
levis: levĭter, *lightly,* levius, levissime;
bonus: bene, melius, optime, *well, better, best.*

82. The Comparative sometimes has the meaning of *rather* or *too much,* and the Superlative, of *very:* thus **propior** is *rather near,* or *too near;* and **proximus,** *very near;* **quam proximus,** *as near as possible.*

XIV. *The Second Journey to Egypt.*

Postquam consumpti-sunt cibi quos attúlerant,
were-consumed had-brought

Jacóbus iterum misit filios in Ægyptum: qui
sent

respondérunt, "Non póssumus adire præfectum
can go-to governor

Ægypti sine Benjamino: [49] ipse enim jussit illum
ordered

ad se addúci. Tandem victus pater ánnuit: "Quó-
to-be-brought   *overcome*   *consented*

niam necesse est," inquit, "proficiscatur [27] Benja-
necessary   *let-go*

minus vobiscum; deferte [28] viro [34] múnera et duplum
carry   *double*

prétium ne forte erróre factum-sit ut vobis red-
price   *lest*   *mistake*   *happened*   *was-*

derétur prior pecúnia."
returned   *money*

Nunciatum est Josépho eosdem viros advenisse,
was-told   *had-come*

et cum eis párvulum fratrem: et jussit eos introduci
little   *to-be-led-in*

domum suam, et lautum parari convivium; et
splendid   *prepared*   *feast*

Simeonem, qui retentus-fúerat jubet ad eos redúci.
kept   *orders*   *brought-back*

Deinde ingressus-est in conclave [50] ubi fratres eum
entered   *chamber*

exspectabant, et clementer [59] eos salutavit; interro-
waited-for   *kindly*   *saluted*

gavítque, "Salvús-ne [55] est senex pater vester?
vivit-ne adhuc?" Qui respondérunt, "Salvus est [54]
pater noster; vivit adhuc." Ille autem, conjectis in
having-cast

Benjamínum óculis, dixit, "Iste est frater vester
eyes

mínimus, qui domi remánserat apud patrem?" et
rursus; "Deus sit [27] tibi propitius, fili mi." Et ábiit
favorable   *went-away*

festínans, quia commótus-erat ánimo, et lacrimavit.
hastening   *disturbed*   *mind*   *wept*

Mox, lotâ facie, regressus contínuit se, et jussit
washed   *returning*   *restrained*

appóni cibos. Tum distríbuit escam unicuique fra-
to-be-set   *distributed*   *to-each*

trum suorum; sed pars Benjamini erat quintuplo
share   *five-times*

major quàm ceterórum. Peracto convívio, Josephus
others   *finished*

dat negotium dispensatóri, ut saccos eorum ímpleat
gives   *business*   *steward*   *bags*   *fill*

frumento, pecuniamque simul repónat, et ínsuper
<small>put-back   besides</small>

póculum suum argenteum in sacco Benjamini re-
<small>cup   of-silver</small>

cóndat.   Ille diligenter facit quod erat imperatum.
<small>hide   diligently   ordered</small>

Quum fratres sese in viam dedissent, necdum
<small>journey   had-given</small>

procul ab urbe essent, vocavit dispensatorem domûs
<small>called</small>

suæ, ei-que dixit, "Perséquere viros, et ubi eos
<small>pursue</small>

assecutus-fúeris, dícito *Quare* [60] *injuriam pro*
<small>have-overtaken   say   wrong</small>

bonis rependistis? subripuistis póculum argénteum,
<small>have-paid   have-stolen</small>

quo [41] *dóminus meus útitur: ímprobè fecistis."*
<small>uses   wrong</small>

Dipensátor mandata perfécit; ad eos celériter con-
<small>orders   fulfilled   swiftly   has-</small>

tendit; furtum exprobravit; rei [38] indignitatem ex-
<small>tened   theft   charged   unworthiness   set-</small>

pósuit.
<small>forth</small>

Fratres Josephi respondérunt, "Istud scéleris
longè a nobis aliénum est; ut tute scis, retúlimus
<small>foreign   as   know   brought-back</small>

bonâ fide pecuniam in saccis repertam; tantum
<small>found   so-much</small>

abest ut furati-simus póculum dómini tui, apud
<small>is-far   have-stolen</small>

quem furtum deprehensum fúerit, is morte multé-
<small>discovered   be-pun-</small>

tur." [27]   Continuò depónunt saccos et apériunt;
<small>ished   at-once   lay-down   open</small>

quos ille scrutatus, [69] invenit póculum in Benjamini
<small>having-searched   found</small>

sacco.

Lesson 21.

ante . . . quam, *before.*	propius, *nearer.*
aut, *or.*	quasi, *as if.*
demum, *at last.*	satis, *enough.*
interea, *in the mean time.*	unice, *especially.*
nequāquam, *by no means.*	vix, *scarcely.*
nisi, *unless.*	dignus, a, um, *worthy.*
primum, *first;* primo, *at first.*	liber, libera, liberum, *free.*

COMPOUNDS OF esse, *to be.*

83. The verb **posse** (**potis esse**), *to be able,* is inflected nearly like **esse**:

PRESENT.		IMPERFECT.		FUTURE.	
possum	possŭmus	potĕram	poterāmus	potĕro	poterĭmus
potes	potestis	potĕras	poterātis	potĕris	poterĭtis
potest	possunt	potĕrat	potĕrant	potĕrit	potĕrunt

PERF. potui. PLUP. potuĕram. FUT. PERF. potuĕro. (25.)
SUBJ. PRES. possim. IMP. possem.
PERF. potuĕrim. PLUP. potuissem.
INFINITIVE. posse, *to be able;* potuisse, *to have been able.*
PARTICIPLE. potens, potentis, *able* or *powerful.*

Decline **potens** like **amans** (Table 4).

84. The verb **esse** is compounded also with the prepositions **ab, ad, de, in, inter, ob, præ, pro, sub, super.**

Thus the verb **prodesse**, *to benefit,* is inflected like **esse**, with **pro** (or **prod**) before it:

PRES. prosum, prodes, prodest, prosŭmus, prodestis, prosunt.
IMPERF. prodĕram. FUT. prodĕro.
PERF. profui. PLUP. profuĕram. FUT. PERF. profuĕro. (25.)
SUBJ. PRES. prosim. IMPERF. prodessem.
PERF. profuĕrim. PLUP. profuissem.
INFIN. prodesse, profuisse. FUT.-PARTICIPLE. profuturus.

All these compounds except **abesse** are followed by the Dative: as, adĕro tibi, *I will be near you;* profuit mihi, *he helped me.*

The adjectives **absens**, *absent,* **præsens**, *present,* are used as participles of **absum** and **adsum.**

xv. *Joseph declares himself.*

Tunc fratres Joséphi, mærore[41] oppressi, rever-
     grief   cast-down

tuntur[69] in urbem.   Adducti ad Joséphum, sese[57]
return   brought

abjecérunt ad pedes ejus.   Quibus ílle, "Quómodo"
     threw   feet   to-whom

inquit "potuistis hoc scelus admittere ?"[29] Judas
                                commit

respondit, "Fateor; res est manifesta; nec audémus
           confess   plain   dare

pétere véniam, aut sperare; omnes érimus servi."
to-seek   favor   to-hope   slaves

"Nequáquam," ait Josephus : "Sed ille apud quem
inventum est póculum erit mihi servus; vos autem
     found

abíte[28] líberi ad patrem vestrum."

Deinde Judas, propiùs accédens ad Joséphum,
                   approaching

"Te oro" inquit "ut bonâ cum veniâ me audias.[27]
Pater noster únicè díligit púerum : primò nolébat
                 loves   refused

eum dimittere :[29] non pótui id ab eo impetrare, nisi
    let-go   obtain

postquam spopondi eum tutum ab omni perículo
           pledged   safe   anger

fore.[29] Si rediérimus ad patrem sine púero, ille
             return

mærore confectus moriétur.   Te oro atque óbsecro,
grief   worn-out   beseech

ut sinas púerum abire, meque pro eo addícas in
   permit   for   bind

servitútem : ego pœnam quâ[42] dignus est mihi sumo,
slavery   take

et exsolvam."
    will-pay

Interea Josephus vix[59] se continére póterat:
                               restrain

quare jussit omnes Ægyptios discédere.   Tum
                               depart

flens, magnâ voce[41] dixit "Ego sum Joséphus;
weeping   voice

vivit-ne adhuc pater meus ? Non póterant respondére fratres ejus, nímio timore perturbati.
too-great fear disturbed
Quibus[34] ille amícè "Accédite"[28] inquit "ad me:
kindly
ego sum Josephus frater vester, quem vendidistis
you-sold
mercatóribus euntibus in Ægyptum. Nolíte timére:
traders going do-not fear
Dei providentiâ id factum-est, ut ego saluti vestræ
providence was-done safety
consúlerem."
might-consult

Hæc locútus, Josephus complexus-est Benjamí-
having-spoken embraced
num, fratrem suum; deinde céteros quoque fratres
lácrimans osculatus-est. Tum demum illi cum eo
fidenter[59] locuti-sunt. Quibus Josephus "Ite" in-
confidently go
quit: "properate ad patrem meum, ei-que nuntiate
hasten
filium suum vívere,[29] et apud Pharaonem plurimam
lives very-great
potentiam habére; et persuadéte ei ut in Ægyptum
power has persuade
cum omni familiâ cómmigret."
family remove
Ita festinantes reversi-sunt ad patrem, ei-que
nuntiavérunt, Josephum vivere, et príncipem esse
prince
totíus Ægypti. Ad quem nuntium, Jacobus, quasi
message
e gravi somno experrectus, obstúpuit; nec primùm
heavy roused was-dumb
filiis rem narrántibus fidem adhíbuit. Sed post-
faith gave
quam vidit plaustra et dona sibi[57] a Josepho missa,
wagons sent
recepit ánimum: et "Mihi satis est" inquit "si vivit
recovered courage enough
adhuc Josephus meus: ibo et vidébo eum ante
still will-go see
quám moriar."

Lesson 22.

adventus, ūs, M., *coming.*
conspectus, ūs, M., *sight.*
locus, i, M., *place*; pl., loca, N.
corpus, ŏris, N., *body.*
opus, ĕris, N., *work, trade.*
pecus, ŏris, N., *herd-of-cattle.*
majores, tm (pl.), *ancestors.*

coram, *in-the-presence-of.*
diu, *long-time.*
obviam, *to meet.*
certo, *certainly.*
confestim, *at-once.*
scilicet, *namely, to-be-sure.*
si-quis, si-qua, si-quod, *if-any.*

Learn the Numerals from one to ten (Lesson 29).

ACCUSATIVE AND INFINITIVE.

85. In English we often use the Infinitive in such sentences as these: "I think it to be right;" "I know it to be so;" "he is said to be rich;" "you ordered it to be done;" where we might say, "I think *that* it is right," and so on. In Latin, we use the Accusative and Infinitive in this way, after any verb of Knowing, Thinking, and Telling; as,

spopondi eum tutum fore, *I promised that he should be safe;*
dixit patrem suum advenisse, *he said that his father had come;*
responderunt se esse pastōres, *they replied they were shepherds;*
sensit mortem sibi imminēre, *he felt that death was near to him.*

In these sentences, the accusative is the Subject of the infinitive. The Accusative with the Infinitive is called a Substantive Clause, and is the Object of the verb of knowing, thinking, or telling.

86. With a verb which means to hope or promise, we generally, in English, use the infinitive without a subject: thus we say, "I hoped to come;" "he promised to do this." But in Latin the accusative me, te, se, is almost always used with such verbs: as,

speravi me esse venturum, *I hoped to come;*
promisit se id [esse] facturum, *he promised to do it.*

87. The Present Infinitive Active of most verbs ends in are, ere, or ire: the Perfect Infinitive ends in isse; but very often in asse, or esse, instead of avisse or evisse.

The Infinitive Passive ends in i; often in āri, ēri, or īri

XVI. *Jacob goes into Egypt.*

Jacóbus, cum filiis nepótibus-que in Ægyptum

grandsons

pervénit; et præmísit Judam ad Josephum, ut eum

came   sent-forward

certiórem-fáceret de adventu suo. Confestim Jose-

might-inform

phus processit óbviam patri,[36] quem ut vidit, in

went-forward to-meet   when

collum ejus procúbuit, et flens flentem [30] complexus-

neck   fall   weeping   embraced

est. Tum Jacobus "Satis diu vixi" inquit; "nunc

have-lived

æquo ánimo moriar, quóniam conspectu [42] tuo frui

calm   mind   will-die since   to-enjoy

mihi lícuit, et te mihi supérstitem relinquo."

it-was-granted   leave

Josephus ádiit Pharaonem, ei-que nuntiavit pa-

went-to

trem suum advenisse: constítuit etiam quinque e

placed

frátribus suis coram [49] rege. Qui eos interrogavit

quidnam óperis habérent; illi respondérunt, se esse

pastóres. Tum rex dixit Josepho: "Ægyptus in

shepherds

potestate tuâ est: cura [98] ut pater et fratres tui in

power   take-care

óptimo loco hábitent; et si qui sint inter eos gnari

dwell   skilful

et industrii, trade eis curam pécorum meorum."

diligent   give   care

Josephus adduxit quoque patrem suum ad Pha-

brought

raonem, qui salutatus a Jacóbo, percontatus-est ab

being-saluted   asked

eo quâ esset [78] ætáte. Jacobus respondit regi:

"Vixi centum et triginta annos; pauci et míseri

lived a-hundred   thirty

sunt anni vitæ meæ, nec adeptus-sum senectutem

life   have-I-gained   old-age

beatam avorum meorum." Tum, bene precatus

happy ancestors   having-prayed

regi, discessit ab eo. Josephus autem fratres suos
for- departed

collocavit in óptimâ [80] parte Ægypti, eis-que om-
placed

nium rerum abundantiam suppeditavit.
plenty supplied

Jacobus vixit septem et decem annos postquam

demigravit in Ægyptum. Ubi sensit mortem sibi
had-removed felt

imminére, arcessíto Josepho, dixit, "Si me amas,
to-be-near having-called

jura te id facturum-esse quod a te petam, scílicet
swear will-do what ask

ut ne me sepélias in Ægypto, sed corpus meum
bury

tránsferas ex hac regione, et condas in sepulcro
carry lay tomb

majorum meorum." Josephus autem "Fáciam"
will-do

inquit "quod jubes, pater." "Jura ergo mihi," ait
what order

Jacobus, "te certò id esse-facturum." Josephus

juravit in verba patris. Et non multo post, Jaco-

bus mortuus-est.
died

Ut vidit Josephus exstinctum patrem, præcépit
dead ordered

médicis [36] ut condírent corpus, et ipse, cum frátribus
physicians embalm

multis-que Ægyptiis, patrem deportavit in regionem
many carried

Canaan. Ibi funus fecérunt cum magno planctu;
funeral made lament

sepeliérunt corpus in speluncâ, ubi jacébant Abra-
buried cave lay

hámus et Isaácus, reversi-que sunt in Ægyptum.
returned

Lesson 23.

REGULAR VERBS.

Learn the inflection of the four Conjugations (Tables **7–11**); also, study the lists of comparative endings in Table **12**.

N.B. This may occupy the time of several lessons; during which the Reading Exercises previously learned should be constantly practised.

88. The Present, Imperfect, and Future tenses of regular verbs are inflected in four different ways. These are called the Four Conjugations.

89. The First and Second conjugations, and the Third and Fourth conjugations, are inflected nearly alike. But most of the tenses of the first have the vowel **a** before the ending; those of the second, **e**; those of the third, **e** or **i**; and those of the fourth, **i**. These are called the Characteristic or Connecting Vowels.

90. In the Subjunctive Present these vowels are changed, in the first conjugation to **e**, and in the others to **a**: in the Imperfect, the verb-ending (**67**) is added to the Present Infinitive (**87**) in all verbs, regular or irregular.

91. The Perfect Tense and the Perfect Participle Passive are generally formed from the Present, thus :

	PRESENT.	INFINITIVE.	PERFECT.	PERF.-PART.
1st CONJUGATION.	o	āre	āvi	ātus
2d ,,	eo	ēre	ēvi or ui	ētus or ĭtus
3d ,,	o	ĕre	si (xi)	tus (sus)
4th ,,	io	īre	īvi	ītus

NOTE. — Those formed differently are given in Tables **13, 14.** The perfect, &c., are often contracted; as, amârat for amaverat.

92. Most Latin verbs have four Participles, called the Present and Future Active; the Perfect Passive; and the Gerundive, sometimes called the Future Passive Participle.

93. The Present Participle ends in **ans** or **ens**, and has the same meaning as the English participle in *ing:* as, **amans**, *loving;* **regens**, *ruling.*

94. The Future Participle ends in **ūrus**. It generally means what is likely to happen, or what one expects or intends to do; as, **venit auditurus**, *he came to hear*.

95. The Perfect Participle ends in **tus** or **sus (xus)**. It is inflected like **bonus**, and often has the meaning of an adjective: as, **amātus**, *beloved;* **acceptus**, *acceptable*.

96. The Gerundive (or Future Passive Participle) ends in **dus**. It has the meaning of *what should be done:* as, **amandus**, *lovely* or *that ought to be loved;* and it is followed by the Dative, as in the sentence

fides servanda est nobis, *we must keep our word (faith is to be kept by us).*

The Gerundive is often translated as if it were an active participle, governing the word it agrees with: as,

ad hauriendam aquam, *for drawing water;* (Lesson 8);
consilium ejus occidendi, *the design of killing him* (Lesson 14).

97. The Gerund has the same meaning, but *governs* the object-word, while the Gerundive *agrees with* it: thus the last examples might be,

ad hauriendum aquam; consilium eum occidendi.

98. The Supine ending in **um** is used after verbs of motion to tell what one is *going to do;* as, **venit audītum**, *he came to hear* (44). The supine ending in **u** is used after adjectives; as, **terribĭle audītu**, *dreadful to hear*.

Lesson 24.

IRREGULAR VERBS.

Learn the Irregular Conjugations given in Tables **15, 16**.

99. In several verbs, the Present tense, with some of the parts formed from it, is not inflected like either of the regular conjugations. These are called Irregular Verbs.

100. The tenses of the Perfect Stem (18) are always inflected regularly, as given in Lesson 5. But in many verbs (as **fero**), they are not formed, as in the regular conjugations, from the Present (see Tables **13, 14**).

Lesson 25.

plurĭmi, æ, a (pl.), *very many.*	aliquando, *at-length.*
proxĭmus, a, um, *very near.*	deinde, *then.*
os, ossis, N., *bone.*	etiam, *also, even.*
placĭde, *calmly.*	illuc, *to that place.*
postĕri, ōrum (pl.), *posterity.*	lenĭter, *gently.*
in dies, *day by day.*	quidem, *indeed.*
metus, ūs, M., *fear.*	seu (sive), *or.*

non est quod timeam, *there is nothing for me to fear.*

PERSONAL PRONOUNS.

Decline the Pronouns ego, nos, tu, vos (Table 5).
Decline the Possessives meus, tuus, noster, vester.
Learn the Numerals from ten to one hundred.

101. The Possessive adjectives, meus, tuus, noster, vester, are used like the Genitive of the Personal Pronouns, and may agree with a genitive in any case: as,

nostra omnium patria, *the country of us all.*

102. Nouns or adjectives ending in ŏlus, ŭlus, or llus, mean that a thing is *little* or *tender.* They are called Diminutives: as,

parvŭlus (from parvus), *little;* puerŭlus (from puer), *little boy;* puer misellus (from miser), *poor little boy.*

103. The verb esse, *to be,* with the dative of persons, is very often used instead of *have:* est mihi liber (*there is a book to me*) means *I have a book.*

104. A second dative is often used after esse (or verbs of giving, sending, &c.), to show *of what use* a thing is to some one: est mihi præsidio means *it is a defence to me.* This use is sometimes called the Double Dative.

XVII. *The Hebrews in Egypt.*

Post mortem patris, Josephi fratres timebant ne
    feared   *lest*
ulcisceretur [69] injuriam quam acceperat. Misérunt
should-revenge   *injury*   *had-received*   *sent*

ígitur ad eum, rogantes, nómine patris, ut eam
<small>asking   name</small>

obliviscerétur, sibi-que [57] condonáret.   Quibus
<small>would-forget   them   pardon   to-whom</small>

Josephus respondit: "Non est quod timeátis: vos
<small>may-fear</small>

quidem malo in me ánimo fecistis; sed Deus
<small>evil   towards   mind   did</small>

convertit illud in bonum; ego vos alam, et vestras
<small>turned   will-feed</small>

omnium [101] famílias." Consolatus-est eos plúrimis [82]
<small>families   comforted</small>

verbis, et léniter [59] cum eis locutus-est.
<small>spoke</small>

Josephus vixit annos centum et decem; et, quum
<small>lived</small>

jam esset morti próximus,[82] convocavit fratres suos,
<small>called-together</small>

et admónuit eos se brevi esse moritúrum.[86] "Ego"
<small>admonished   shortly   would-die</small>

inquit "jam mórior: Deus vos non déseret, sed erit
<small>am-dying   will-forsake</small>

vobis præsidio,[104] et dedúcet vos aliquando ex Ægyp-
<small>defence   will-lead</small>

to in regionem quam pátribus nostris promísit.   Oro
<small>promised   I-pray</small>

vos atque obtestor, ut illuc ossa mea deportétis."
<small>beseech   carry</small>

Deinde placidè obiit: corpus ejus condítum-est,[68] et
<small>died   was-embalmed</small>

in féretro pósitum.
<small>on   bier   put</small>

Interea pósteri Jacobi, seu Hebræi, número aucti-
<small>were-en-</small>

sunt [68] mirum in modum; et eorum multitudo, in
<small>larged   wonderful   manner   multitude</small>

dies crescens, metum incutiebat Ægyptiis.[36] Et
<small>growing   struck</small>

rex novus sólio [42] potítus-est, qui Josephum non
<small>new   throne   possessed</small>

víderat, nec cognóverat, nec mérita ejus recorda-
<small>knew   merits   remembered</small>

batur. Is igitur, ut Hebræos opprímeret, primùm
<small>might-crush</small>

duris labóribus [41] eos conficiébat ; et cómpulit eos
hard   labors   wore-down   forced

láteres fácere, temperantes stípulâ et páleâ pro
bricks   moulding   stubble   chaff

stramentis. Deínde, quum vidéret eos mirè cres-
straw

centes número, edixit etiam ut parvuli [102] eorum
creasing   ordered

púeri, recenter nati, in flumen projicerentur.
newly   born   river   should-be-cast

Lesson 26.

arundo, ĭnis, F., *reed.*
ripa, æ, F., *river-bank.*
comes, ĭtis, C., *companion.*
famĭla, æ, F., *maid-servant.*
mensis, mensis, M., *month.*
apertā fiscellā, *when the basket was opened.*

diutius, *longer.*
intus, *within, inside.*
mox, *presently.*
quare, *wherefore.*
merces, ēdis, F., *pay, wages.*

DEMONSTRATIVE PRONOUNS.

		this	SINGULAR.		*that*	
NOM.	hic	hæc	hoc	is	ea	id
GEN.		hujus			ejus	
DAT.		huic			ei	
ACC.	hunc	hanc	hoc	eum	eam	id
ABL.	hoc	hac	hoc	eo	ea	eo

		these	PLURAL.		*those*	
NOM.	hi	hæ	hæc	ii (ei)	eæ	ea
GEN.	horum	harum	horum	eorum	earum	eorum
DAT.		his			eis or iis	
ACC.	hos	has	hæc	eos	eas	ea
ABL.		his			eis or iis	

Decline ille, *that,* ipse, *self,* and idem, *same* (Table 5) ; also iste, *that, yonder,* like ille.

Observe that these Demonstratives are used as Adjectives ; and that none of them can have a Vocative, except ipse.

4

105. Many adjectives ending in **eus, ius, anus,** or **inus,** are formed from nouns, and have nearly the meaning of the genitive, showing *to whom a thing belongs*, or *what it is made of*; those in **ensis** mean *of a town*, or *place* : as,

scirpeus (from **scirpus**), *of rushes*; **patrius** (from **pater**), *of a father*; **montānus** (from **mons**), *mountaineer*; **bombycīnus** (from **bombyx**), *silken*; **byssīnus** (from **byssus**), *of fine cotton*; **Atheniensis**, *Athenian*.

106. Verbs ending in **sco** (called Inceptives) are formed from nouns, adjectives, or other verbs; and mean that a thing is *beginning* or *coming to be* : thus **cognovi** means *I know*, **cognosco**, *I find out*; **caleo**, *I am hot*, **calesco**, *I grow hot*; **vesper est,** *it is evening*, **vesperascit,** *it is growing late*.

XVIII. *Birth of Moses.*

Post multos annos, una ex mulieribus Hebræis

Hebrew

habuit filium; quem ut vidit formósum et vigentem

             saw   handsome   vigorous

voluit servare. Quare abscondit eum très ménses;

wished save   hid

sed, quum non posset eum diutiús occultare, sumpsit

                      conceal   took

fiscellam scirpeam,[105] quam linívit bitúmine et pice;

basket of-rushes   smeared with-slime   pitch

deinde pósuit intus infántulum,[102] et expósuit eum

             baby   exposed

inter arúndines ripæ flúminis. Hábuit se-cum unam

          river   had

cómitem, sororem púeri, quam jussit stare procul,

                  ordered stand   afar

ut eventum rei [38] cognósceret.[106]

result   learn

Mox filia Pharaonis venit ad flumen, ut sese [57]

lavaret in aquis. Prospexit fiscellam in arundínibus

might-bathe   saw

hærentem, misit-que illuc ùnam e famulabus [47] suis.

sticking   sent

Apertâ fiscellâ, cernens párvulum [102] vagientem,

      perceiving   crying

miserta-est illíus:[39] "Iste est" inquit "unus ex
<small>pitied</small>

infántibus Hebræorum." Tunc soror púeri, accé-
<small>children   coming-</small>

dens, "Vis-ne" inquit "ut arcessam múlierem
<small>near   wish   send-for</small>

Hebræam, quæ nútriat párvulum?" Et vocavit
<small>   may-nurse   called</small>

matrem, cui filia Pharaonis dedit púerum alendum,[96]
<small>   to-feed</small>

promissâ mercéde. Itaque mater nutrívit púerum,
<small>having-promised   pay   nursed</small>

et adultum [30] réddidit filiæ [34] Pharaonis, quæ eum
<small>when-grown   returned</small>

adoptavit, et nominavit Mosem, — id est, *servatum*
<small>adopted   called   saved</small>

ex aquis.

Lesson 27.

nubes, nubis, F., *cloud.*	**brevi**, *shortly.*
plāga, æ, F., *plague, stripe.*	**enim**, *for.*
vulgus, i, N., *people, crowd.*	**interdiu**, *by day.*
desum, deesse, defui, *to fail.*	**noctu**, *by night.*
jubente Deo, *by God's command.*	**nihilomĭnus**, *nevertheless.*
ad unum, *to a man (every one).*	**quod**, *because, that.*
unā ex parte, *on one side.*	**tamquam**, *as-it-were.*
alterā ex parte, *on the other side.*	**tot**, *so many.*
hinc et illinc, *on both sides.*	**super**, *above.*

RELATIVE PRONOUNS.

107. The Relative *who, which,* or *that,* refers to some word before it, which is called the Antecedent. If I say, "The book that I was reading," *book* is the antecedent of *that.*

	SINGULAR.			PLURAL.		
Nom.	qui	quæ	quod	qui	quæ	quæ
Gen.		cujus		quorum	quarum	quorum
Dat.		cui			quibus	
Acc.	quem	quam	quod	quos	quas	quæ
Abl.	quo	qua	quo		quibus	

Decline **quis, aliquis,** and **quidam** (Table **6**).

Learn the Numerals from one hundred to one thousand.

108. Many verbs in Latin are used only in the third person singular, and are called Impersonal Verbs. Examples of these are —

libet mihi ludĕre, *I like (it pleases me) to play ;*

licet tibi ire, *you may go ;*

pœnĭtet me culpæ, *I repent (it repents me) of the fault ;*

miseret eum tui, *he pities you.*

In the first of these examples, **ludere** is the Subject of **libet.**

109. If a verb governs the dative, it must be impersonal in the Passive :

nocet tibi, *he harms you (does harm to you).*

nocētur tibi, *you are harmed (harm is done to you).*

110. A verb which does not govern an object in the active is often impersonal in the passive : as, **pugnātur,** *there is* (or *they are*) *fighting ;* **ventum est,** *they came.*

NOTE. — Such verbs are called Neuter or Intransitive. A verb which governs a direct object is called Transitive.

XIX. *The Red Sea.*

Moses jam senex, jubente Deo, ádiit Pharaonem,
commanding went-to

ei-que [36] præcépit, nómine [41] Dei, ut dimitteret
instructed name let-go

Hebræos. Sed rex ímpius parére [29] mandatis Dei
wicked to-obey commands

recusavit. Moses, ut Pharaonis pertinaciam vín-
refused obstinacy might-

ceret, multa et stupenda édidit prodígia, quæ
conquer many amazing wrought wonders

vocantur plagæ Ægypti. Quum nihilóminus
are-called

Pharao in sententiâ perstaret, Deus interfécit primo-
his-purpose persisted killed

génitum ejus filium, et omnes primogénitos Ægyp-

tiorum. Tandem metu victus rex páruit, dedit-que
conquered obeyed gave

Hebræis discedendi [97] facultatem.
of-departing power

Profecti-sunt Hebræi ex Ægypto, ad sexcenta
went-away   about

millia virorum, præter párvulos, et promiscuum vul-
                   besides   mixed

gus. Eis[36] egrediéntibus præibat colúmna nubis
         going-out   went-before   pillar

intérdiu, et columna ignea[105] noctu, quæ esset dux
              of-fire

viæ; nec umquam, per quadraginta annos défuit[84]

illa columna. Post paucos dies multitudo Hebræo-

rúm pervenit ad littus maris Rubri, íbique castra
    arrived   shore   red   camp

pósuit.

Regem brevi pœnítuit[108] quòd tot millia hóminum
            repented   so-many

dimisisset; et, collecto ingenti exércitu, eos perse-
had-let-go   gathered   vast   army   pur-

cutus-est. Hebræi, quum viderent ex unâ parte se
sued

mari[41] interclusos-esse,[85] ex alterâ parte instare[85]
by-   were-cut-off   was-near

Pharaonem cum ómnibus cópiis, magno timore
                          troops

correpti-sunt.[68] Tunc Deus Mosi "Protende" in-
were-seized   stretch-forth

quit "déxtram tuam super mare, et dívide aquas, ut
        right-hand   above   divide

Hebræis progrediéntibus iter siccum præbeant."
        advancing   dry   afford

Fecit Moses quod jússerat Deus: et quum tenéret
did   had-ordered   held

manum extensam super mare, aquæ divísæ-sunt,[68]
       outstretched   were-parted

et intumescentes hinc et illinc pendebant.[21] Flavit
   swelling   hung   blew

etiam ventus véhemens, quo[41] exsiccatus-est álveus.
      wind   violent   was-dried   channel

Tunc Hebræi ingressi-sunt in mare siccum: erat
             entered

enim aqua tamquam murus a dextrâ eorum et a
                    wall

lævâ. Et omnes ad unum tuti sunt-transgressi.
left   safe   crossed

Rex quoque Ægyptius,[105] insecutus Hebræos,
<small>following</small>

non dubitavit, mare quâ patebat, íngredi[29] cum
<small>hesitated · · · was-open · · · to-enter</small>

universo exércitu. Et quum Ægyptii progrede-
<small>whole · · · advanced</small>

rentur in medio mari, Dóminus subvertit eorum
<small>midst-of · · · overturned</small>

currus, et dejécit équites. Metu perculsi, fúgere
<small>chariots · · cast-down · horsemen · · · struck-through · to-fly</small>

cœpérunt: at Deus dixit Mosi; "Extende rursus
<small>began · · · · · · hold-out</small>

dextram super mare, ut aquæ revertantur in locum
<small>may-return · · · place</small>

suum." Páruit Moses, et statim aquæ refluentes
<small>their · · · · · flowing-back</small>

obruérunt Ægyptios, et eorum currus et équites.
<small>covered · · · · · · horsemen</small>

Deletus-est universus exércitus Pharaonis in médiis
<small>was-destroyed · · whole · · · · · midst-of</small>

flúctibus; nec unus quidem nuntius tantæ cladis
<small>waves · · · · · messenger · so-great · disaster</small>

supérfuit.[84]
<small>survived</small>

Lesson 28.

imāgo, ĭnis, F., *image.*
interdum, *at times.*
lex, legis, F., *law.*
tonitru, ūs, N., *thunder.*
trajecto mari, *when the sea was crossed.*

fulgur, ŭris, N., *lightning.*
radix, īcis, F., *root, foot* (of hill).
porro, *then, further.*
ne, neve, *not, nor* (with imp.).
sive, seu, *whether, or.*

ABLATIVE ABSOLUTE.

111. In the sentence " Charles was sick," the word *Charles*
is Subject, and *sick* Predicate (15). In Latin, the sentence
would be **Carŏlus æger erat**; or, **Carŏlus ægrotabat**: in the
first, the adjective **æger** is called the predicate, and **erat** the
Copula (or *link*); in the second, the neuter verb **ægrotabat**
is the predicate.

Whatever is told of the Subject of a sentence is called the
Predicate.

112. If I wish to say "While Charles was sick," I may use a conjunction, as in English, **dum Carŏlus ægrotabat,** or **quum Carŏlus ægrotaret.** But it is more common to make the predicate a participle or adjective (sometimes a noun), and put it in the ablative, agreeing with the subject (**66**): thus, **Carolo ægrotante,** or **ægro.**

This is called the ABLATIVE ABSOLUTE.

113. When two nouns in a sentence, or a subject and predicate, meaning the same thing, are put in the same case, it is called Apposition. The Ablative Absolute is the apposition of subject and predicate in the ablative. It may be seen in these examples:—

apertā **fiscellā,** *when the basket was opened.*
jubente **Deo,** *(when God commanded) at God's command.*
Josepho præfecto **Ægypti,** *when Joseph was governor of Egypt.*
collecto **exercitu,** *an army having been gathered.*

In translating the last example, it is better to put the participle in the Active Voice, and say, *having gathered an army.*

114. In the following Exercise, the Ten Commandments are given with the Future of the Imperative. This is used especially in Laws and Wills. In examples like these, it is generally translated *thou shalt;* or, with **ne** or **neve,** *thou shalt not.*

With the Imperative **ne** means *not,* and **neve,** *nor.* With the Subjunctive, **ne** generally means *lest,* or *that not.*

xx. *The Ten Commandments.*

Hebræi, trajecto mari[118] Rubro, diu peragrârunt
crossed   wandered-through

vastam solitúdinem.   Déerat[84] panis : at Deus ipse
desolate   wilderness   was-wanting bread

eos áluit; e cælo per annos quadraginta cécidit
fed   fell

cibus, quem appellârunt *Manna.*   Inerat[84] huic
food   called   was-in

cibo[36] gustus símilæ cum melle mixtæ.   Interdum
taste   fine-flour   honey   mixed

etiam défuit aqua : at, jubente Deo,[118] Moses per-

cussit rupem virgâ, et contínuò erupérunt fontes
struck   rock   rod   at-once   broke-out

aquæ dulcis.
     sweet

Mense [42] tertio postquam egressi-sunt ex Ægypto,
                                went-out

pervenérunt ad montem Sinaï.   Ibi Deus dedit eis
arrived   gave

legem cum apparátu terrífico.   Cœpérunt exaudíri
law   display   terrible   began   to-be-heard

tonítrua, micare fúlgura; nubes densa operiebat
          . flash   thick   covered

montem, et clangor búccinæ veheméntiùs perstre-
          noise   trumpet   louder-and-louder sounded

pébat.[21]   Stabat pópulus, præ metu trépidus, ad
stood   people   through   trembling

radíces montis fumantis.[30]   Deus autem locutus-est
                smoking

in monte, e mediâ nube, inter fúlgura et tonítrua.

Hæc porro sunt verba quæ locutus-est Deus:
                    words

"Ego sum Dóminus, qui te eduxi e servitute Ægyp-
                        led-forth   slavery

tiorum. — I. Non erunt tibi [108] dii alieni: ego unus
                              gods strange   alone

sum Deus, et non est alius præter me. — II. Ne
facito [114] neve venerátor imáginem, vel simulácrum
make   worship   likeness

cujúsquam rei, sive in cælo, sive in terrâ, vel in
any

aquis. — III. Ne usurpáto [114] nomen Dei tui témerè
                   employ   rashly

et sine causâ — IV. Diem Sábbati sanctè ágere
        cause   Sabbath   religiously to-spend

memento. — V. Honorato patrem tuum et matrem
remember   honor

tuam, ut vita tua longa sit in terrâ quam Deus tibi
dabit. — VI. Ne hóminem occídito. — VII. Ne
will-give   kill

mœchator. — VIII. Ne fácito-furtum. — IX. Ne
commit-adultery   steal

dícito falsum testimonium adversus proximum [77]
speak   false   witness   against   neighbor

tuum. — x. Ne concupíscito domum, vel uxórem,
<small>covet</small>
vel quidquam quod sit altérius."

Cunctus autem pópulus audivit voces sónitumque
<small>whole   heard   voices   sound</small>
búccinæ, et vidit lámpades montém-que fuman-
<small>flames   smok-</small>
tem; et pertérriti ac pavóre concússi stetérunt pro-
<small>ing   afraid   fear   struck   stood</small>
cul, dicentes Mosi, "Lóquere [28] tu nobis, et audié-
<small>saying   speak   will-</small>
mus; ne [114] loquátur [27] nobis Dóminus, ne [114] forte
<small>hear   lest   perhaps</small>
moriámur." Stetit-que pópulus de-longè. Moses
<small>we-die   stood   far-away</small>
autem accessit ad calíginem in quâ erat Deus; et
<small>approached   darkness</small>
inde prótulit duas tábulas lapídeas, [105] in quibus
<small>brought   tables   of-stone</small>
scripta erat lex.
<small>written   law</small>

Post quadraginta annos profectionis in deserto,
<small>journeying   desert</small>
quum Moses centum et viginti annos natus-esset,
jam-que in conspectu haberet terram a Deo promis-
<small>sight   had   prom-</small>
sam, mortuus-est, — vir sapientiâ, fortitúdine, et
<small>ised   wisdom   courage</small>
multis aliis virtútibus mirè præditus. Et populus
<small>many   virtues   wonderfully   endowed</small>
luxit eum triginta dies.
<small>mourned</small>

Lesson 29.

NUMERALS.

115. The names of the numbers, *one, two, three, &c.*, are called Cardinal Numbers; the adjectives which tell their Order, *first, second, third, &c.*, are Ordinal Numbers. Their Latin names are: —

	CARDINAL.	ORDINAL.	ROMAN NUMERALS.
1.	unus, una, unum, *one*	primus, a, um, *first*	I.
2.	duo, duæ, duo, *two*	secundus (alter), *second*	II.
3.	tres, tria, *three, &c.*	tertius, *third, &c.*	III.
4.	quattuor	quartus	IV.
5.	quinque	quintus	V.
6.	sex	sextus	VI.
7.	septem	septĭmus	VII.
8.	octo	octāvus	VIII.
9.	novem	nonus	IX.
10.	decem	decĭmus	X.
11.	undĕcim	undecĭmus	XI.
12.	duodĕcim	duodecĭmus	XII.
13.	tredĕcim	tertius decĭmus	XIII.
14.	quattuordĕcim	quartus decĭmus	XIV.
15.	quindĕcim	quintus decĭmus	XV.
16.	sedĕcim	sextus decĭmus	XVI.
17.	septendĕcim	septimus decĭmus	XVII.
18.	duodeviginti (octodĕcim)	duodevicesĭmus	XVIII.
19.	undeviginti (novendĕcim)	undevicesĭmus	XIX.
20.	viginti	vicesĭmus (vigesĭmus)	XX.
21.	viginti unus *or* unus et vi-	vicesimus primus, &c.	XXI.
30.	triginta [ginti	tricesimus	XXX.
40.	quadraginta	quadragesimus	XL.
50.	quinquaginta	quinquagesimus	L.
60.	sexaginta	sexagesimus	LX.
70.	septuaginta	septuagesimus	LXX.
80.	octoginta	octogesimus	LXXX.
90.	nonaginta	nonagesimus	XC.
100.	centum	centesimus	C
200.	ducenti, æ, a	ducentesimus	CC.
300.	trecenti	trecentesimus	CCC.
400.	quadringenti	quadringentesimus	CCCC.
500.	quingenti	quingentesimus	IↃ, *or* D.
600.	sexcenti	sexcentesimus	DC.
700.	septingenti	septingentesimus	DCC.
800.	octingenti	octingentesimus	DCCC.
900.	nongenti	nongentesimus	DCCCC.
1000.	mille	millesimus	CIↃ, *or* M.
10,000.	decem millia (milia)	decies millesimus	CCIↃↃ.

116. Unus, una, unum, has the genitive **unius,** and dative **uni** (65). It is sometimes used in the plural, to agree with a noun that means one thing: as, **una castra,** *one camp.*

117. Duo, *two* (also **ambo,** *both*), is thus declined:

	M.	F.	N.
Nom.	duo	duæ	duo
Gen.	duŏrum	duārum	duŏrum
Dat.	duōbus	duābus	duōbus
Acc.	duos (duo)	duas	duo
Abl.	duōbus	duābus	duōbus

118. Tres, tria, *three,* is declined like the plural of **facīlis** (Table 3).

119. The other Cardinal Numbers, up to 100, are not declined. The hundreds, up to 1000, are declined like the plural of **bonus** (Table 3).

120. Mille, *a thousand,* is not declined; **millia (milia),** *thousands,* is declined like the plural of **rete** (Table 1).

Thus we say, **cum mille hominibus,** *with a thousand men;* but,
  cum duobus millibus hominum, or,
  cum bis mille hominibus, *with two thousand men.*

121. The following are called Distributive Numerals, and are inflected like the plural of **bonus:**

1. singuli, *single,* or *one by one*
2. bini, *in pairs,* or *two-and-two*
3. terni or **trini,** *by threes*
4. quaterni
5. quini
6. **seni**
7. **septēni**
8. **octōni**
9. **novēni**
10. **deni,** &c.

122. The following are called Numeral Adverbs:

semel, *once*
bis, *twice*
ter, *three times*
quater, *four times*
quinquies, *five times*
sexies, *six times.*

All the remainder end in **ies** (or **iens**).

Lesson 30.

123. A word is said to Agree with another, when it is in the same gender, number, case, or person; it is said to Govern another, when it requires it to be in a particular Case.

124. That part of Grammar which teaches the Agreement and Government of Words, and their Arrangement in a sentence, is called SYNTAX.

125. Latin Syntax must be learned from a larger Grammar; but the following Rules will be convenient to help in remembering the more common uses of the language.

RULES OF SYNTAX.

1. NOUNS meaning the same thing agree in Case (APPOSITION).

2. ADJECTIVES agree with Nouns in Gender, Number, and Case.

3. RELATIVES agree with their Antecedents in Gender, Number, and Person.

4. A VERB agrees with its Subject in Number and Person.

5. One Noun governs another in the GENITIVE.

6. Words meaning a Part are followed by the Genitive of the word denoting the Whole.

7. Certain Genitives of Quantity, as magni, pluris, and the like, are used to express indefinite Value.

8. Some words of Memory and Feeling, Fullness and Want, govern the Genitive (**39**).

9. Verbs of Accusing and the like take the Genitive of the Charge or Penalty.

10. The DATIVE is generally used for the Indirect Object, or for the Person whose interest is concerned.

11. Verbs signifying to favor, help, command, obey, serve, resist, threaten, be angry, pardon, envy, and trust, govern the Dative.

12. The verb esse, *to be*, with its compounds (except posse and abesse), governs the Dative (**103**).

13. Verbs compounded with ad, ante, con, in, inter. ob, post, præ, pro, re, sub, super, govern the Dative.

14. Verbs of Comparing, Giving, Declaring, and Taking away, govern the Accusative and Dative.

15. The Dative is used to denote Purpose or End, often with another dative of the Person or Thing affected.

16. The Accusative is the case of the Direct Object of a Transitive Verb.

17. The Subject of the Infinitive Mood is in the Accusative.

18. Length of Time and extent of Space are put in the Accusative.

19. Verbs of Asking and Teaching govern two Accusatives.

20. The Ablative is used of Cause, Manner, Means, Instrument, and Price.

21. The Voluntary Agent after a Passive Verb is in the Ablative with **a** or **ab**; after the Gerundive, in the Dative.

22. Words signifying Separation, and Plenty or Want, govern the Ablative.

23. Participles denoting Birth or Origin govern the Ablative.

24. The Adjectives **dignus, indignus, contentus,** and **fretus,** govern the Ablative.

25. The Deponents **utor, fruor, fungor, potior, vescor,** and **dignor** govern the Ablative.

26. The Comparative Degree is followed by the Ablative (*than*)

27. Degree of Difference or Distance is put in the Ablative.

28. Time *when* but in the Ablative.

29. The Subject and Predicate of a subordinate clause are often put in agreement in the Ablative (Ablative Absolute, **112**).

30. The name of the Place *where* is put in what is called the Locative Case: this is generally in form like the Genitive or Dative (see **74**).

31. The name of the Place *whither* is in the Accusative; of the Place *whence* in the Ablative. But with names of Countries, Prepositions are always used to express *where, whither,* or *whence.*

32. One Verb governs another in the Infinitive.

33. The Infinitive is often used for the tenses of the Indicative in narration (Historical Infinitive).

34. Conjunctions which simply connect sentences, or parts of sentences, are followed by the same Case or Mood as that which goes before.

35. Conjunctions — also Relatives — implying Purpose or Result, require the Subjunctive Mood. Thus,

36. Ut (*that*), **ne, quo, quin, quomĭnus;** also **quasi, velutsi, utinam, licet, quum** (*since* or *though*), **dum** (*until*), and **dummŏdo,** — also Indirect Questions — take the Subjunctive.

For the government of Prepositions, see **48, 49, 50.**

Lesson 31.

DERIVATIVES AND COMPOUNDS.

126. In using the Dictionary, it will be a great help to learn carefully the meaning of the following forms:

Feminines in a are formed from masculines in us or er: as, servus, serva, *slave;* magister, magistra, *master, mistress;*

Diminutives in olus, ŭlus, or ellus (a, um), from nouns or adjectives, signifying *little* or *tender* (102);

Nouns ending in tor (M.), or trix (F.), from the Supine of verbs signifying the one who *does a thing:* as, from colo (cultum), *cultivate,* cultor, cultrix;

Adjectives in eus, inus, ilis, anus, ensis, from nouns signifying *possession, material,* or *residence* (105);

Verbal adjectives in bundus, having nearly the meaning of the present participle: as, cogitabundus, *reflecting;*

Adverbs in e or ĭter, formed from Adjectives, and regularly compared (61, 81). For other Derivative forms, see Gr., § 44.

127. Very many Compounds are formed by prefixing a Preposition to a Verb or Adjective. The prepositions most commonly used, with their meaning in the compound, are:

a or ab, *away;*
ad, *to* or *towards;*
ante, *before;*
circum, *around;*
con, *together;*
de, *down, utterly,*
di or dis, *apart;*
e, ex, *out;*
in, *in, on,* or *against* (with adjectives, *not*).

inter, *into* or *to pieces;*
ne, nec, *not;*
ob, *towards, in the way of;*
per or præ, *very;*
re (red), *back* or *again;*
se, *apart;*
sub, *under* or *slightly;*
super, *on, in place of;*

128. A verb is Conjugated, by giving its four Principal Parts: these are, the Indicative Present, the Infinitive, the Perfect, and the Supine: as,

amo, amāre, amavi, amatum, *to love* (1st Conjugation);
cado, cadĕre, cecĭdi, casum, *to fall* (3d Conjugation).

From these parts all the others may be formed; except, in irregular verbs, some of those formed from the Present (99).

DIALOGUES.

NOTE. — The figures in the English column refer to the Foot-notes; in the Latin, to the foregoing Sections; the letter R, to the Rules of Syntax in Lesson 30.

I. — CORDERIUS.

1. *Spending-money.*

Carolus. Abiit-ne [55] pater tuus?

Charles. Is your father gone?

Joannes. Abiit. [54]

John. Yes.

C. Quotâ?

C. At what time? [1]

J. Primâ pomeridianâ. [R. 28]

J. At one in the afternoon.

C. Quid dixit tibi?

C. What did he say to you?

J. Multis verbis me monuit ut diligenter studérem.

J. He said a good deal,[2] and told me to study well.

C. Dedit-ne tibi pecuniam? [R. 14]

C. Did he give you any money?

J. Ut ferè solet.

J. Yes, as usual.

C. Quantum?

C. How much?

J. Nihil ad te.

J. None of your business.

C. Fateor; sed tamen quid fácias istâ pecuniâ?

C. True: but what shall you do with your money?

J. Emam chartam, et alia quæ opus sunt mihi.

J. I shall buy some paper and other things I want.

C. Quid si amíseris?

C. What if you lose it?

J. Animo æquo erit ferendum. [90]

J. I must bear it patiently.

C. Quid si forte egúero; dabis-ne mutuo?

C. What if I happen to want some: will you lend it? [3]

J. Dabo mutuo, et libenter quidem.

J. I will lend it with all pleasure.

C. Ago tibi gratias.

C. Thank you.

---

[1] Understand hora.   [2] He warned me in many words.
[3] Will you give for a loan?

2. *Lending and Borrowing*.

C. Quando exspectas réditum patris?

J. Hinc ad octavum diem.

C. Quî scies diem?

J. Ipse ad me scripsit.

C. Adventus ejus, ut spero, te ditabit.

J. Crœso[R. 20] ditior ero, si bene nummatus vénerit.

C. Tunc reddes mihi[R. 14] mutuum?

J. Ne dúbites, quin si amplius tibi opus erit, non modò mutuum reddam,[R. 36] sed etiam referam gratiam.

C. Quómodo?

J. Vicissim pecuniam mutuam dabo.

C. Nihil opus erit, ut spero.

J. At nescis quid accídere possit.[78]

C. Ago tibi gratias: saluta patrem, meo nomine, ubi redíerit.

J. Ita fáciam: vale.

C. Tu quoque vale.

C. When do you expect your father back?

J. A week from to-day.[1]

C. How will you know the day?

J. He wrote me himself.

C. His coming, I hope, will make you rich.

J. I shall be richer than Crœsus, if he comes with plenty of money.

C. Will you return me the loan then?

J. Do not doubt, but if you need more I will not only repay the loan, but return the favor.

C. How?

J. I will lend you money in turn.

C. I hope there will be no need.

J. But you don't know what may happen.

C. I thank you: when your father comes give him my respects.[2]

J. I will: good-bye.

C. Good-bye to you.

3. *A Sick Mother*.

Magister. Quid sibi vult, quod hac totâ hebdómade[R. 28] abfúeris.

Discipulus. Oportuit[106] me domi[74] manére.

M. Quamobrem?

Master. What does it mean,[3] that you have been away all this week?

Scholar. I had to stay at home.

M. What for?

[1] At the eighth day from here.   [2] Salute in my name.   [3] Wish for itself.

D. Ut adessem matri,[R. 13] quæ ægrotabat.

S. To be with my mother, who was sick.

M. Quid officii[R. 6] ei præstabas?

M. What service did you do for her?

D. Sæpiùs[88] ei legébam.

S. I would often read to her.

M. Quid legebas?

M. What did you read?

D. Aliquid ex litteris sacris, aliis-que bonis libris.

S. Something from the Bible and other good books.

M. Sanctum et laudábile ministerium istud erat: sed quid, nihil aliud agebas?

M. A right and praiseworthy service: but what, did you do nothing else?

D. Quoties erat opus, ministrabam ei[R. 13] cum ancillâ.

S. As often as there was need, I waited on her, with the maid.

M. Sunt-ne hæc vera?

M. Is this true?

D. Ecce[88] testimonium.

S. Here is a certificate.

M. Quis scripsit?

M. Who wrote it?

D. Fámulus noster, nomine matris.

S. Our man-servant, in mother's name.

M. Agnosco manum ejus, quia sæpe mihi litteras ab illo attulisti.

M. I know his hand: as you have often brought me notes from him.

D. Licet-ne[105] ígitur in sedem redire?

S. May I go back to my seat, then?

M. Quidni licet, quum mihi[80] satisféceris?[R. 80]

M. Why not, since I am satisfied?

4. *A Morning Walk.*

M. Heus,[83] puer!

M. Halloo boy!

D. Hem præceptor, quid vis?

S. Ah, teacher! what do you want?

M. Pone libros: totum diem[R. 18] satis studuisti: para te ut eamus ambulatum.[96]

M. Put by your books: you have studied hard all day: get ready for a walk.

D. Nonne præstaret post cenam?

S. Wouldn't it be better after supper?

M. Exercitatio córporis salubrior est ante cibum.

M. Active[1] exercise is wholesomer before eating.

[1] Of the body.

D. Sed quò prodíbimus ?

M. Extra urbem.

D. Mutabo-ne cálceos ?

M. Muta, ne conspergas [a.86] is-tos novos púlvere : sume umbellam, ne ardor solis faciem tibi [a.10] obfuscet.

D. Adsum,[64] jam paratus.

M. Nunc sanè prodeamus.

D. Vocabo-ne unum aut alte-rum cómitem ex viciniâ ?

M. Rectè ádmones : sic enim deambulatio jucundior erit; nam sermónes inter vos per viam conferétis, et alícubi sub umbrâ col-ludetis.

D. Quid si nullos cómites invé-nero ?

M. Nihilóminus séquere [88] me : audîsti-ne ?

D. Audivi,[54] præceptor.

S. But where shall we go ?

M. Out of town.

S. Shall I change my shoes ?

M. Yes, so as not to soil your new ones with dirt : and take an umbrella, so that the glare of the sun may not tan your face.

S. I am on hand, all ready.

M. Now, then, let us go.

S. Shall I call a companion or two from the neighbor-hood ?

M. A good idea[1] : for so the walk will be pleasanter ; for you can have a talk on the way, and play together here and there in the shade.

S. What if I find no play-fellows ?

M. Follow me all the same : do you hear ?

S. Yes, sir.

5. *Luncheon.*

Guilielmus. Quid mater tibi dedit in merendam ?

Jacobus. Vide.

G. Est caro : sed quænam ?

J. Búbula.

G. Utrùm est recens, an salíta ?

J. Est búbula salíta.

G. Utrùm est pinguis, an macra ?

J. Eho [83] inepte ! nonne vides esse [85] macram ?

William. What did your mother give you for lunch ?

James. See.

W. It is meat : but what sort ?

J. Beef.

W. Is it fresh, or salt ?

J. It is salt beef.

W. Is it fat, or lean ?

J. You stupid ! don't you see it is lean ?

---

[1] You advise rightly.

G. Annon malis esse vituli-nam, aut vervecínam ?

W. Hadn't you rather it would be veal, or mutton ?

J. Utraque bona est, sed præ céteris hædina mihi pla-cet, præsertim assa.

J. Either is good ; but I like kid's meat best, espe-cially roasted.

G. Hem delicátule ![103] habes-ne tam doctum palátum ?

W. Oh you dainty fellow ! have you such a choice palate ?

J. Dico ut sentio : non enim est mentiendum.[97]

J. I say as I think : for we must not lie.

G. At ego contrà suillam amo, módico sale adspersam, et bene coctam.

W. But for my part, I like pork, sprinkled with a little salt, and well done.

J. Quot paúperes in hac urbe putas esse,[85] qui pane hor-deáceo solo víctitant, nec tamen ad saturitatem !

J. How many poor people do you think there are in town, who live on nothing but barley-bread, and not enough of that ?[1]

G. Non dúbito esse[86] multos, præsertim tantâ caritate[113] annonæ.

W. No doubt there are many, especially now that pro-visions are so dear.

J. Itaque quantas gratias Deo ágere debemus, in tantâ copiâ bonarum rerum !

J. What thanks, then, we ought to pay God, in such plenty of good things !

6. *A Mote in the Eye.*

Edvardus. Obsecro te da mihi óperam paulisper.

Edward. Pray, help me a little while.

Georgius. Quid est illud ?

George. What is that ?

E. Nescio quid íncidit in ocu-lum meum, quod me valde malè habet.

E. Something[2] has fallen into my eye, which hurts me very badly.[3]

G. In utrum óculum íncidit ?

G. Which eye did it fall into ?

E. In dextrum.

E. Into the right.

G. Vis inspíciam ?

G. Do you wish me to look at it ?

E. Inspice, obsecro te.

E. Do, I beg you.

G. Aperi quantum potes, et tene immótum.

G. Open it as wide as you can, and hold still.

---

[1] Nor yet to fulness.   [2] I know not what.   [3] Has me very ill.

E. Non possum a nictu con-tinére.

E. I can't keep from winking.

G. Mane, égomet sinistrâ manu [R. 20] tenébo.

G. Stop, I will hold it with **my** left hand.

E. Ecquid vides?

E. Do you see any thing?

G. Video àliquid minútum.

G. I see some little thing.

E. Exime, quæso, si potes.

E. Pray take it out if you **can**.

G. Exémi.

G. I have got it out.

E. O bene factum! quid est?

E. Good! what is it?

G. Cerne tu ipse.

G. Look yourself.

E. Est mica púlveris.

E. It is a speck of dust.

G. Est quidem adeò exigua, ut vix cerni possit. [R. 86]

G. In fact it is so small it can hardly be seen.

E. Vide quantum dolóris tam exigua res ásferat! [78] Nonne óculus rubet?

E. See how much pain such a little thing gives. Isn't my eye red?

G. Aliquántulum, [108] quòd fricu-isti.

G. A little, because you rub-bed it.

E. Credin' mihi adhuc do-lére? [108]

E. Do you think it pains me now?

G. Quidni credam, qui talem molestiam tóties sum expertus?

G. Why not? since I have felt the same trouble so often?

E. Quid præmii médico dabo pro labore?

E. What fee shall I pay the doctor for his trouble?

G. Quantum pacti-sumus. [69]

G. What we agreed on.

E. Nihil ergo: sed tamen maximas tibi gratias habeo.

E. Nothing, then: but I thank you with all my heart.

II. — ERASMUS.

1. *A Morning Call and Walk.*

Carolus. Heus, heus, puer! [88] nemon' huc prodit?

Charles. Halloo boy! will nobody show his head? [1]

Henricus. Hic, opínor, effrin-get fores. Familiarem oportet [108]

Henry. I think that fellow will break down the door. He

[1] Come forth hither.

esse. O lepidum caput! Quid affers,[20] mi Carole?

C. Meipsum.

H. Næ tu rem haud magni pretii huc attulisti.

C. Atqui magno[R.20] cónstiti patri meo.

H. Credo, pluris[R.7] quàm revendi possis.

C. Céterùm, Jacóbus estne domi?

H. Incertus sum : sed visam.

C. Quin potius abi, et roga ipsum an velit nunc esse domi.

H. Abi tu potiùs, sisque tibi ipsi Mercurius.

C. Heus Jacobe, num[12] es domi?

Jacóbus. Non sum.[54]

C. Impudens : non ego audio te loquentem?

J. Immo, tu impudentior : nuper ancillæ[R.11] tuæ crédidi te non esse[85] domi, et tu non credis mihi ipsi?

C. Æquum dicis : par pari relatum.

J. Equidem ut non omnibus dormio, ita non omnibus sum domi : tibi posthac semper ero.

C. Sed tu mihi vidéris cochleæ ágere vitam.

J. Quî sic?

C. Quia perpetuò domi láti- tas, nec usquam prorépis. Nec

ought to be on easy terms here. My dear fellow![1] What have you got here, Charley?

C. Only myself.

H. Truly, you bring what isn't worth much.[2]

C. At any rate I cost some- thing to my father.

H. More than you will ever sell for, I reckon.

C. Well—is James at home?

H. I don't know : I'll go see.

C. Better[3] go and ask him whether he chooses to be at home.

H. Go yourself, and be your own errand-boy.[4]

C. Halloo James! are you at home.

James. No.

C. That's cool :[5] don't I hear you say so?

J. You are cooler yet : I believed your maid-servant, when she said you were not in, and now you won't believe me!

C. Very good : a very fair hit.[6]

J. In fact, I am not asleep to everybody, and not at home to everybody : but I shall always be at home *to you.*

C. It seems to me you lead a snail's life.

J. How so?

C. Because you are always hiding at home, and never

---

[1] O pleasant head. [2] Of no great price. [3] Nay, but.
[4] Mercury (the messenger of Jupiter). [5] Shameless. [6] Like returned for like.

secus atque claudus sutor, ju-
giter domi[74] désides. Tu tibi
domi situm cóntrahis.

J. Est quod agam[2. 36] domi,
foris nihil est negotii. Et siquid
esset,[37] tamen hoc cælum me
dies áliquot a público cohibu-
isset.

C. At nunc sudum est, et
invitat ad deambulandum.[97]
Vide, ut blandítur.

J. Si prodeambulare lubet, non recúso.

C. Planè videtur hoc uten-
dum[97] cælo.[2. 36]

J. Súperest[84] ut locum di-
spícias amœnum.

C. Ego verò tibi locum os-
tendam, ubi nec némoris[2. 6]
umbram, nec pratorum sma-
rágdinum virorem, nec fon-
tium vivas scátebras desidera-
bis. Dices dignam Musis[2. 84]
sedem.

J. Magnfficè polliceris.

C. Nimiùm affixus es libris:[86] nimiùm ássides libris:
immódico studio[2. 90] teipsum
máceras.

J. Malim studio macres-
cere[100] quam amóre.

C. At non ideo vívimus ut
studeámus; ideo studémus ut
suáviter vivámus.

J. Mihi verò vel ímmori
chartis[2. 18] dulce est.

crawl out any where: always
stay at home, just like[1] a lame
cobbler. You are getting all
rusty here.

J. I have plenty to do here,
and no business out-doors.
And if I had, such a day as
this would have kept me out of
the street these many days.

C. But it is fair now, and
tempts one to a walk. See how
soft it is!

J. If you like to stroll about,
I am willing.

C. We certainly ought to
take advantage of this weather.

J. Then[2] you have to look
out for a pleasant place.

C. I will show you a place
where you will not lack the
shade of trees, nor the emerald
green of meadows, nor the
fresh bubbling of springs: you
will call it a seat fit for the
muses.

J. You promise famously.

C. You are too tied to your
books: you stick too close to
books: you are getting lean
with immoderate study.

J. I'd rather pine with study
than love.

C. Pooh! we don't live for
the sake of study: we study
so as to live agreeably.

J. As for me, I should like[3]
to die amongst my papers.

---

[1] Not otherwise than.   [2] It remains that.

[3] It is sweet to me.

C. Equidem immorari probo: ímmori non probo. — Ecquid voluptati [104] fuit hæc deambulatio ?

J. Me quidem vehementer oblectavit.

2. *A Trial of Jumping.*

Ricardus. Libetne [108] decertare saltu ?

Joannes. Ludus iste non cónvenit pransis.[96]

R. Quamobrem ?

J. Quia ventris suburra gravat corpus.

R. Non ádmodum sanè iis [B. 10] qui pransi sunt in pædagogio : nam hi plerumque cænaturiunt priusquàm absólverint prandium.

J. Quod ígitur saliendi [97] genus placet ?

R. Auspicemur [97] ab eo quod est simplicissimum, — a saltu locustarum, sive mavis [90] ranarum, — utrâque tibiâ, sed junctis pédibus.[112] Qui longissimè promóverit cíngulum, coronam feret. Hujus ubi erit satietas, aliud atque aliud genus experiemur.

J. Equidem nullum recusabo genus, nisi quod géritur cum periculo tibiarum : nolim mihi [103] esse rem cum chirurgis.

C. I like staying among them well enough : dying, I don't like that. — Well, how have you enjoyed the walk ?

J. I was perfectly charmed [1] with it.

Richard. Should you like a match at jumping ?

John. That's no game for after dinner.[2]

R. Why not ?

J. Because the ballast inside [3] weighs you down.

R. Not very much those that dine at the school-table : they generally want their supper before they have done dinner.

J. What sort of jumping do you like ?

R. Let's begin with the easiest, — grasshoppers' jump, or frogs' jump if you like it better, — with both legs, and feet together. The one that gets his belt furthest takes the prize. When we have had enough of that, we'll try another sort, and then another.

J. I shan't object to any, unless it [4] is dangerous to my shins ; I don't want any thing to do with the doctors.

---

[1] It greatly delighted me.　[2] Those who have dined.　[3] Of the stomach.
[4] What is done.

R. Quid si certemus unâ tibiâ?

J. Iste ludus est Empusæ: valeat.

R. Hastæ innixum salire cum primis est elegans.

J. Liberalius est certare cursu. En, designa stadium: hoc loco sit carcer, quercus ista sit meta.

R. Sed útinam adesset Ænéas, qui propónat et præmia victori.

J. Victori [108] abundè magnum præmium est gloria.

R. Victo potius dandum [96] erat præmium, solatii gratiâ.

J. Sit ígitur victo præmium, ut lappâ coronatus redeat in urbem.

R. Equidem non recusârim, si tu præcédas tibiâ canens.

J. Est ingens æstus.

R. Nec mirum, cùm sit [2, 36] solstítium æstivum.

J. Præstíterat natare.

R. Mihi non placet ranarum vita. Animal sum terrestre, non amphibium.

J. Sed tamen hoc exercitamenti genus olim cum primis habebatur liberale.

R. Immo etiam utile.

J. Ad quid?

R. Si fugiendum [97] sit in bello, ibi potíssimùm valent qui

R. What if we try on one leg?

J. That's hop-scotch: none of that.

R. Jumping with a pole is first-rate.[1]

J. A foot-race[2] is more manly. Here, mark out the course: let the bounds be just here, and the goal yonder oak.

R. I wish Æneas was here, to give prizes to the one that beats.

J. Glory is prize enough for the conqueror.

R. The prize should rather be given to the one that's beaten, to comfort him.

J. Let him have the prize, then, of going back to town with a wreath of burrs.

R. I am willing,[3] if you will go ahead playing on a whistle.

J. It's tremendously hot.[4]

R. No wonder, as it is midsummer.[5]

J. It would have been better to swim.

R. I don't like a frog's life. I am a land animal, and not amphibious.

J. But that sort of exercise used to be reckoned particularly manly.

R. Yes, and very useful too.

J. Useful for what?

R. If you want to run away in battle, those have the best

---

[1] Elegant among the first.　　[2] To strive in running.　　[3] May not refuse.
[4] Great heat.　　[5] Summer solstice.

sese cursu pedum et natatu exercuérunt.

J. Artem narras haudquaquam aspernandam.⁹⁸ Neque enim minus laudis est aliquando bene fugere, quam fortiter pugnare.

R. Sum planè rudis et imperítus natandi ; nec sine perículo versamur in alieno elemento.

J. Sed assuéscere oportet.¹⁰⁸ *Nemo náscitur ártifex.*ᵃˑ¹

R. At ego istíus géneris artífices⁹⁵ permultos audio natâsse, sed non enatâsse.

J. Experiéris primùm innixus súberi.⁹⁶

R. Nec súberi fido magis quàm pedibus. Si vobis cordi¹⁰⁴ est natatio, spectator esse malo⁹⁰ quàm certator.

of it¹ who have practised running and swimming.

J. It is an art not to be despised. Sometimes there is no less glory in running well, than in fighting bravely.

R. I am quite raw and unskilful in swimming: and it is dangerous to venture in a strange element.

J. But you must get used to it. "Nobody is born a workman."

R. But a good many who have practised that way, I hear, have swum out and never swum back.

J. You will begin by trying with a cork-belt.

R. I trust a cork no more than I do my feet. If you like swimming,² I had rather be a looker-on than in the game.

3. *The Young Sportsmen.*

Paulus. "*Trahit sua quemque voluptas.*" Mihi⁹⁸ placet venatio.

Thomas. Placet et mihi: sed ubi canes? ubi venábula? ubi casses?

P. Valeant apri, ursi, cervi et vulpes; nos insidiemur⁹⁹ cuniculis.

Richardus. At ego laqueos injiciam locustis: insidiabor gryllis.⁹⁸

Paul. "*Every one to his liking.*" I like hunting.

Thomas. So do I: but where are the dogs? where are the guns?³ where are the traps?

P. No matter for boars and bears, deer and foxes: let's hunt rabbits.

Richard. But I will go noose grasshoppers: I'll set traps for crickets.

¹ Prevail most of all.   ² If swimming is to your heart.   ³ Hunting-spears.

Joannes. Ego ranas captabo.

Guilielmus. Ego papiliones venabor.

J. Difficile est sectari[60] volantia.

G. Difficile, sed pulchrum: nisi pulchrius[79] esse ducis sectari lúmbricos aut cochleas, quia carent alis.

J. Equidem malo insidiari piscibus: est mihi[108] hamus élegans.

G. Sed unde parabis escam?

J. Lumbricorum ubique est magna copia.

G. Est, si tibi velint prorépere e terrâ.

J. At ego mox efficiam ut multæ myríades prosiliant.

G. Quo pacto? incantamentis?

J. Videbis artem. Imple hanc sítulam aquâ. Hos juglandium summos córtices virentes confractos immítito. Hac aquâ perfunde solum. Nunc observa paulisper: vides emergentes?

G. Rem prodigiosam vídeo. Sic olim, opínor, exsiliebant armati ex satis * serpentis dentibus. Sed pleríque pisces delicatioris[79] et elegantioris sunt paláti, quàm ut escâ tam vulgari capiantur.

J. Novi quoddam insecti genus quo talibus insidiari soleo.

John. And I will catch frogs.

William. I will hunt butterflies.

J. It is hard to chase things that fly.

W. Hard, but glorious: unless you think it finer to chase worms and snails, because they have no wings.

J. I had rather catch fish: I've got a splendid hook.

W. But where will you get your bait?

J. There's plenty of worms everywhere.

W. Yes, if they will only crawl out of the ground for you.

J. But I will make thousands of them jump out in a minute.

W. How? by witchcraft?

J. You shall see the way. Fill this bucket with water. Put in these broken bits of green walnut-hulls. Drench the ground with this water. Now watch awhile: do you see them coming up?

W. I see an astonishing thing. Just so, I suppose, the armed men sprang up once from the sowing of serpents' teeth. But most fishes have too dainty and nice a palate to be taken with such vulgar bait.

J. I know a sort of fly, that I generally catch that kind with.

---

* Participle of *sero*, to sow.

G. Tu vide an possis impó-
nere píscibus : [20] ego ranis faces-
sam negotium.

J. Quómodo ? reti ?

G. Non, sed arcu.

J. Novum piscandi genus.

G. At non injucundum. Videbis et fatéberis.

R. Quid si nos duo micemus
dígitis.

P. Ignavum est ac rústicum
lusûs genus. Ad focum desi-
déntibus magis cónvenit, quàm
in campo versántibus.

R. Quid si certemus núcibus.

P. Nuces ádmodum púeris
relinquamus : nos grandiús-
culi [102] sumus.

R. Et tamen nihil aliud
adhuc quàm púeri sumus.

P. Sed quibus decórum est
lúdere núcibus, iisdam non in-
decórum est equitare in arún-
dine longâ.

R. Tu ígitur præscríbito [114]
lusûs genus : sequar quocum-
que vocâris.

P. Et ego futurus sum ómnium horarum homo.

W. You see if you can take
in the fish : I'll do the business
for the frogs.

J. How ? with a net ?

W. No — with a bow-and-
arrows.

J. A new style of fishing.

W. But it's jolly, as you
will own when you see it.

R. Suppose we two play
odd-or-even.

P. That is a mean and lub-
berly sort of game — more fit
for idlers by the fire than for
playing out-of-doors.

R. Suppose we play marbles.

P. Let us leave that to little
boys ; we are rather too big.

R. And yet we are nothing
else but boys.

P. But those who are suited
with playing marbles, might as
well ride horseback on a long
stick.

R. You then direct the sort
of play : I will follow, wherever you say.

P. And I will be your man
for any thing.

4. *A Shipwreck.*

Antonius. Horrenda narras !
Est istuc navigare ? Prohíbeat
Deus, ne mihi quidquam un-
quam tale veniat in mentem.

Bernardus. Immo quod hác-
tenus memoravi, lusus merus
est, præ his quæ nunc audies.

Antonio. A dreadful story !
Is that going to sea ? God forbid any such thing should ever
come into my mind.

Bernardo. But what I have
told you so far, is mere sport to
what you shall hear now.

A. Plus satis malorum audivi: inhorresco te memorante,[112] quasi ipse periculo[B. 13] intersim.

B. Immo mihi jucundi sunt acti[95] labores. Eâ nocte quiddam áccidit, quod magnâ ex parte spem salutis adémit naucléro.[B. 14]

A. Quid, obsecro.

B. Nox erat sublustris: et in summo malo stabat quidam e nautis in galeâ, — sic enim vocant, opínor, — circumspectans, si quam terram vidéret: huic[96] cœpit adsístere sphæra quædam ignea: id nautis tristissimum ostentum est, si quando solitárius ignis est; felix, quum gémini. Hos vetustas crédidit Castorem et Pollucem.

A. Quid illis[106] cum nautis, — quorum alter fuit eques, alter pugil ?

B. Sic visum est poetis. Nauclérus, qui clavo[96] assidebat, "Socie,"[88] inquit (nam eo nomine se mutuò compellant nautæ), "videsne quod sodalitium tibi claudat latus?" "Video," respondit ille, "et precor ut sit felix." Mox globus igneus,[105] delapsus per funes, devolvit sese usque ad nauclerum.

A. Num ille exanimatus est metu ?

B. Nautæ assuevêre mon-

A. I have heard more than enough of horrors: I shudder while you speak, as if I myself were in the same danger.

B. Nay, but past dangers are pleasant to me. That night a thing happened which almost took from the captain any hope of safety.

A. What was that, pray ?

B. It was a glimmering night; and at the mast-head stood one of the sailors on the round-top — I think they call it — looking round if he could see any land. Near him a ball of fire began to rest; this is a very unlucky sign for sailors, if ever it is a single flame, but lucky when there are two. These the ancients thought were Castor and Pollux.

A. What have they to do with sailors, — one of them a horseman, and one a boxer?

B. So the poets saw it. The captain, who stood by the helm calls out, "Ho, shipmate," says he (for sailors hail one another by that name), "do you see what company you have got, hiding your side?" "Yes, sir," he answered, "and I pray it may be good luck." Presently the fire-ball slid down the rigging, and rolled close up to the captain.

A. He wasn't out of breath with fear ?

B. Sailors get used to strange

stris. Ibi paulisper commoratus, volvit se per márgines totíus [65] navis : inde per medios foros dilapsus evanuit. Sub meridiem cœpit magis ac magis incrudescere tempestas. Vidistine [66] unquam Alpes ?

A. Vidi.[54]

B. Illi montes verrúcæ sunt, si conferantur ad undas maris. Quoties tollebamur in altum, licuisset [108] lunam dígito [R. 20] contíngere : quoties demittebamur, videbamur, dehiscente terrâ,[112] rectâ ire in Tártara.

A. O insános, qui se credunt mari ! [R. 11]

B. Nautis frustra luctantibus [R. 20] cum tempestate, tandem nauclerus totus pallens nos ádiit.

A. Is pallor præságit aliquod magnum malum.

B. "Amici" inquit, "desii esse dóminus [15] navis meæ : réliquum est ut spem nostram collocemus in Deo, et quisque se paret ad extrema."

A. O veré Scythicam concionem !

B. "In primis autem," inquit, "exoneranda [96] est navis ; sic jubet necessitas, durum telum : [R. 1] præstat consúlere vitæ, dispendio [R. 20] rerum, quàm simul cum rebus interire." Persuasit véritas : projecta sunt in

things. After staying there a while, it rolled all along the ship's bulwarks, then went down the main hatchway and disappeared. Towards noon, the storm began to rage more and more. Did you ever see the Alps ?

A. Yes.

B. Those mountains are warts, if you compare them to the sea-waves. Whenever we were lifted up, we might have touched the moon with a finger : whenever we went down, it seemed as if the earth were gaping, and we were going straight to the bottomless pit.

A. Madmen, who trust themselves to the sea !

B. As the sailors were fighting in vain against the storm, at last the captain comes to us, all pale.

A. That paleness means some great mischief.

B. "Friends," said he, "I am no longer master of my ship : for the rest, we must put our hope in God, and every one make ready for the end."

A. Truly, a speech fit for a wild Indian.

B. "But first of all," said he, "we must lighten the ship ; so necessity compels — a hard weapon : it is better to look out for your life at the cost of the goods, than go to the bottom with them." The truth

mare plurima[98] vasa plena pretiosis mércibus.[R. 28]

A. Hoc erat verè jacturam fácere.

B. Aderat Italus quidam, qui legatum égerat apud regem Scotiæ; huic[108] erat scrínium plenum vasis argenteis,[105] annulis, panno, ac vestimentis séricis.

A. Is nolebat decídere cum mari ?

B. Non: sed cupiebat aut perire cum amícis ópibus suis, aut simul cum iis servari. Itaque refragabatur.

A. Quid nauclerus ?

B. "Per nos," inquit, "licéret[108] cum tuis perire solum: sed æquum non est, ut nos omnes tui scrinii causâ periclitemur:[R. 38] aļíoqui te unà cum scrinio dábimus in mare præcípitem."

A. Orationem verè naúticam.

B. Sic Italus quoque jactúram fecit, multa mala precans et súperis et ínferis, quod suam vitam elemento tam bárbaro credidisset.

A. Agnosco vocem Italicam.

B. Paulo[R. 27] post venti, nihilo mitiores facti nostris muneribus, rupère funes, disjecère vela.

A. O calamitatem !

B. Ibi rursus nos adit nauta.

persuades: very many bales of precious wares are thrown overboard.

A. That was an overthrow, indeed !

B. There was an Italian fellow, who had been envoy with the king of Scotland : he had a chest full of silver plate, rings, cloth, and silk dresses.

A. Wasn't he willing to make terms with the sea ?

B. No: he chose to be lost with his darling treasures, or else be saved with them. And so he held back.

A. What said the Captain ?

B. "For all me," says he, "you might go to the bottom alone, with your goods : but it is not fair for all of us to risk our lives for that chest of yours ; and so we will pitch you overboard head-first, chest and all."

A. Truly a sailor's speech.

B. So the Italian, too, lost his goods, with many imprecations to saints and devils, that he had trusted his life to so wild an element.

A. I know the Italian style.

B. Presently the winds, made none the kinder by our gifts, broke the rigging, and tore the sails to pieces.

A. What a misfortune !

B. Here a sailor comes up to us again.

A. Concionaturus ?[94]

B. Salutat : " Amici," inquit, "tempus hortatur ut unusquisque se Deo commendet, ac morti se præparet."

A. Hæc concio durior etiam erat priore.[B. 26]

B. Hæc ubi locutus est, jubet incídi funes omnes, ac malum usque ad thecam, cui inséritur, incídi serrâ, ac simul cum antennis devolvi in mare.

A. Cur hoc ?

B. Quoniam, sublato aut lacero velo,[B. 39] erat oneri[104] non usui : tota spes erat in clavo.

A. Quid interea vectores ?

B. Ibi vidisses míseram rerum faciem : nautæ canentes *Salve Regina !* implorabant matrem Vírginem, appellantes eam *Stellam maris, Dominam mundi, Portum salutis,* aliisque multis títulis illi[36] blandientes. Nonnulli, procumbentes in tabulas, adorabant mare, quidquid erat olei effundentes in undas, non áliter illi blandientes, quàm[B. 34] solémus irato príncipi.

A. Quid aiebant ?

B. " *O clementissimum mare ! O generosissimum mare ! O ditissimum mare ! O formosissimum mare ! mitesce, serva !* " hujúsmodi multa occinebant surdo mari. . . .

A. To make a speech ?

B. He hails us : " Friends," says he, " the time warns every man to commit himself to God, and prepare for death."

A. A harder speech than that before.

B. When he had said this, he orders all the ropes to be cut, and the mast to be sawed off close to the socket it is set into, and to be hove overboard, spars and all.

A. Why was that ?

B. Because, as the sail was carried off or torn, it was a burden and no use : the only hope was in the helm.

A. How about the passengers ?

B. There you might see a sad state of things : the sailors, singing " Hail Queen ! " besought the Virgin Mother, calling her *Star of the sea, Mistress of the world, Port of safety,* and flattering her with many other titles. Some, falling on deck, prayed to the sea, pouring upon the waves whatever oil there was, and flattering it just as we do an angry prince.

A. What did they say ?

B. " Oh most merciful sea ! Oh most noble sea ! Oh most wealthy sea ! Oh most beauteous sea ! grow calm and save us ! " many things like that they shouted to the deaf sea.

Unum audívi, non sine risu, qui clarâ voce, ne non exaudiretur, pollicebatur Christóphoro, qui est Lutetiæ in summo templo — mons veriùs quàm statua — cereum tantum quantus esset ipse. Hæc cùm vociferans quantùm poterat, idéntidem inculcaret, qui forté proximus adsistebat, illi notus, cúbito tétigit eum, ac submónuit: "Vide quid pollicearis:[18] etiam si rerum omnium tuarum auctionem facias, non fúeris solvendo."[W] Tum ille, voce jam pressiore, ne vidélicet exaudiret Christóphorus: "Tace," inquit, "fátue: an credis me ex animi sententiâ loqui? Si semel contígero terram, non daturus sum illi candélam sebaceam." . . .

Inter omnes, nullus se tranquilliùs agebat, quàm mulier quædam, cui erat infantulus[108] in sinu, quem lactabat.

A. Quid illa?

B. Sola nec vociferabatur, nec flebat, nec pollicitabatur: tantùm, complexa puellum, precabatur tácitè. Intereà dum navis subinde illideretur vado, nauclerus, metuens ne tota solveretur, rudentibus eam cinxit a prorâ et a puppi.

A. O miserum præsidium!

B. Interim exóritur quidam sacríficus senex, annos[2,18] natus

I couldn't help laughing to hear one, who in a loud voice, lest he might not be heard, promised St. Christopher in the great church at Paris (more a mountain than a statue), a wax-candle as big as himself. As he kept shouting this, as loud as he could bawl, an acquaintance of his, who happened to be standing close by, nudged him with his elbow, and gave him a hint: "Look out what you promise; you couldn't pay if you should make an auction of all your goods." Then he, in a lower voice, so that Christopher might not hear him, "Hold your tongue," says he, "you fool: do you suppose I mean what I say? If I once reach land, I don't mean to give him a single tallow candle." . . .

Among all, there was none kept calmer than a woman with a baby at her breast, which she was nursing.

A. What did she do?

B. She alone neither cried out, nor wept, nor made promises: only hugging the child she prayed silently. Meantime, as the ship struck bottom now and then, the captain, for fear she would all go to pieces, bound her, stem and stern, with ropes.

A. A wretched shift!

B. Presently an old priest gets up, a man of sixty, named

sexaginta; nomen erat Ad-ámus: is abjectis vestibus [R. 29] usque ad indusium, abjectis etiam ocreis et calceis, jussit ut omnes pararemus nos ad natandum.[97] Dum hæc aguntur, redit ad nos nauta lacrimabundus. "Paret," inquit, "se quisque; nam navis non erit nobis usui[104] ad quartam horæ partem." Jam enim, locis áliquot convulsa, hauriebat mare. Paulo post, nauta renuntiat nobis, se vidére [95] procul turrim sacram, adhortans ut divi,[R. 5] quisquis esset ejus templi præses, auxilium imploremus. Procumbunt omnes, et orant ignotum divum.

A. Si nómine compellâssetis eum, fortassis audîsset.

B. Erat ignotum. Interim nauclerus, quantum potest, eò navim dírigit — jam laceram, jam úndique combibentem undas; ac planè dilapsuram,[94] ni rudentibus fuisset succincta.

A. Dura rerum conditio!

B. .. Jam mare totam navim occupârat, ut nihilo [R. 27] tutiores essemus futuri [96] in navi quàm in mari.

A. Hîc ad sacram áncoram confugiendum erat.[97]

B. Immo ad miseram. Nautæ scapham exónerant aquâ,[R. 98] ac dimittunt in mare. In hanc

Adam: he strips to the shirt, throws off his shoes and leather hose, and bids us all get ready to swim. Meantime, the sailor comes back to us, all in tears. "Every one get ready," says he; "the ship will not serve us a quarter of an hour more." For already it was leaking in several places, and taking in the water. A little after, the sailor calls out that he sees a church-spire at a distance, and tells us to pray for the help of the saint, whoever it was, the guardian of that church. All fall down, and pray to the unknown saint.

A. If you had called him by his name, perhaps he would have heard.

B. We did not know it. Meantime the captain steers the ship as well as he can towards it — already breaking up and leaking every where: and it would have gone quite to pieces, unless it had been undergirt with ropes.

A. A hard state of things!

B. .. Now the sea had filled the whole ship, so that we were likely to be no safer aboard than overboard.

A. Here you must take to your sheet-anchor.

B. A poor one at that. The sailors bale out the long-boat and let her down into the

omnes sese conantur conjícere: nautis magno tumultu reclamantibus, scapham non esse[85] capacem tantæ multitudinis; arríperet sibi quisque quod posset, ac nataret. Res non patiebantur lenta consilia: alius árripit remum, alius contum, alius alveum, alius sítulam, alius tábulam; ac suo quisque præsidio nitentes, committunt se flúctibus.

A. Quid ínterim áccidit illi muliérculæ,[102] quæ sola non ejulabat?

B. Illa omnium prima pervénit ad littus.

A. Quî potuit?

B. Imposueramus eam repandæ tabulæ,[R. 18] et sic alligaveramus, ut non fácilè posset decídere: dédimus illi tabellam in manu, quâ[R. 36] vice remi uteretur: ac bene precantes exposúimus in fluctus, conto protrudentes, ut abesset a navi, unde erat perículum; illa lævâ tenens infántulum,[102] dextrâ remigabat.

A. O viráginem! scapha pervénit incólumis?

B. Nulli priùs periêre. Porro triginta sese in eam conjécerant.

A. Quo malo fato id factum est?

B. Priùs quàm posset se liberare a magnâ navi, illíus vacillatione subversa est.

water. Every body tries to force himself aboard of her: the sailors calling out in great confusion that the boat can never hold such a crowd; every one must catch hold of what he can, and swim. The affair suffers no long debate: one man snatches an oar, one a pole, one a pump, one a bucket, one a plank; every man helps himself, and so they plunge into the waves.

A. Meantime, what happened to that poor woman— the only one that did not cry?

B. She was the very first that got to land.

A. How could she?

B. We had put her on a wide plank, and fastened her on so that she could not well fall off: we put a board in her hand, to use for an oar: and with our blessing launched her into the waves, pushing her off with a pole to keep clear of the ship, where the danger was: and so, holding the child in her left hand, she rowed with her right.

A. O the heroine! and did the long-boat get through safe?

B. They were lost first of all. Why, thirty men had crowded aboard of her.

A. By what unlucky chance did that happen?

B. Before she could get clear of the great ship, she was swamped by the swaying of it.

A. O factum malè! Quid tum?

B. Ubi jam aliquámdiu sic natantes nónnihil promovissemus, sacrificus, quoniam erat miræ proceritatis, "Bono" inquit "es[28] animo! sentio vadum." Ego non ausus tantum sperare felicitatis, "Longiùs" inquam "ábsumus a littore, quàm ut vadum sperandum[96] sit." "Immo," inquit, "sentio pédibus terram." "Est" inquam "fortassis e scriniis aliquod, quod huc devolvit mare." "Immo," inquit, "scalptu digitorum planè sentio terram." Cùm adhuc aliquamdiu natâssemus, ac rursus sentiret vadum, "Tu fac"[30] inquit "quod tibi videtur factu[96] optimum; ego tibi cedo malum totum, et vado me credo:" simulque, exspectato flúctuum decessu,[112] pedibus secutus est quanto potuit cursu. Rursus accedentibus undis,[112] utrâque manu complexus utrumque genu, obnitebatur fluctui,[36] occultans sese sub undis, quemádmodum solent mergi ac ánates: rursus, abeunte fluctu, promicabat et currebat. Ego, videns hoc illi succédere,[108] sum imitatus.[69] Stabant in arenâ, qui, porrectis inter se prælongis hastilibus, fulciebant sese adversus ímpetum undarum, — viri robusti, et fluctibus adsueti — sic ut ultimus hastile

A. Oh, cruel misfortune! But what next?

B. When by dint of swimming we had made some headway, the priest — for he was marvellous tall — calls out, "Courage! I touch bottom!" I did not venture to hope any such good luck, and said, "We are too far from shore to expect to find bottom." "But in fact," said he, "I feel the ground with my feet." "Perhaps," said I, "it is one of the chests, that the sea has washed this way." "Nay," says he, "I plainly feel the ground by the scraping of my toes." We had swum a little further, and again he touched bottom: then "You do," says he, "what you think best: I give you all the mast, and trust the bottom:" at the same time he waited for the ebb, and ran afoot as far as he could. As the waves came up again, he hugged both his knees with both hands, and so braced himself against the undertow, hiding under water as gulls and ducks do: again, as the wave fell back, he came up and ran forward. Seeing him succeed, I followed suit. Some men standing on the beach reach out very long poles to one another, and hold themselves firm against the sweep of the waves — stout men, used to water — so that the furthest

porrígeret adnatanti. Eâ con-
tactâ, omnibus in littus se
recipientibus, tutè pertraheba-
tur in siccum. Hac ope servati
sunt aliquot.

A. Quot?

B. Septem : verum ex his
duo soluti sunt tepóre, admoti
igni.

A. Quot erátis in navi ?

B. Quinquaginta octo.

A. O sævum mare! Ex
tanto numero tam paucos réddidit!

B. Ibi experti sumus⁰⁰ in-
credíbilem gentis humanitatem,
omnia nobis mira alacritate
suppeditantis,ᴿ ² — hospitium,
ignem, cibum, vestes, viáticum.

A. Quæ gens erat ?

B. Hollándica.

A. Istâ ᴿ ²⁶ nihil humanius,
cùm ᴿ ²⁶ tamen feris nationibus
cincta sit. Non répetes, opi-
nor, posthac Neptunum.

B. Non, nisi mihi Deus
adémerit sanam mentem.

A. Et ego malim audire tales
fabulas, quàm experiri.

reached his pole to the swim-
mer. Taking hold of this, and
all pulling back to the shore, he
was got safe to dry land. In
this way some few were saved.

A. How many ?

B. Seven : but, out of these,
two fainted with the heat when
they reached the fire.

A. How many of you were
on board ?

B. Fifty-eight.

A. O cruel sea! To give
back so few from such a number !

B. Here we felt the incredible kindness of the people, who
with wonderful eagerness supplied us everything — shelter,
fire, food, clothes, and supplies
for travelling.

A. What people was it ?

B. Dutch.

A. There is none kinder
than that — though it is sur-
rounded with fierce nations.
You'll not try the sea again, I
fancy, after this.

B. Not unless God takes
away my sober senses.

A. And I would rather hear
such tales, than try it myself.

CHARADE

(Such as may have been addressed by the young Virgil to a fair maid of Mantua)

From " Day-dreams of a Schoolmaster."

BY D'ARCY W. THOMPSON.

O mea bellula cara puellula,
In meo pectore quod micat *Primulom*
 Est et erit tui plenom amore :
O si calfâr' io primuli ignibus
Illud *Secundulom*, quod gremi' in tuo
 Urit me frigidiore nitore !
Dom mea carmina vesperi pérlegis,
Mal' ominato ne *Totulom* impleat
 Crudelitate te, meque dolore ;
Sed te, puellul', Amoris aucellula *
Prætrevolans tuom impleat gremiom
 Debito tu' amatoris amore.

NOTE.—The answer to this Charade may be found, page 6 of the Vocabulary. The learner will observe the antique and rustic form of several words. Something of its movement and spirit is given in the following:

O little maiden, my dearest and prettiest,
Here in my bosom my *First* that is quivering
 Is and shall ever be faithful to thee :
Ah ! might I melt with its flames that are scorching me
That frozen *Second*, which still in thy colder breast,
 Frostily glittering, desolates me !
While to my lay thou at even art listening,
Let not my *Whole*, dear, with croak evil-ominous,
 Fill thee with cruelty — fill me with pain ;
But, little maiden, may Love's light-winged messenger,
Fluttering over, shed into thy bosom
 A love which thy lover's due renders again !

* Diminutive of avicella. *little bird.*

NURSERY SONGS

1. *Bye, Baby Bunting.*

Bye, Baby Bunting!
Father's gone a hunting;
Mother's gone a milking;
Sister's gone a silking:
Brother's gone to buy a skin
To wrap Baby Bunting in.

2. *Hey my Chickie.*

Hey, my chickie, my chickie,
  Hey, my chickie, my deary!
Such a sweet birdie as this
  Was neither far or neary.
Here we go up, up, up,
  Here we go down, down, downy:
Here we go backwards and forwards,
  And here we go round, round, roundy.

3. *Poor Robin.*

The North wind doth blow,
And we shall have snow:
And what will poor Robin do then
                    Poor thing?

He'll sit in a barn,
And keep himself warm,
And hide his head under his wing,
                    Poor thing!

IN LATIN.

[From " Arundines Cami."]

1. *Dormias.*

Dormias bellule, care puellule!
Pater erraticus abît venaticus;
Lacte matercula apparat fercula;
Soror cum fiscinâ quærit bombycina;
Frater, his gravior — frater, his suavior —
Redît cum vellere, quo sciat pellere
Frigus a bellulo fratre puellulo.

2. *O mea Pullula.*

O mea pullula blandula,
   O mea pullula suavis!
Procul in terris, aut prope,
   Non est, ut hæc rara avis!
Hîc sursum, et sursum, et sursum
   Deorsum, deorsum, hîc imus:
Hîc rursum et prorsum cursamus,
   Et circum et circum redimus.

3. *Rubicilla.*

Stridet ventus Borealis,
Imber ingruet nivalis;
Quo se vertet horâ in illâ
     Rubicilla?

In granario sedebit,
Plumeâ tepens fovebit
Molle caput sub axillâ,
     Rubicilla!

4. *Mistress Mary.*

Mistress Mary, quite contrary,
   How does your garden grow?
With silver bells, and cockle-shells,
   And hyacinths, all of a row.

5. *A Solemn Dirge.*

Ding dong bell!
The cat's in the well.
   Who put her in?
   Little Johnny Green.
What a naughty boy was that
To drown poor harmless pussy-cat!

6. *Twinkle, Twinkle.*

Twinkle, twinkle, little Star!
How I wonder what you are!
Up above the world so high
Like a diamond in the sky.

When the blazing Sun is gone,
When he nothing shines upon,
Then you show your little light
Twinkle, twinkle, all the night.

Then the traveller in the dark
Thanks you for your tiny spark:
He could not see which way to go
If you did not twinkle so.

In the dark blue sky you keep,
And often through my curtains peep:
For you never shut your eye
Till the sun is in the sky.

4. *O mea Maria.*

O mea Maria, tota contraria,
    Quid tibi crescit in horto?
Testæ et crotali sunt mihi flosculi,
    Cum hyacínthino [105] serto.

5. *Carmen Luctuosum.*

Æs sacrum sonet: æs mæstum tonet!
Obît in luteo Felis puteo.
Quis sic, mihi dic, merserit illîc?
Quisnam hoc facinus?—puer est Prasinus.
Proh cor durum, miserum puerum!
Proh ridiculum Johanniculum,
Immergere tam felem immeritam!

6. *Mica, Mica.*

Mica, mica, parva Stella!
Miror quænam sis, tam bella!
Splendens eminus in illo,
Alba velut gemma, cælo.

Quando fervens Sol discessit,
Nec calore prata pascit,
Mox ostendis lumen purum,
Micans, micans, per obscurum.

Tibi, noctu qui vagatur,
Ob scintillulam gratatur:
Ni micares tu, non sciret
Quas per vias errans iret.

Meum sæpe thálamum luce
Specularis curiosâ;
Neque carpseris soporem
Donec venit Sol per auram.

HIAWATHA

BY H. W. LONGFELLOW.

1. *Hiawatha's Childhood.*

Then the little Hiawatha
Learned of every bird its language,
Learned their names and all their secrets,
How they built their nests in Summer,
Where they hid themselves in Winter;
Talked with them whene'er he met them,
Called them " Hiawatha's Chickens."

Of all beasts he learned the language,
Learned their names and all their secrets,
How the beavers built their lodges,
Where the squirrels hid their acorns,
How the reindeer ran so swiftly,
Why the rabbit was so timid;
Talked with them whene'er he met them,
Called them " Hiawatha's Brothers."

Then Iagoo, the great boaster,
He the marvellous story-teller,
He the traveller and the talker,
Made a bow for Hiawatha;
From a branch of ash he made it,
From an oak-bough made the arrows,
Tipped with flint, and winged with feathers,
And the cord he made of deerskin.

Then he said to Hiawatha;
" Go, my son, unto the forest,
Where the red deer herd together,
Kill for us a famous roebuck.
Kill for us a deer with antlers!"

Forth into the forest straightway,
All alone walked Hiawatha
Proudly, with his bow and arrows;

TRANSLATION

BY F. W. NEWMAN.

1. *Hiawathæ Pueritia.*

Deinde parvus ille Hiawatha
Avium omnigenûm sermonem didicit,
Harumque et nomina et artes arcanas;
Quo pacto æstate nidificarent;
Ubinam hieme se absconderent.
Hisce quoties obviàm fieret, colloquebatur,
*Pullos*que *Hiawathæ* appellabat.
    Ferarum mox itidem didicit sermonem,
Nominaque earum et artes arcanas:
Ut fibri casulas contabularent,
Ubinam sciuri glandes conderent;
Tum, quàm velox curreret tarandus,
Quare metueret adeò cunículus.
Hosce, si quando forent obvii, compellabat,
Indiditque nomen, *Fratres Hiawathæ.*
    Deinceps Iago, summus jactator,
Mirandarum narrator fabularum,
Peregrinator, loquax nimiùm,
Arcum confecit Hiawathæ
E ramo fraxineo figuratum,
Cum sagittis e quernâ virgâ,
Silice præfixis, ponè pennatis,
Proque nervo intendit pellem cervinam:
    Atque ille Hiawathæ dixit,
"In silvam abi mi puer,
Eò ubi cervi congregantur.
Grandem tu capream occidito,
Cornutum nobis damam afferto."
    Foras protinus in silvam
Solívagus incessit Hiawatha
Exsultanter, cum arcu et sagittis:

And the birds sang round him, o'er him,
"Do not shoot us, Hiawatha!"
Sang the robin, sang the blue-bird,
"Do not shoot us, Hiawatha!"
   Up the oak-tree sprang the squirrel,
In and out among the branches,
Coughed and chattered from the oak-tree,
Laughed, and said between his laughing,
"Do not shoot me, Hiawatha!"
   And the rabbit from his pathway
Leaped aside, and at a distance
Sat erect upon his haunches,
Half in fear and half in frolic,
Saying to the little hunter,
"Do not shoot me, Hiawatha!"
   Hidden in the alder-bushes,
There he waited till the deer came,
Till he saw two antlers lifted,
Saw two eyes look from the thicket,
Saw two nostrils point to windward,
And a deer came down the pathway,
Flecked with leafy light and shadow.
And his heart within him fluttered,
Trembled like the leaves above him,
Like the birch-leaf palpitated,
As the deer came down the pathway.
   Then, upon one knee uprising,
Hiawatha aimed an arrow;
Scarce a twig moved with his motion,
Scarce a leaf was stirred or rustled,
But the wary roebuck started,
Stamped with all his hoofs together,
Listened with one foot uplifted,
Leaped as if to meet the arrow;
Ah! the singing, fatal arrow,
Like a wasp it buzzed and stung him!

Circùmque ac suprà aves
"Ne nos tu ferias!" canebant.
Iterabat rubecula, cyáneola,
"Ne nos tu ferias, Hiawatha!"
    Super quercum exsiluit sciurus,
Seque induens exuens frondibus
Tussivit, garrivit e quercu,
Ridens; atque inter ridendum
"Ne me ferias, Hiawatha!" inquit.
    Jamque e semitâ cunículus
In obliquum prósilit: ibi longè
Natibus insidit erectus,
Et metuens et simul lusurus;
Isque juveni inquit venatori,
"Ne tu me ferias, Hiawatha!"
    Inter alnorum dumos recónditus
Cervorum adventum opperiebatur,
Donec cornua duo sensit sublevari,
Duo oculos e dumeto prospicere.
Duo nares ad ventum dírigi:
Mox désilit dama in semitam
Umbris foliorum distinctam.
Sanè palpitabat cor venatoris,
Velut supernè tremebant circà
Betularum folia ac frondes,
Dum fera semitam decurrit.
    At uno suffultus genu
Hiawatha emisit sagittam.
Vix virgula dimovebatur,
Vix folii excitabatur sonus;
Tamen résilit dama prævigil,
Conjuncto pedum nisu supplodens;
Uno pede sublato auscultat,
Dein prosilit, ut sagittæ occursurus.
Heu! canorâ illâ ac dirâ sagittâ,
Velut a vespâ stridente, pungitur!

2. *Hiawatha's Sailing.*

"Give me of your bark, O Birch-Tree!
Of your yellow bark, O Birch-Tree!
Growing by the rushing river,
Tall and stately in the valley!
I a light canoe will build me,
That shall float upon the river,
Like a yellow leaf in Autumn,
Like a yellow water-lily!

"Lay aside your cloak, O Birch-Tree!
Lay aside your white-skin wrapper!
For the Summer-time is coming,
And you need no white-skin wrapper!"
Thus aloud cried Hiawatha
In the solitary forest,
When the birds were singing gayly,
In the Moon of Leaves were singing,
And the sun, from sleep awaking,
Started up and said, "Behold me!"

And the tree with all its branches
Rustled in the breeze of morning,
Saying, with a sigh of patience,
"Take my cloak, O Hiawatha!"
With his knife the tree he girdled;
Just beneath its lowest branches,
Just above the roots, he cut it,
Till the sap came oozing outward;
Down the trunk, from top to bottom,
Sheer he cleft the bark asunder;
With a wooden wedge he raised it,
Stripped it from the trunk unbroken.

"Give me of your boughs, O Cedar!
Of your strong and pliant branches,
My canoe to make more steady,
Make more strong and firm beneath me!"

2. *Hiawathæ Cymba.*

I. Betulæ dixit Hiawatha,
" Gilvam da mihi corticem tu,
Quæ amnem juxta rapidum in valle
Excelsa et procera crescis !
Cymbam volo levem contexere,
Quæ summo amni ínnatet
Velut Auctumni folium,
Velut luteum aquatile lilium.
    " Quare, O Betula ! pellem tuam,
Albæ cutis involucrum, exue ;
Nam adest, ecce ! æstas ;
Neque jam tegumento est opus."
    Talia magnâ voce Hiawatha
Solum per saltum insonuit,
Dum aves supernè hilariter
Mense florifero cantillabant ;
Et cælorum lumen maximum
Sol, experrectus somno,
Exsiliens clamabat, " Ecce me ! "
    At arbor in aurâ matutínâ
Cunctos per ramos agitata,
Cum suspirio dixit patiens,
" Ergo capias tu pellem meam."
    Tum cultro amputavit corticem
Infimis sub ramis suprà,
Summis super radicibus infrà,
Donec exsudaret succus.
Mox truncum désuper ad imum
Dissecuit planè corticem,
Quam, ligneo sublevatam cuneo,
Integram trunco detraxit.
    II. " Ramorum, Cedre ! tuorum aliquot
Validorum da mihi, ac flexilium,
Qui cymbam mihi constabiliant,

Through the summit of the Cedar
Went a sound, a cry of horror,
Went a murmur of resistance;
But it whispered, bending downward,
" Take my boughs, O Hiawatha!"
    Down he hewed the boughs of cedar,
Shaped them straightway to a framework,
Like two bows he formed and shaped them,
Like two bended bows together.
    " Give me of your roots, O Tamarack!
Of your fibrous roots, O Larch-Tree!
My canoe to bind together,
So to bind the ends together
That the water may not enter,
That the river may not wet me!"
    And the Larch, with all its fibres,
Shivered in the air of morning,
Touched his forehead with its tassels,
Said, with one long sigh of sorrow,
" Take them all, O Hiawatha!"
    From the earth he tore the fibres,
Tore the tough roots of the Larch-Tree,
Closely sewed the bark together,
Bound it closely to the framework.
    " Give me of your balm, O Fir-Tree!
Of your balsam and your resin,
So to close the seams together
That the water may not enter,
That the river may not wet me!"
    And the Fir-Tree, tall and sombre,
Sobbed through all its robes of darkness,
Rattled like a shore with pebbles,
Answered wailing, answered weeping,
" Take my balm, O Hiawatha!"
    And he took the tears of balsam,
Took the resin of the Fir-Tree,

Addantque infrà firmitatem."
Cedrum pertentavit summam
Horror atque ejulans querela,
Quasi contumaciam mussitans:
Tamen deflexa susurravit,
" Ramos meos, si vis, capias."
   Jam cedrinos ramos succídit,
Atque in compaginem fabricatur
Instar parium compositorum arcuum.
   III. " E contortis tuis radicibus,
O Larix! da mihi aliquot,
Quæ cymbæ bene cólligent
Oras, ne madefiam,
Irrumpente undâ fluvii!"
   Tum cunctas per fibras Larix
Aurâ matutínâ inhorrescens,
Cirris suis fronte ejus tactâ,
Longùm suspiravit mærens:
" Ergo cunctas, Hiawatha, capias."
   Ille tenaces láricis fibras
Vi multâ érutas ex humo
Cum cortice ipsâ consuit,
Cum compagine astrictè colligat.
   IV. " Balsamum da mihi," inquit,
" Resinamque tuam, O Abies!
Quâ suturas arctè conjungam
Fluvii undam exclusuras,
Ne irrumpens me madefaciat"
   Atque Abies procéra et pullata
Per nigrantia sua vestimenta suspiravit,
Instarque littoris lapillis plangentis
Fletu luctuoso respondit:
" Ergo balsamum tu capias meum."
   Itaque balsami cepit lacrimas,
Et resinam ex abiete multam,
Quibus óblita, unaquæque sutura

7

Smeared therewith each seam and fissure,
Made each crevice safe from water.
  "Give me of your quills, O Hedgehog!
I will make a necklace of them,
Make a girdle for my beauty,
And two stars to deck her bosom!"
  From a hollow tree the Hedgehog
With his sleepy eyes looked at him,
Shot his shining quills, like arrows,
Saying, with a drowsy murmur,
Through the tangle of his whiskers,
"Take my quills, O Hiawatha!"
  From the ground the quills he gathered,
Stained them red and blue and yellow,
With the juice of roots and berries;
Into his canoe he wrought them,
Round its waist a shining girdle,
Round its bows a gleaming necklace,
On its breast two stars resplendent.
  Thus the Birch Canoe was builded
In the valley, by the river,
In the bosom of the forest;
And the forest's life was in it,
All its mystery and its magic,
All the lightness of the birch-tree,
All the toughness of the cedar,
All the larch's supple sinews;
And it floated on the river
Like a yellow leaf in Autumn,
Like a yellow water-lily.
  Paddles none had Hiawatha,
Paddles none he had or needed,
For his thoughts as paddles served him
And his wishes served to guide him;
Swift or slow at will he glided,
Veered to right or left at pleasure.

Ac rima excluderet aquam.

    v. " Spinas mihi tuo ex corpore,
O Erinaceë," inquit, " da cunctas ;
Quibus collarem fabricer catellam
Ac cingulum Veneri meæ,
Duasque stellas thoraceas."

    Ex cavâ árbore Erinaceüs
Oculis circumspectans veternosis,
Spinas, sagittarum instar projecit,
Per implexam narium barbam
Inter sopores murmurans,
" Ergo capias tu spinas meas."

    Ille ex humo collectas spinas
Radícum ac baccarum succo
Tinxit in rubrum, cæruleum, croceum :
Has cymbæ interstinxit,
Lucidum ventri cingulum,
Proræ fulgentem torquem,
Par stellarum pro mammis micans.

    Sic betulea cymba in valle
Propter amnem est contexta,
Ipso in gremio silvæ.
Ergo vita inerat silvestris,
Horrenda sanè ac magica ;
E Betulâ sua levitas,
E Cedro suum robur,
E Lárice nervorum lentitudo.
Jamque innatabat amni
Velut auctumnale folium.
Velut luteum aquatile lilium.

    Neque erant remi Hiawathæ,
Neque rémige omnino opus erat.
Nam ipsius voluntate cymba,
Et nutu animi, movebatur ;
Velociter, lentè, dextrâ, sinistrâ,
Progrediens, recedens, se convertens.

FABLES OF ÆSOP.

1. *Quarrel of the Oxen.*

In eodem prato pascebantur tres boves in maximâ concordiâ, et sic ab omni ferarum incursione tuti erant. Sed, dissidio inter illos orto,[R. 29] singuli[121] a feris petiti et laniati sunt.

2. *The Fox and Grapes.*

Vulpes uvam in vite conspicata,[69] ad illam subsiliit omnium virium suarum contentione, si eam fortè attingere posset. Tandem, defatigata inani labore, discédens dixit, "At nunc etiam acerbæ sunt, nec eas in viâ repertas * tollerem."

3. *The Wolf and the Crane.*

In faucibus lupi os inhæserat. Mercéde igitur conducit gruem, qui illud extrahat. Hoc grus longitudine colli facilè effecit. Cùm autem mercedem postularet, subridens lupus et dentibus infrendens, "Num tibi" inquit "parva merces videtur, quòd caput incolume ex lupi faucibus extraxisti ?"

4. *Union is Strength.*

Agricola senex, cùm mortem sibi appropinquare sentiret, filios convocavit, — quos, ut fieri solet, interdum discordare noverat, — et fascem virgularum afferri jubet. Quibus allatis, filios hortatur, ut hunc fascem fràngerent. Quod cùm facere non possent, distribuit singulas virgas; iisque celeriter fractis, docuit filios, quàm firma res esset concordia, quàmque imbecillis discordia.

* *If I found them.*

5. *The Lion's Share.*

Societatem junxerant leo, juvenca, capra, ovis. Prædâ autem quam ceperant in quattuor partes divisâ,[113] leo "Prima" ait "mea est; debetur enim hæc præstantiæ[34] meæ. Tollam et secundam, quam meretur robur meum. Tertiam vindicat sibi egregius labor meus. Quartam qui sibi adrogare voluerit, is sciat, se habiturum me inimicum sibi." Quid facerent imbecilles bestiæ? aut quæ sibi leonem infestum habere vellet?

6. *The Fox that lost his Tail.*

Vulpes quædam cassibus capta erat, sed posteà, amissâ caudâ, effugit. Convocavit igitur omnes vulpes, et suasit eis, ut ipsæ quoque absciderent caudas, quippe quæ non modò indecoræ essent, sed merum inutile pondus. Sed una ex iis, "At tu" inquit "non ita moneres,[27] nisi ista calamitas ipsi tibi accidisset."

7. *King Log and King Stork.*

Ranæ, dolentes propter turbatam civitatem, legatos miserunt, qui a Jove* regem postularent. At ille, videns earum simplicitatem, demisit trabem in paludem ubi habitabant. Primò igitur ranæ, sonitu territæ, in imâ palude sese abdiderunt. Mox autem, cùm vidérent trabem immotam innoxiamque, paullatim ad tantum audaciæ pervenêre, ut insilientes in eam, ibi subsíderent. Tum, dedignantes se talem habere regem, iterum ad Jovem convenêre; orantes ut sibi regem alterum daret; primum enim inertem esse, atque nequam. Sed Jupiter, iratus, immisit ciconiam, a quâ captæ sunt ac devoratæ.

* Ablative of Jupiter, the King of the Gods.

THE GOLDEN EGG.

[Translated from " Dream Children."]

Olim gallina, errans præter limites agelli, intrârat * fundum divitis agricolæ. Ubi cùm deambularet, temptans fimum, aut scalpturiens in horto, invenit Phœnicópterum † stantem, ut mos est ei volucri,[103] uno in pede — altero alicubi reposito [R. 29] — quasi in terram defixum.[R. 2]

Gallina stetit aliquamdiu intuens, incerta utrùm mirum hoc animal vivum esset,[78] necne: stans et ipsa pede in uno, intorquens digitos alterius. Flamingo vidit eam, conivitque: tum gallina ausa est loqui.

"Salve!" inquit; "pace tuâ dicam:[27] sed quomodo vadis uno pede? an es verè infixus humo?"[R. 13] Gallina autem admodum erat simplex, et omnino ignara consuetudinum mundi; aliter, nimis impudenter locuta esset.

"Satis bene vivo," respondit Flamingo, magnâ cum dignitate: "Est mihi gravius aliquid faciendum,[96] quàm ut semper hinc illinc circumvager: multa revolvo, cogitabundus mecum de omnibus rebus."

Gallina, his vocibus auditis, cepit subitum consilium, — unicum, pæne dixerim, ‡ quod gallinis umquam venit in mentem, nisi quod pertineat [R. 35] ad quotidianum [105] victum. "Esne" rogavit "avis sapiens?"

Adnuit Flamingo: "Næ," inquit, "licet[106] quidem istud dicere."

* Pluperfect, for intraverat.
† A Greek word, meaning *scarlet-wing*: i. e. *a Flamingo.*   ‡ *As I may say.*

"Potesne igitur docere quomodo gallina aurea
pepererit [78] ova?"

"Prorsus intelligo," respondit Flamingo: "a
Ciconiis didici, quæ Orientem et Ægyptum et Per-
sida visunt. Nam in iis maximè regionibus factum
est. Anus quædam habuit gallinam—"

"Id planè memoriâ teneo," inquit pennigera
comes: "oro ut ad rem venias; nam valde cupio
audire."

"Ab initio oportet [108] exordiri," refert Flamingo.
"Anus quædam habuit gallinam—"

"Immo, intelligo," gallina inquit, "et ova aurea
peperit. Sed quomodo? hæc res est."

"Suadeo tibi ut discas bonos mores," respondet
Flamingo: "Anus quædam habuit gallinam, quæ ova
aurea peperit, singula singulis diebus. Anus autem
cogitabat, *Singula singulis diebus—hau sat est:
satius erat dissecare gallinam, et cuncta simul ova
habere.* Cepit ergo cultrum, eamque dissecuit:
sed ecce! nulla ova inerant. Hinc intelligendum—" [96]

"Num quomodo ova pepererit?" interpellat
gallina.

"Hinc intelligendum" iterat Flamingo, "ut sis
contentus [R. 24] eo quod habes."

"Sed quomodo ova parta sunt?" ait gallina,
insistens.

"Istud numquam compertum est," respondet
Flamingo.

"At promisisti te mihi dicturum." [86]

"Vin' ergo me sinere ad finem venire?" ait alter,
iratus: "est mihi [103] in animo nil amplius dicere.
At tu saltem" inquit, fastidiosè, "numquam poteris [88]

aurea ova párere.   Volo tamen quod ciconiæ mihi
dixerunt id tibi referre : sed cave interpelles."

"Perge modò" inquit gallina.

"Ciconiæ autem omnia nôrunt; quotannis veniunt
in Septemtrionem, et de hac re narrant.   Sed non
huc migrant : hæc audivi, cùm aliàs peregrinabar.
Ne existimâris [27] me semper hîc habitâsse :" et Flamingo superbiosè circumspectavit.

"In isto colle ergo habitâsti ?" interrogavit gallina : "unus e gallis nostris dehinc commigravit."

"Quem mihi collem narras ? trans mare huc
demigravi."

"Ego scio," gallina interpellat, alacriter : "Anas
noster omnia me docuit : longè, longissimè natavit.
Sed perge, quæso : non interpellabo."

Primò igitur Flamingo sibi proposuit nihil ultrà
dicere : sed magnopere cupivit sapientiam suam
ostentare ; itaque progressus est :

"Ciconiæ mihi dixerunt rem denuo vel pluries
esse factam,—ad hunc modum.   Eundum [97] est
foras, sub vesperum frigidissimum totius [65] hiemis,
horâ [R. 28] quâ aliæ gallinæ ad perticam eunt, et ovum
pariendum [96] inter vepres.   Ibi usque ad mane
vigilandum, juxta stanti ; [96] solis [R. 5] orientis primi
radii ovum in aurum convertent.   Sic audivi, et
haud dubiè verum est.   De hac re præceptum
composui : *Semper —*"

"Vive, vale," inquit gallina ; "perlibenter ma-
nerem te auditura [94] loquentem ; sed jam advesperascit." [106]   Hæc locuta, abiit.

"Animal verè rusticum !" ait Flamingo : et,
altero pede reposito, hic quoque in alteram partem
spatiatur.

Hiems jam venerat, et nox erat frigidissima: quod ánates intellexêre; nam aquarum frígore noscitabant. Facilè credas [27] gallinam retinuisse [85] ea quæ ex Flamingone audierat: et nemini alteri [65] dixisse. Cùm igitur ceteræ gallinæ in perticâ con--sedissent, ea nusquam est inventa: sed aër frigidior erat quàm ut speculatum irent. Manè autem, dum ceteri hortum circumibant, aliquantulum [102] cibi passim carpentes, vel terram gelu duram rimantes, ad vepres tandem pervenêre. Quid illic appáret? inter vepres, aureum ovum! at propter ovum conspexêre gallinam congelatam, rigentem. Ovum quidem pepererat; fortiter, fideliter, vigilârat; sed, cùm radii matutini ovum in aurum verterunt, gallinam glacialem recalefacere nequiverunt.

Tum gallinæ omnes, congregatæ, cum pullis gallisque, circumstetêre veneranter. Princeps gallorum juxta ovum constitit, et magnâ voce cantavit. Cantum en quàm clarum! quàm velut tubâ sonantem! quàm resonantem, quàm diuturnum, quàm triumphantem! Singulis pedibus pulli circumstetêre; alterum præ frigore retraxerant: obstupuêre, conticuêre omnes! Tandem gallinæ inter se dicere cœperunt: "Nec quidquam ista nos docuit! quî nunc cognosci potest, quâ ratione sit factum?"

Quid autem ovo [41] faciendum erat? Decrevit gallus. Gallinæ [R. 11] maculentæ imperat, ut ovo in nido insideat, videatque quid foret partum. Ita gallina maculata sedebat. Per quinquaginta dies sedebat — viginti diebus [R. 27] ampliùs quàm gallinis [103] mos est: sed statutum erat ut aliquid ex ovo gigneretur. Sedebat usque dum moreretur: nam, quinquagesimo die, [R. 28] cùm gallus jam ediceret ne diutiùs consideret, obiit: et usque adhuc ecce aureum ovum! Ipse rostro tútudit, sed non valebat testam frangere. Universi rostris tutudêre, quàm multi multæque circumsistere poterant; sed testa perfringi recusavit. Tum volverunt ovum extra nidum, in lapideum pavimentum. Volvitur longiùs quàm destinabant; nam non destitit volvi, donec in impluvium cecidit; et anas fortissimus, immersus in undas, nequidquam quæsivit.   J. H. A.

CRŒSUS AND SOLON.

[From Herodotus, Book I, chapters 30-32; 86, 87.]

SOLON, the wisest of the Athenians, lived about six hundred years before Christ. After establishing laws and a constitution for Athens, he went upon a journey to the East, and visited Crœsus, the wealthy and powerful king of Lydia, a district of Asia Minor. It is of his visit here that the following story is told.

Peregrè profectus Solon in Ægyptum, se cóntulit Sardes,* [R. 31] ad Crœsum. Quò ut advenit, in regiâ hospitio acceptus est a Crœso. Tum, tertio aut quarto post die, jussu Crœsi, ministri regis circumduxêre Solonem, ostentantes thesauros omnes, et quidquid ibi magni [R. 6] et opùlenti inerat.[84]

Quæ cùm ille spectâsset, et cuncta esset[69] contemplatus, tali modo eum percunctatus est Crœsus: "Hospes Atheniensis," [105] inquit, "incessit me cupído ex te sciscitandi,[97] quem tu adhuc víderis [78] omnium hominum [R. 6] beatissimum." Nempe, quòd se ipsum hominum beatissimum esse putaret,[R. 35] idcirco hanc illi quæstionem proposuit.

At Solon, nullâ usus adsentatione,[R. 25] sed ut res erat, "Ego verè," inquit "beatissimum vidi Tellum Atheniensem."

* Sardis, the capital of Lydia.

Quod miratus Crœsus, quærit, "Quâ tandem ratione Tellum beatissimum judicas?"

Cui ille: "Tellus," inquit, "florente civitate,[112] filios habuerat bonos viros honestosque, et eorum liberos viderat, omnes superstites; idemque vitæ finem habuit splendidissimum: nam in prœlio postquam fortiter pugnavit, hostemque in fugam vertit, honestissimâ morte[R. 25] defunctus est; et, eodem loco quo cecidit, publicè sepultus est, et magnificè honoratus."

Ita cùm Solon Crœsum admonuisset, interrogare hic institit, quemnam secundum ab illo vidisset[78] beatissimum; existimans utique secundas certè partes sese laturum.[94] At ille "Cleobin," inquit, "et Bitonem; de quibus hæc etiam narratur historia. Cùm festus dies ageretur Junonis Argivæ,* oporteretque matrem horum bigis in templum vehi, nec in tempore ex agro adessent boves; tunc juvenes, jugum ipsi subeuntes, plaustrum traxerunt quo mater vehebatur; eoque[112] per quadraginta quinque stadia tracto,[112] ad templum pervenerunt. Quo facto,[112] optimus eisdem[R. 13] obtigit vitæ exitus; ostenditque in his Numen, melius esse hominibus mori, quàm vivere. Nam mater, stans ante simulacrum, precata est deam, ut filiis[R. 14] suis id daret, quod optimum esset contingere homini. Post hanc precationem, peracto sacrificio, juvenes, cùm in ipso templo somno se dedissent, non ampliùs resurrexerunt; sed hoc vitæ exitu[R. 25] sunt perfuncti."

Tum vero subiratus Crœsus, "Hospes Atheniensis," ait, "nostra verò felicitas adeò abs te in

* Juno (Queen of the Gods) at Argos.

nihilum projicitur, ut ne privatis quidem hominibus
æquiparandos [93] nos existimes ? "

Cui ille "Crœse," inquit, "in diuturno tempore
multa videre est * quæ quis nolit,[R. 36] atque etiam
tolerare multa. Jam te quidem ego et opulentum
video, et multorum hominum regem ; istud vero,
quod ex me quærebas, de te non prædicabo, priusquàm te vitâ bene defunctum audiero. In omni re
respiciendus [96] finis est, in quem sit res exitura :
multos enim Deus, postquam felicitatem eis ostendit,
funditus dein evertit."

Post Solonis discessum, gravis divinitus vindicta
Crœsum excepit : hac causâ, ut conjicere licet,[108]
quòd se ipsum hominum beatissimum judicaret.
Nam multos post annos, captus a Persis,† ad regem Cyrum ductus est : qui Crœsum, compedibus
vinctum, jussit imponi ingenti rogo,[R. 13] ut vivus com-
bureretur.[R. 36] Tum vero aiunt in mentem Crœso [34]
venisse illud Solonis, *Neminem viventem esse
beatum.* Dicitur ergo, post longum silentium, ex
imo péctore vocem edidisse, et ingemiscens ter
clamâsse *Solonem!*

Tum Cyrus, hoc audito, jussit interpretes e Crœso
quærere, quis ille esset [78] quem invocaret ; illique
accedentes quæsiverunt. Sed Crœsus initio nihil
iis respondit. At iis instantibus, et operosè urgen-
tibus, dixit demum quod res erat : quo pacto olim
Solon ad se venisset,[78] Atheniensis ; qui, cùm omnes
suas opes esset contemplatus, pro nihilo eas dux-
isset ; nec verò ea illum in se magis dixisse, quàm
in universum genus hominum, et in eos maximè qui
sibi ipsis viderentur esse beati.

* *There is occasion, or one is likely to see,* &c.   † The Persians.

Hæc dum Crœsus referebat, jam incenso rogo, arsêre extrema circumcirca; Cyrus verò, ubı ex interpretibus cognovit ea quæ Crœsus dixisset, — pœnitentiâ ductus, et cogitans quid esset [78] quòd (cùm ipse homo esset) alium hominem, qui sese [R. 28] non inferior fuisset felicitate, vivum igni traderet; ad hæc veritus deorum vindictam, reputansque quàm nihil esset in rebus humanis stabile, — ociùs restingui jussit accensum ignem, Crœsumque inde deduci; verùm ii quibus id mandatum erat vim flammæ non ampliùs superare potuerunt.

Tum inter lácrimas Deum invocante Crœso,[R. 29] repente nubes, cùm serenum et tranquillum adhuc fuisset cælum, contrahebatur, coörtâque tempestate, et vehementissimo effuso imbre, ignis exstinctus est.

ROMAN STORIES.

1. *How Horatius kept the Bridge.*

[Lívy, Book II. chap. 10]

After the kings had been expelled from Rome, the city was besieged and almost taken by the Etruscans, who held the ground beyond the Tiber.

Pons sublicius iter pæne hostibus dedit: ni unus vir fuisset, Horatius Cocles; qui, positus forte in statione pontis, reprehensans singulos, obsistens, obtestansque deûm et hominum fidem, testabatur: "Nequidquam, deserto præsidio,[R. 29] fugitis. Si tránsitum pontem a tergo relinquétis, jam plus hostium in Palatio Capitolioque, quàm in Janiculo, erunt.* Itaque moneo, prædíco vobis, ut pontem

---

* The Palatium and Capitolium are hills in the heart of the city: the Janiculum is beyond the bridge.

ferro, igni, quâcumque vi poteritis, interrumpatis. Ego impetum hostium, quantùm corpore uno obsisti [110] potest, excipiam."

Vadit inde in primum áditum pontis; insignisque inter conspecta cedentium * terga, ipso miraculo [R. 20] audaciæ obstupefecit hostes. Duos tamen cum eo pudor tenuit, Spurium Lartium ac Titum Hermi-nium, ambos claros genere factisque. ·Cum his primam periculi procellam parumper sustinuit; deinde eos quoque ipsos, exiguâ parte pontis relictâ, cedere in tutum coëgit.

Circúmferens inde truces minaciter oculos ad proceres Etruscorum, nunc singulos provocare,[R. 33] nunc increpare omnes: "Servitia regum super-borum! vestræ libertatis [R. 8] immémores, alienam oppugnatum [98] huc venistis?"

Cunctati aliquamdiu sunt, dum alius alium cir-cumspectant: pudor deinde cómmovet aciem; et, clamore sublato, undique in unum hostem tela con-jiciunt. Quæ cùm in objecto scuto hæsissent, neque ille minùs obstinatus pontem obtinéret, jam impetu conabantur detrudere virum; cùm simul fragor rupti pontis, simul clamor Romanorum, alacritate perfecti operis sublatus,† pavore subito impetum sustinuit.

Tum Cocles, "Tiberine pater!" inquit, "te sancte precor, hæc arma et hunc militem propitio flumine accipias." Ita, sic armatus,‡ in Tiberim desiluit, incolumisque ad suos tranavit, — rem ausus plus famæ habituram § ad posteros, quàm fidei. Grata erga tantam virtutem civitas fuit: statua in comitio posita; agri quantum uno die circumaravit, datum.

---

* Of those who fled.   † Raised for joy when the work was done.
‡ Armed as he was.   § Likely to have.

2. *Coriolanus and his Mother.*

[Valerius Maximus, Book V. ch. 4.]

Coriolanus was a brave general, but haughty, and hated by the people, who banished him from the city.

Coriolanus, maximi vir animi, et altissimi consilii, optimèque de Republicâ meritus, iniquissimæ damnationis ruinâ prostratus, ad Volscos, infestos tunc Romanis, confugit. Magno ubique pretio [R.20] virtus æstimatur. Itaque, quò latebras quæsitum [98] vénerat, ibi brevi summum adeptus est imperium: evenitque, ut [eum] quem pro se salutarem imperatorem cives habere noluerant, pæne pestiferum adversùs se ducem experirentur. Frequenter enim fusis exercitibus nostris, victoriarum suarum gradibus, áditum juxta moenia urbis Volsco militi struxit. Missi ad eum deprecandum legati nihil profecérunt. Missi deinde sacerdótes, cum infulis, æquè sine effectu rediérunt. Stupebat senatus; trepidabat populus: viri páriter ac mulieres exitium imminens lamentabantur.

Tunc Veturia, Coriolani mater, Volumniam uxorem ejus, et liberos, secum trahens, castra Volscorum petiit. Quam ubi filius adspexit, "Expugnâsti," inquit, "et vicisti iram meam, patria,[31] precibus hujus admotis; [112] cujus amori [R.14] te, quamvis meritò mihi invisam, dono." Continuòque Romanum agrum hostilibus armis [R.22] liberavit.

3. *How Cincinnatus was called to Power.*

[Livy, Book III. chap. 26.]

Spes única imperii Romani, L. Quinctius, trans Tiberim, contra eum ipsum locum ubi nunc navalia sunt, quattuor jugerum colebat agrum, quæ prata

Quinctia vocantur. Ibi ab legatis — seu fossam
fodiens palæ innisus, seu cùm araret; operi certè
agresti intentus, — salute datâ invicem, redditâque,
rogatus ut mandata senatûs audiret, admiratus,
rogat, "Satin' salva sunt omnia?" Tum togam
properè e tugurio proferre uxorem Raciliam jubet.
Quâ * simul, absterso pulvere ac sudore, velatus *
processit, Dictatorem eum legati gratulantes consa-
lutant: in urbem vocant; qui terror sit in exercitu
exponunt. Navis Quinctio publicè parata fuit;
transvectumque † tres obviàm egressi filii excipiunt;
inde alii propinqui atque amici; tum Patrum ‡
major pars.

Eâ frequentiâ stipatus, antecedentibus lictoribus,
deductus est domum. Et plebis concursus ingens
fuit: sed ea nequâquam tam læta Quinctium vidit; §
et imperii nimium, et virum in ipso imperio vehe-
mentiorem,[82] rata. Et illâ quidem nocte nihil
præterquam vigilatum est[110] in urbe.

4. *How the Capitol was saved by Geese.*

[Livy, Book v. chap. 47.]

In the year 389, B. C., Rome was taken and burnt by the
Gauls, who then held the north of Italy. A garrison remained
on the steep hill of the Capitol, but this was nearly surprised
by the enemy, who climbed the rocky side of the hill by night.

Interim arx Romæ Capitoliumque in ingenti
periculo fuit. Namque Galli tanto silentio in summum evasêre, ut non custódes[R. 16] solùm fállerent,
sed ne canes quidem, ‖ sollícitum animal ad nocturnos

---

* *Clad in this.*   † *When he had crossed.*   ‡ The Senators.

§ Cincinnatus had suppressed with great severity a revolution attempted by the
people.   ‖ ne. . . quidem, *not even.*

strepitus, excitarent.[R. 36]   Anseres[R. 16] non fefellêre,
quibus,[41] sacris Junoni, in summâ inopiâ cibi, tamen
abstinebatur.[110] * .

Quæ res saluti[104] fuit.   Namque clangóre[R. 20]
eorum, alarumque crepitu, excitus M. Manlius, —
qui triennio[R. 27] ante consul fúerat, vir bello[R. 20] egregius, — armis arreptis,[112] simul ad arma céteros
ciens, vadit; et, dum ceteri trépidant, Gallum, qui,
jam in summo constíterat, umbone ictum,[96] deturbat.
Cujus casus prolapsi cùm proximos[R. 16] sterneret,
trepidantes alios, armisque omissis saxa quibus[R. 13]
adhærebant manibus[R. 20] amplexos, trucídat.

Jamque et alii congregati telis missilibusque saxis
proturbare[R. 33] hostes, ruinâque tota prolapsa acies
in præceps deferri.   Sedato deinde tumultu, reli-
quum noctis quieti datum est.

Luce ortâ, vocatis clássico[R. 20] ad consilium mili-
tibus ad tribunos (cùm et rectè et pérperam facto
pretium deberétur), Manlius primùm ob virtutem
laudatus donatusque, — non ab tribunis solùm militum, sed consensu etiam militari: cui universi
selibras farris, et quartarios vini ad ædes ejus, quæ
in arce erant, contulérunt, — rem dictu[98] parvam,
ceterùm inopia fécerat eam argumentum ingens
caritatis; cùm, se quisque victu[R. 22] suo fraudans,
detractum † corpori[R. 14] atque usibus necessariis ad
honorem unius viri conferret.

Tum vígiles ejus loci, quâ feféllerat adscendens
hostis, citati.   Et cùm in omnes (more militari) se
animadversurum[96] Q. Sulpicius tribunus militum
pronuntiâsset — consentiente clamore[R. 20] militum,

* Which they refrained from eating.   † *That which was taken*, or *spared*.

8

in unum vigilem conjicientium culpam, deterritus —
a ceteris abstinuit : reum haud dubium [66] ejus noxæ,
approbantibus cunctis, de saxo dejecit.

5. *How Curtius leaped into the Gulf.*

[Livy, Book VII. chap. 6.]

Eodem anno, seu motu terræ, seu quâ vi aliâ,
Forum medium, ferme specu vasto, collapsum in
immensam altitudinem dicitur : nec ea vorago con-
jectu terræ, cùm pro se quisque gereret, expleri
potuit, priùs quàm, deûm monitu, quæritur, *Quo
plurimùm populus Romanus posset.** Id enim illi
loco [R. 14] dicandum vates canebant, si rempublicam
perpetuam esse vellent.

Tum M. Curtius, juvenis bello egregius, casti-
gavit dubitantes † an ullum magis Romanum bonum ‡
esset, quàm arma virtusque. Silentio facto, intuens templa deorum immortalium, quæ Foro imminent, Capitoliumque, et porrigens manus nunc in
cælum, nunc in patentes terræ hiatus ad deos
Manes, § se devovit. Equo [R. 13] deinde quàm poterat
maximè exornato insidens, armatum se in specum
immisit : donaque ac fruges super eum a multitu-
dine virorum ac mulierum sunt congestæ ; lacusque
Curtius ab hoc est appellatus.

STORY OF A DOLPHIN.

[From Pliny's Letters, Book ix. 33, written about A.D. 100]

Est in Africâ Hipponensis colonia mari [R. 10] prox-
ima : ádjacet navigabile stagnum : ex hoc in

---

* *In what the Roman people were strongest.*
† *Those who doubted* (acc.). ‡ *Any good thing more truly Roman.*
§ The spirits of the dead below.

modum fluminis æstuarium emergit, quod vice
alternâ, prout æstus aut repressit aut ímpulit, nunc
infertur mari,[R. 13] nunc redditur stagno. Omnis hîc
ætas piscandi,[107] navigandi, atque etiam natandi
studio tenetur,—maximè pueri, quos otium lusus-
que sollícitat. His[103] gloria et virtus, altissimè
provehi; victor ille, qui longissimè ut littus, ita
simul natantes, reliquit.

Hoc certamine puer quidam, audentior ceteris,[R. 26]
in ulteriora tendebat. Delphínus occurrit; et nunc
præcedere[33] puerum, nunc sequi, nunc circumire,
postremò subire, deponere, iterum subire, trepidan-
temque perferre primùm in altum; mox flectit ad
littus, redditque terræ[R. 14] et æqualibus.

Serpit per coloniam fama: concurrere[R. 88] omnes;
ipsum puerum tamquam miraculum adspícere,
interrogare, audire, narrare. Postero die óbsident
littus, prospectant mare, et si quid est mari simile.
Natant pueri: inter hos ille, sed cautiùs. Delphinus rursus ad tempus, rursus ad puerum venit.
Fugit ille, cum ceteris. Delphinus, quasi invitet[R. 36]
et revocet, éxsilit; mérgitur, variosque orbes implí-
citat expeditque.

Hoc altero die, hoc tertio, hoc pluribus; donec
homines innutritos mari[R. 14] subíret timendi[97] pudor.
Accédunt, et adludunt, et appellant; tangunt etiam,
pertrectantque [se] præbentem.* Crescit audacia
experimento.[R. 20] Maximè puer, qui primus expertus
est, adnatantis ínsilit tergo;[R. 13] fertur referturque;
agnosci[85] se, amari putat, amat ipse; neuter timet,
neuter timétur; hujus fiducia, mansuetudo illius

* i. e. the dolphin.

augétur. Necnon alii pueri, dextrâ lævâque, simul eunt, hortantes monentesque.

Ibat unâ (id quoque mirum) delphinus alius, tantùm spectator et comes. Nihil enim simile aut
faciebat aut patiebatur; sed alterum illum ducebat
reducebatque, ut puerum ceteri pueri. Incredi-
bile,—tam verum tamen quàm priora,—del-
phinum [R. 17] gestatorem conlusoremque puerorum in
terram quoque extrahi solitum; * arenisque siccatum,
ubi incaluisset, in mare revolvi. Constat Octavium
Avitum, legatum pro consule, in littus educto, †
religione pravâ superfudisse [R. 18] unguentum: cujus
illum novitatem odoremque in altum refugisse; nec
nisi post multos dies visum, languidum et mæstum;
mox, redditis viribus, priorem lasciviam et sólita
ministeria repetisse.

Confluebant omnes ad spectaculum magistratus,
quorum adventu et morâ módica respública novis
sumptibus atterebatur. Postremò locus ipse quie-
tem suam secretumque perdebat. Placuit [108] occultè
intérfici [animal] ad quod coibatur.[110]

STORIES OF THE MIDDLE AGE.

1. *A Frank at the Eastern Court.*

[From St. Gall's Life of Charlemagne, written about A.D. 885.]

CHARLEMAGNE (Karl or Charles the Great), King of the
Franks, was crowned Emperor of the West in the year 800.
This story is told of an officer of his, sent as envoy to the
Greek Emperor's court, at Constantinople.

Non videtur occultanda [96] sapientia, quam sapienti
Græciæ [R. 10] idem missus aperuit. Quum, autumnáli

---

* Understand esse: *was accustomed.* † Understand delphino, *on the dolphin.*

témpore, ad urbem quamdam regiam cum sociis
venisset, aliis alió divísis, ipse cuidam epíscopo
commendatus est: qui quum jejuniis et orationibus
incessanter incúmberet, legatum illum pæne con-
tinuâ mortificavit inediâ.

Vernali autem temperie jam aliquantulùm arri-
dente,[112] præsentavit eum Regi.* Qui et interrogavit
eum qualis sibi idem videretur epíscopus. At ille,
ex imis præcordiis alta suspiria trahens, "Sanc-
tissimus est" ait "ille vester episcopus, quantùm
sine Deo possíbile est." Ad quod stupefactus Rex
"Quómodo" inquit "sine Deo aliquis sanctus esse
potest?" Tum ille "Scriptum est" inquit "*Deus
cáritas est*, quâ[R. 29] iste vacuus est."

Tunc rex vocavit eum ad convivium suum, et
inter medios próceres collocavit. A quibus talis
lex constituta erat, ut nullus in mensâ regis,
indígena sive ádvena, aliquod animal, vel corpus
animális, in partem aliam convérteret; sed ita
tantùm, ut pósitum erat, de superiore parte man-
ducaret.

Adlátus est autem piscis fluvialis, et pigmentis
infusus, in disco pósitus. Quumque hospes idem,
consuetúdinis illíus ignárus, piscem illum in partem
alteram giraret, exsurgentes omnes dixérunt ad
Regem: "Domne,† ita estis inhonorati, sicut nunquam anteriores vestri."

At ille, ingemiscens, dixit ad legatum illum,
"Obstare non possum ístis,[R. 13] quin morti continuò
tradaris.[R. 36] Alíud pete, quodcumque volúeris, et
complébo."

---

* That is, the Greek Emperor.
† For domine: the plural (estis) is used in addressing the sovereign.

Tunc, parumper deliberans, cunctis audientibus, in hæc verba prorúpit : "Obsecro, domne Imperator, ut secundùm promissionem vestram concedatis mihi unam petitionem parvulam."

Et Rex ait, "Postula [31] quodcumque volueris, et impetrabis ; præter quòd contra legem Græcorum vitam tibi concedere non possum."

Tum ille, "Hoc" inquit "unum moriturus [94] flagito, ut quicumque me piscem illum girare conspexit, oculorum lumine [B. 22] privetur."

Obstupefactus ad talem conditionem, Rex juravit quòd ipse hoc non vidisset, sed tantùm narrantibus credidisset. Deinde regina ita se cœpit excusare, "Per sanctam Mariam, ego illud non adverti." Post réliqui próceres, alius ante alium, tali se perículo exúere cupientes, ab hac se noxâ terribilibus sacramentis absólvere conabantur, Tum sapiens ille Francigena,* vanissimâ Hellade † in suis sedibus exsuperatâ, victor et sanus in patriam suam reversus est.

2. *The Court of Charlemagne.*

[Continuation of the foregoing.]

Post annos autem aliquot, direxit illuc indefessus Károlus quemdam epíscopum, præcellentissimum mente et córpore visum, adjuncto ei comite nobilissimo duce. ‡ Qui diutissimè protracti, tandem ad præsentiam Regis perducti, et indignè hábiti, per diversissima sunt loca divisi. Tandem verò, aliquando dimissi, cum magno navis et rerum dispendio rediérunt.

---

* *Frank, or Frenchman.* † *Hellas, Greece.* ‡ *Duke.*

Non post multum autem direxit idem Rex legatorios suos ad gloriosissimum Károlum. Fortè verò cóntigit, ut tunc idem epíscopus, cum duce præfáto, apud Imperatorem esset.[R. 36] Nuntiatis igitur venturis,* dederunt consilium sapientissimo Karolo, ut circumducerentur per Alpes et invia, donec, attritis omnibus et consumptis, ingenti penuriâ confecti, ad conspectum illius venire cogerentur.

Quumque venissent, fecit idem episcopus, vel socius ejus, comitem stabuli, in medio subjectorum suorum, throno sublimi considere, ut nequâquam alius quàm imperator credi posset. Quem ut legati viderunt, corruentes in terram, adorare voluerunt. Set a ministris repulsi, ad interiora prógredi sunt compulsi.

Quò quum venirent, videntes comitem palatii in medio procerum concionantem, Imperatorem † suspicati, terrâ[49] tenus sunt prostrati. Quumque et inde colaphis propellerentur, — dicentibus [eis] qui aderant *Non hic est Imperator!* — in ulteriora progressi, et invenientes magistrum mensæ regiæ, cum ministris ornatissimis, putantes Imperatorem, devoluti sunt in humum.

Indeque repulsi, repererunt in consistorio cubicularios Imperatoris circa magistrum suum, de quo non videretur dubium, quin ille princeps posset esse mortalium. Qui quum se quod non erat abnegâsset, ostendebat tamen, quâtenus, si fieri potuisset, in præsentiam Imperatoris augustissimi pervenire deberent.

* *When it was told that they were coming.*
† *Supposing it was the emperor.*

Tunc ex latere Cæsaris * directi sunt [homines] qui eos honorificè introducerent. Stabat autem gloriosissimus regum Karolus juxta fenestram lucidissimam, radians sicut sol in ortu suo, gemmis et auro conspicuus, innixus super Heittonem. Hoc quippe nomen erat episcopi ad Constantinopolim quondam destinati. In cujus undique circuitu consistebat instar militiæ cœlestis, tres videlicet juvenes filii ejus, jam regni participes effecti; filiæque cum matre non minùs sapientiâ vel pulchritudine quàm monilibus ornatæ; pontifices formâ et virtute incomparabiles; præstantissimique nobilitate simul et sanctitate abbates; duces verò, tales qualis quondam apparuit Josue in castris Galgalæ; † exercitus verò, talis qualis de Samariâ Siros ‡ cum Assyriis effugavit.

Tunc consternati missi Græcorum, deficiente spiritu, et consilio perdito, muti et exanimes in pavimentum decidérunt: quos benignissimus Imperator elevans, consolatoriis allocutionibus animare conatus est. Tandem itaque recreato spiritu, quum exosum quondam et abjectum a se Heittonem in tali gloriâ viderent, iterum pavefacti, tamdiu volutabantur humi,[74] donec eis rex per Regem cœlorum juraret, nihil se illis mali in nullo aliquo § facturum. Quâ sponsione relevati, aliquantulùm fiducialiùs agere cœperunt; patriæmque reversi, non sunt ulteriùs ad nostra ‖ progressi.

* A title of the Emperor.   † Joshua in the camp at Gilgal.   ‡ Syrians.
   § *In nothing at all*: this is not good Latin.   ‖ Our country.

NOTE. — The teacher will observe, in this and the preceding section, several phrases not belonging to classical Latin: particularly, *dixerunt ad regem* (p. 117), and *juravit quod non vidisset* (p. 118), where we should say *regi*, and *se non vidisse*; also, *præsentavit* for *adduxit*, and *aliquis* for *quisquam* (p. 117).

3. *How Queen Philippa saved the Burghers of Calais.*

[Translated from the Chronicles of Froissart.]

In the year 1347, King Edward III., of England, after the battle of Crécy, had forced the city of Calais, by a long and painful siege, to ask for conditions of surrender. The story begins when the terms of the conqueror are first made known to the citizens, in the market square.

Ad sonum campanæ omnes convenêre, viri atque mulieres, valde cupientes aliquid novi [R. 6] audire, ut fit * eis qui famem tamdiu tolerârunt, ut nihil possint ampliùs. Quibus congressis, et in magnum atrium congregatis, viris [R. 1] atque mulieribus, Johannes quidam Viennensis, quàm humanissimè [82] poterat, significavit omnia verba jam ante narrata: "Res" inquit "non aliter se habere potest; et necesse est ut quàm brevissimè consulatis atque respondeatis."

Quo audito, cœpêre omnes tam vehementer plorare ac flere, ut nemo, quamvis ferreus, non simul mæreret. Et per spatium horæ, nec respondére nec loqui poterant; quin ipse Johannes Viennensis tantâ misericordiâ commotus est, ut abundè lacrimaret.

Paullo post, oppidanus gravis surrexit, ditissimus totius urbis — cui nomen Eustachio Sancti Petri — et coram [49] omnibus sic locutus est: "Miserum, cives mei, atque nefandum foret, si tantus populus fame sive aliter periret, aliquâ viâ salutis apparente; et magnum ejus meritum erit, qui talem calamitatem defendet. Immo, tantam habeo spem gratiæ veniæque, apud Deum Dominum nostrum, si pro hoc

---

* *As usually happens.*

populo moriar, ut velim primus omnium[R.6] mori; et libenter me tradam, cum merâ tunicâ, nudo capite, laqueo circa collum dato, misericordiæ[R.14] Regis Anglicani."

Hæc ubi dixit, cuncti circumvenêre plorantes: complures, viri 'mulieresque, ei[R.10] se projecêre ad pedes; maximèque flebile erat illic stare, illa audire, attendere, videre.

Deinde alter fortis oppidanus, dives et ipse admodum, cui duæ filiæ pulcherrimæ, ipse quoque óbtulit se comitem; tum tertius, homo locuples supellectile heredioque,[R.20] addidit se comitem propinquis;[R.14] fraterque ejus, quartus; deinde quintus; tum sextus. Hi omnes nudati, cum meris tunicis braccisque, et laqueis circum colla datis, ut a rege edictum erat, egressi sunt, portantes claves castelli et urbis: quisque manu tenuit aliquid clavium. . . .

Rex fortè tum in conclavi sedebat, magnâ cum frequentiâ comitum, baronum, equitum.* Certior factus 'oppidanos appropinquare,[85] cum præscripto apparatu, exiit in spatium ante castellum, omni cœtu nobilium comitante, magnâque insuper turbâ cupientium oppidanos videre.† Regina quoque Regem, dominum suum, secuta est.

Tum Gualterus quidam, qui oppidanos eò duxerat, cum multis aliis, accessit ad Regem, dixitque: "Rex domine noster, ecce obsides oppidanorum, utì jussisti." Rex paulisper sese continuit, sæviter eos intuens: nam omnes oppidanos magnopere óderat, propter immensa damna stragesque, jam ante ab eis in se facta.

---

* Observe that these are the modern titles, *counts, barons,* and *knights.*
† *Of those eager to see the burghers.*

Et sex oppidani, in genua coram rege procumbentes, junctis manibus, ita locuti sunt: "Domine noster, Rex clementissime, ecce nos hîc præsentes, nobilissimi natu [98] omnium civium, magni mercatores: huc attulimus, tradimusque tibi, claves urbis et castelli; sic vestiti utì vides, voluntati tuæ prorsus dediti, ut reliquos oppidanos servemus, tanta tamque dura jamdiu passos. [69] Placeat ergo tibi misereri nostri,[R. 8] pro virtute nobilitateque tuâ."

Neque verò quisquam aderat — princeps, eques, aut miles — qui præ misericordiâ lacrimis abstinere poterat; diuque omnes loqui nequiverunt. Nec mirum quidem; multum enim habet in se miserationis, homines videre tam prostratos, in tantum periculum lapsos.

Rex interea conspexit, admodum iratus; nam adeò durus erat, tantâque iracundiâ commotus, ut loqui non posset. Quum primùm loqui poterat, imperavit ut statim securi ferirentur.* Tum omnes principes equitesque qui aderant, instanter, magno cum fletu, obsecrârunt ut rex casum eorum miseraretur; sed noluit quidquam morari.

Deinde Gualterus, de quo suprà dictum est, ita loquitur: "O Rex clementissime, cóhibe iracundiam tuam. Est tibi fama ac laus summæ mansuetudinis atque nobilitatis: noli [99] igitur facinus patrare, quo laus tua obscuretur, aut quod quis tibi ut scelus objiciat. Nisi hominum [R. 8] horum eris miseritus, omnes nimiam tuam sævitiam incusabunt, qui tam crudeliter viros fortes interfeceris,[R. 35] ultrò sese offerentes misericordiæ tuæ, ut alios tutarentur."

* *That they should be instantly beheaded.*

Ad hoc dictum Rex, dentibus frendens, "Gualtere," inquit, "noli me frænare: ita esse oportet, et nequâquam aliter: carnifex statim adesto: isti oppidani tot militum meorum occiderunt, ut eis quoque profectò sit moriendum." [96]

Tunc generosa Regina Angliæ humiliter, demisso vultu, flensque tam luctuosè ut vix se sustinere posset, in genua sese prosternens ante Regem dominum suum, ita locuta est: "Domine mi benigne, ex eo tempore quum mare transivi, magno (ut ipse scis) cum periculo meo, nihil umquam a te poposci vel postulavi: hoc ergo humillimè oro, et pro meâ parte deposco — solum et unicum munus tum pio filio sanctæ Mariæ, tum pro tuo in me amore — ut horum sex hominum te misereat."

Rex paulisper reticuit, contemplans formosam uxorem, in genibus tam miseriter flentem: tandem aliquantulùm mitigatus — noluit enim irasci mulieri [R. 11] tam teneræ tamque humili — respondit: "At malim, mulier, te úbivis esse terrarum quam hîc: adeò instanter me hoc rogas, ut recusare non ausim: et, quamvis invitus, ecce, tibi istos libero: tu eis [R. 10] facito quodcumque voles."

Generosa Regina respondit: "Domine mi, maximas gratias ago."

Tum Regina surrexit: sex oppidanos resurgere jussit: laqueisque de collis detractis, in conclave eos gaudenter duxit: deinde, quum vestiti essent, paravit amplissimam cœnam, eosque securos de tecto dimisit: unde discessêre alius aliò, habitaturi in urbibus Picardiæ.*   J. H. A.

* *Picardie*, the northern part of France.

MEDIÆVAL HYMNS.

1. *Dies Iræ.*

[Written by Thomas of Celano, a Franciscan monk of the Thirteenth Century. The
entire hymn consists of eighteen stanzas.]

Dies iræ, dies illa
Solvet sæclum in favillâ:
Teste David cum Sibyllâ.

Quantus tremor est futurus,
Quando judex est venturus,
Cuncta strictè discussurus!

Tuba, mirum spargens sonum,
Per sepulcra regionum,
Coget omnes ante thronum.

Mors stupebit et natura,
Quum resurget creatura,
Judicanti responsura.

Liber scriptus proferetur,
In quo totum continetur,
Unde mundus judicetur.

Judex ergo quum sedebit,
Quidquid latet apparebit:
Nil inultum remanebit.

Quid sum miser tunc dicturus?
Quem patronum rogaturus,
Quum vix justus sit securus?

Rex tremendæ majestatis,
Qui salvandos salvas gratis,
Salva me, fons pietatis!

2. *Stabat Mater.*

[Composed in prison, about the year 1300, by Jacopone da Todi, a brilliant lawyer, who after his wife's death became a monk.   The hymn consists of ten stanzas.]

Stabat mater dolorosa
Juxta crucem lacrimosa,
   Dum pendebat filius:
Cujus animam gementem,
Contristantem et dolentem
   Pertransivit gladius.

O quàm tristis et afflicta
Fuit illa benedicta
   Mater unigeniti!
Quæ mærebat, et dolebat,
Et tremebat, dum videbat
   Nati pœnas incliti.

Quis est homo qui non fleret,
Christi matrem si videret,
   In tanto supplicio?
Quis non posset contristari,
Piam matrem contemplari,
   Dolentem cum filio?

Pro peccatis suæ gentis
Vidit Jesum in tormentis,
   Et flagellis subditum!
Vidit dulcem suum natum
Moriendo desolatum,
   Dum emisit spiritum.

Sancta mater! istud agas:
Crucifixi fige plagas
   Cordi meo validè:

Tui nati vulnerati,
Tam dignati, pro me pati,
   Pœnas mecum divide!

Fac me verè tecum flere,
Crucifixo condolere,
   Donec ego vixero!
Juxta crucem tecum stare, .
Te libenter sociare
   In planctu desidero.

EVENING HYMN.

[By Bishop Heber.]

God that madest earth and heaven,
   Darkness and light:
Who the day for toil hast given,
   For rest the night:
May thine angel guards defend us:
Slumber sweet thy mercy send us:
Holy dreams and hopes attend us
   This livelong night!

HYMNUS VESPERTINUS.

[" Arundines Cami."]

Qui terras, cælumque, Deus, sublime parâsti,
   Quique diem et tenebras:
Qui rigidum tolerare jubes sub luce laborem,
   Otia nocte refers:
Angelicis functos operum tueare ministris,[R. 20]
   Dum sopor altus habet:
Spesque hilares adstent, et longâ noctis in horâ
   Somnia sancta toris.

LINES

OF THE EMPEROR HADRIAN ADDRESSED TO HIS SOUL.

Hadriani morientis ad animam suam.

Animula, vagula, blandula,
Hospes comesque corporis,
Quæ nunc abibis in loca?
Pallidula, rigida, nudula,
Nec, ut soles, dabis joca.

PRAYER

[Written by Mary, Queen of Scots, on the morning of her execution, Feb. 8, 1587.]

O domine Deus!
  Speravi in te:
O care mi Jesu,
  Nunc libera me!
In durâ catenâ,
In miserâ pœnâ,
  Desidero te:
Languendo, gemendo,
Et genu flectendo,
Adoro, imploro,
  Ut liberes me!

TABLES.

Table 1.

INFLECTION OF NOUNS.

1. Vowel Stems.

Sing.	I. Wing, F.	II. Grandfather, M.	II. Boar, M.	III. Bird, F.	III. Bag, M.	IV. Lake, M.	V. Day, M.
N.	a'la	a'vus	a'per	a'vis	u'ter	la'cus	di'es
G.	a'læ	a'vi	a'pri	a'vis	u'tris	la'cus	die'i
D.	a'læ	a'vo	a'pro	a'vi	u'tri	lac'ui	die'i
A.	a'lam	a'vum	a'prum	a'vem	u'trem	la'cum	di'em
V.	a'la	a've	a'per	a'vis	u'ter	la'cus	di'es
A.	a'la	a'vo	a'pro	a've	u'tre	la'cu	di'e

Plur.							
N.	a'læ	a'vi	a'pri	a'ves	u'tres	la'cus	di'es
G.	ala'rum	avo'rum	apro'rum	a'vium	u'trium	lac'uum	die'rum
D.	a'lis	a'vis	a'pris	av'ibus	u'tribus	lac'ubus	die'bus
A.	a'las	a'vos	a'pros	a'ves(is)	u'tres(is)	la'cus	di'es
V.	a'læ	a'vi	a'pri	a'ves	u'tres	la'cus	di'es
A.	a'lis	a'vis	a'pris	av'ibus	u'tribus	lac'ubus	die'bus

Sing.	I. Comet, M.	II. Cave, N.	III. Net, N.	III. Spur, N.	IV. Horn, N.
N.	come'tes	an'trum	re'te	cal'car	cor'nu
G.	come'tæ	an'tri	re'tis	calca'ris	cor'nu (us)
D.	come'tæ	an'tro	re'ti	calca'ri	cor'nu
A.	come'ten	an'trum	re'te	cal'car	cor'nu
V.	come'ta	an'trum	re'te	cal'car	cor'nu
A.	come'ta	an'tro	re'ti	calca'ri	cor'nu

Plur.					
N.	come'tæ	an'tra	re'tia	calca'ria	cor'nua
G.	cometa'rum	antro'rum	re'tium	calca'rium	cor'nuum
D.	come'tis	an'tris	ret'ibus	calcar'ibus	cor'nibus
A.	come'tas	an'tra	re'tia	calca'ria	cor'nua
V.	come'tæ	an'tra	re'tia	calca'ria	cor'nua
A.	come'tis	an'tris	ret'ibus	calcar'ibus	cor'nibus

2. Consonant Stems.

Sing.	Consul, M.	Lion, M.	Father, M.	Tree, F.	Maiden, F.	Burden, N.
N.	con'sul	le'o	pa'ter	ar'bor	vir'go	o'nus
G.	con'sulis	leo'nis	pa'tris	ar'boris	vir'ginis	on'eris
D.	con'suli	leo'ni	pa'tri	ar'bori	vir'gini	on'eri
A.	con'sulem	leo'nem	pa'trem	ar'borem	vir'ginem	o'nus
V.	con'sul	le'o	pa'ter	ar'bor	vir'go	o'nus
A.	con'sule	leo'ne	pa'tre	ar'bore	vir'gine	on'ere

Plur.						
N.	con'sules	leo'nes	pa'tres	ar'bores	vir'gines	on'era
G.	con'sulum	leo'num	pa'trum	ar'borum	vir'ginum	on'erum
D.	consu'libus	leon'ibus	pat'ribus	arbor'ibus	virgin'ibus	oner'ibus
A.	con'sules	leo'nes	pa'tres	ar'bores	vir'gines	on'era
V.	con'sules	leo'nes	pa'tres	ar'bores	vir'gines	on'era
A.	consu'libus	leon'ibus	pat'ribus	arbor'ibus	virgin'ibus	oner'ibus

Sing.	Beam, F.	Wealth, F.	Age, F.	Art, F.	Light, F.	Journey, N.
N.	trabs	(ops)	æ'tas	ars	lux	i'ter
G.	tra'bis	o'pis	æta'tis	ar'tis	lu'cis	itin'eris
D.	tra'bi	o'pi	æta'ti	ar'ti	lu'ci	itin'eri
A.	tra'bem	opem	æta'tem	ar'tem	lu'cem	i'ter
V.	trabs	(ops)	æ'tas	ars	lux	i'ter
A.	tra'be	o'pe	æta'te	ar'te	lu'ce	itin'ere

Plur.						
N.	tra'bes	o'pes	æta'tes	ar'tes	lu'ces	itin'era
G.	tra'bium	o'pum	æta'tum	ar'tium	lu'cum	itin'erum
D.	trab'ibus	op'ibus	ætat'ibus	ar'tibus	lu'cibus	itiner'ibus
A.	tra'bes	o'pes	æta'tes	ar'tes	lu'ces	itin'era
V.	tra'bes	o'pes	æta'tes	ar'tes	lu'ces	itin'era
A.	trab'ibus	op'ibus	ætat'ibus	ar'tibus	lu'cibus	itiner'ibus

Table 2.

TERMINATIONS OF NOUNS.

DECL. I. (a)	II. (o)	III. (i)	IV. (u)	V. (e)
N. **a, ĕ**, *as, es*	**us, ŏs,** *eus*, **um,** *ŏn*	**s, &c.** (See § 11, IV.).	**us, u** *ŏ*	**es**
G. **ae** (ai), *es*	**i** (ius), *ei* *o*	**is,** *ŏs*	**us** (uis) *ûs*	**ei** (e)
D. **ae** (ai)	**o** (i) *ei*	**i**	**ui** (u) *o*	**ei** (e)
A. **am,** *an, en*	**um,** *on, ea*	**em** (im), *in* *yn* *ă*	**um** *o*	**em**
V. **a,** *ĕ*	**e** (i), *eu*	(as nom.) *ĭ* *y*	**us** *o*	**es**
A. **a,** *ā*	**o**	**e** (i), *i*	**u** *o*	**e**
Plural.				
N.V. **ae**	**i** *a*	**es, a, ia** *ĕs*	**us, ua**	**es**
G. **arum** (um)	**orum** (um, om), *ŏn*	**um, ium**	**uum**	**erum**
D.A. **is** (abus)	**is** (obus)	**ibus**	**ibus** (ubus)	**ebus**
A. **as**	**os,** *a*	**es** (is), **a, ia** *ăs*	**us, ua**	**es**

1. Unusual forms are in parenthesis; Greek forms in *Italics*.

2. In the Second Declension, when the stem ends in **er, ir**, the terminations of the nom. and voc. singular are not added.

3. In vowel-stems of the Third Declension, the characteristic vowel (**i**) is in several of the cases absorbed in the termination; but it remains in the gen. pl. **ium**, and in some words in the acc. and abl. sing. **im, i**, and the acc. plur. **is (eis)**.

4. The accusative **im** and abl. **i** are found in names of rivers in **is**; also in **ămussis**, † **ăquālis**, **būris**, **cannăbis**, † **clāvis**, † **febris**, **mĕphītis**, † **messis**, † **nāvis**, **pelvis**, **praesēpis**, † **puppis**, **rāvis**, † **restis**, **sĕcūris**, † **sēmentis**, **sĭtis**, † **strĭgĭlis**, † **turris**, **tussis**, **vis**.

5. The following also have the abl. sometimes in **i**: **amnis, civis, finis, fustis, ignis, imber, orbis**.

6. The gen. plur. **ium** is found (rarely with acc. pl. in **is**), in—

a. Vowel-stems, including neuters in **al** and **ar**, and the masculines **imber, linter, ūter, venter**:—except **ăpis, cănis, fŏris, jŭvĕnis, mūgĭlis, prōles, strĭgĭlis, strues, vātes**, and **vŏlucris**, and occasionally a few others, which have **um**;

b. Mute-stems ending in two consonants, except some in **nt**;

c. Local names (adjectives) in **as**, as **nostras**, *of our country*; also **Quĭris, Samnis, Penātes, optĭmātes**, and sometimes other nouns in **as**, as **aetas, civitas**;

d. And the following:—**dos, fauces,** † **fraus,** † **fur, glis,** † **lar lis, mas,** † **mus, nix,** † **ren, strix, trabs, vis**.

7. Nouns in **io**, abstract and collective,—as **rătio**, *reason*; **lĕgio**, *legion*,—are feminine. The following, denoting material objects, are masculine:—**curcŭlio**, *weevil*; **păpĭlio** *butterfly*; **pūgio**, *dagger*; **scīpio**, *staff*; **septemtrio**, *the north*; **stellio**, *lizard*; **struthio**, *ostrich*; **tĭtio**, *firebrand*; **unio**, *pearl*; **vespertilio**, *bat*.

8. The following in **ūs** are feminine:—**incus**, *anvil*; **jŭventus**, *youth*; **pălus**, *marsh*; **pĕcŭs**, *sheep*; **sălus**, *safety*; **sĕnectus**, *old age*; **servĭtus**, *slavery*; **subscus**, *dovetail*; **tellus**, *earth*; **virtus**, *virtue*.

† Sometimes.

Table 3.

INFLECTION OF ADJECTIVES. — I.

FIRST AND SECOND DECLENSION.

Bonus, *good.* | | | **Solus,** *alone, only.*

Sing.	M.	F.	N.	M.	F.	N.
N.	bo'nus	bo'na	bo'num	so'lus	so'la	so'lum
G.	bo'ni	bo'næ	bo'ni	soli'us	soli'us	soli'us
D.	bo'no	bo'næ	bo'no	so'li	so'li	so'li
A.	bo'num	bo'nam	bo'num	so'lum	so'lam	so'lum
V.	bo'ne	bo'na	bo'num	so'le	so'la	so'lum
A.	bo'no	bo'na	bo'no	so'lo	so'la	so'lo

Plur.						
N.	bo'ni	bo'næ	bo'na	so'li	so'læ	so'la
G.	bono'rum	bona'rum	bono'rum	solo'rum	sola'rum	solo'rum
D.	bo'nis	bo'nis	bo'nis	so'lis	so'lis	so'lis
A.	bo'nos	bo'nas	bo'na	so'los	so'las	so'la
V.	bo'ni	bo'næ	bo'na	so'li	so'læ	so'la
A.	bo'nis	bo'nis	bo'nis	so'lis	so'lis	so'lis

Miser, *wretched.* | | | **Ater,** *black.*

Sing.	M.	F.	N.	M.	F.	N.
N.	mi'ser	mis'era	mis'erum	a'ter	a'tra	a'trum
G.	mis'eri	mis'eræ	mis'eri	a'tri	a'træ	a'tri
D.	mis'ero	mis'eræ	mis'ero	a'tro	a'træ	a'tro
A.	mis'erum	mis'eram	mis'erum	a'trum	a'tram	a'trum
V.	mi'ser	mis'era	mis'erum	a'ter	a'tra	a'trum
A.	mis'ero	mis'era	mis'ero	a'tro	a'tra	a'tro

Plur.						
N.	mis'eri	mis'eræ	mis'era	a'tri	a'træ	a'tra
G.	misero'rum	misera'rum	misero'rum	atro'rum	atra'rum	atro'rum
D.	mis'eris	mis'eris	mis'eris	a'tris	a'tris	a'tris
A.	mis'eros	mis'eras	mis'era	a'tros	a'tras	a'tra
V.	mis'eri	mis'eræ	mis'era	a'tri	a'træ	a'tra
A.	mis'eris	mis'eris	mis'eris	a'tris	a'tris	a'tris

THIRD DECLENSION.

1. ADJECTIVES OF TWO AND THREE TERMINATIONS (*Vowel Stems*).

Facilis, *easy.* | | | **Celeber,** *famous.*

Sing.	M.	F.	N.	M.	F.	N.
N.	fac'ilis	fac'ilis	fac'ile	cel'eber	cel'ebris	cel'ebre
G.	fac'ilis	fac'ilis	fac'ilis	cel'ebris	cel'ebris	cel'ebris
D.	fac'ili	fac'ili	fac'ili	cel'ebri	cel'ebri	cel'ebri
A.	fac'ilem	fac'ilem	fac'ile	cel'ebrem	cel'ebrem	cel'ebre
V.	fac'ilis	fac'ilis	fac'ile	cel'eber	cel'ebris	cel'ebre
A.	fac'ili	fac'ili	fac'ili	cel'ebri	cel'ebri	cel'ebri

Plur.						
N.	fac'iles	fac'iles	facil'ia	cel'ebres	cel'ebres	cele'bria
G.	facil'ium	facil'ium	facil'ium	cele'brium	cele'brium	cele'brium
D.	facil'ibus	facil'ibus	facil'ibus	cele'bribus	cele'bribus	cele'bribus
A.	fac'iles(is)	fac'iles(is)	facil'ia	cel'ebres(is)	cel'ebres(is)	cele'bria
V.	fac'iles	fac'iles	facil'ia	cel'ebres	cel'ebres	cele'bria
D.	facil'ibus	facil'ibus	facil'ibus	cele'bribus	cele'bribus	cele'bribus

Like **celĕber** are declined **acer,** *keen;* **alăcer,** *eager;* **campester,** *of the field;* **equester,** *of horsemen;* **paluster,** *marshy;* **pedester,** *on foot;* **puter,** *rotten;* **salūber,** *wholesome;* **silvester,** *wooded;* **terrester,** *of the land;* **volūcer,** *winged;* also, **celer, celĕris, celere,** *swift.*

Table 4.

INFLECTION OF ADJECTIVES. — II.

ADJECTIVES OF ONE TERMINATION (*Consonant Stems*).

Sing.

	M. F.	N.	M. F.	N.	M. F.	N.
N.	u'ber, *fertile*		ve'tus, *old*		par, *equal*	
G.	u'beris		vet'eris		pa'ris	
D.	u'beri		vet'eri		pa'ri	
A.	u'berem	uber	vet'erem	ve'tus	pa'rem	par
V.	u'ber		ve'tus		par	
A.	u'bere (i)		vet'ere (i)		pari	

Plu.

	M. F.	N.	M. F.	N.	M. F.	N.
N.	u'beres	u'bera	vet'eres	vet'era	pa'res	pa'ria
G.	u'berum		vet'erum		pa'rium	
D.	uber'ibus		veter'ibus		par'ibus	
A.	u'beres	u'bera	vet'eres	vet'era	pa'res	pa'ria
V.	u'beres	u'bera	vet'eres	vet'era	pa'res	pa'ria
A.	uber'ibus		veter'ibus		par'ibus	

Sing.

	M. F.	M. F.	M. F.	N.	M. F.	N.
N.	in'ops, *poor*	sos'pes, *safe*	di'ves, *rich*		e'dax, *greedy*	
G.	in'opis	sos'pitis	div'itis		eda'cis	
D.	in'opi	sos'piti	div'iti		eda'ci	
A.	in'opem	sos'pitem	div'item	di'ves	eda'cem	e'dax
V.	in'ops	sos'pes	di'ves		e'dax	
A.	in'opi	sos'pite	div'ite (i)		eda'ci	

Plu.

	M. F.	M. F.	M. F.	N.	M. F.	N.
N.	in'opes	sos'pites	div'ites	(ditia)	eda'ces	eda'cia
G.	in'opum	sos'pitum	div'itum		eda'cium	
D.	inop'ibus	sospit'ibus	divit'ibus		edac'ibus	
A.	in'opes	sos'pites	div'ites	(ditia)	eda'ces	eda'cia
V.	in'opes	sos'pites	div'ites	(ditia)	eda'ces	eda'cia
A.	inop'ibus	sospit'ibus	divit'ibus		edac'ibus	

Sing. — PARTICIPLES. — COMPARATIVES.

	M. F.	N.	M. F.	N.	M. F.	N.
N.	a'mans, *loving*		i'ens, *going*		al'tior	al'tius, *higher*
G.	aman'tis		eun'tis		altio'ris	
D.	aman'ti		eun'ti		altio'ri	
A.	aman'tem	a'mans	eun'tem	i'ens	altio'rem	al'tius
V.	a'mans		i'ens		al'tior	al'tius
A.	aman'te (i)		eun'te (i)		altio're (i)	

Plur.

	M. F.	N.	M. F.	N.	M. F.	N.
N	aman'tes	aman'tia	eun'tes	eun'tia	altio'res	altio'ra
G	aman'tium (um)		eun'tium		altio'rum	
D	aman'tibus		eun'tibus		altior'ibus	
A.	aman'tes	aman'tia	eun'tes	eun'tia	altio'res	altio'ra
V.	aman'tes	aman'tia	eun'tes	eun'tia	altio'res	altio'ra
A.	aman'tibus		eun'tibus		altior'ibus	

The ablative singular commonly ends in i. Many adjectives, as, Inops, have only i; some, as sospĕs, only e. Comparatives, and participles in ns, when used as participles, have usually e; so also have adjectives used as nouns, as inops, *a poor man*, inŏpe.

Liquid stems, and a few mute stems, as dīves, inops, supplex, partĭceps, with those that have abl. sing. e, have gen. pl. um.

Some adjectives, as inops, sospes, are found only in the masc. and fem., and may be called adjectives of Common Gender.

Plus, *more* (N.), has gen. plūris; plur., nom. plures, plura; gen. plurium, etc. : complūres, *several*, has sometimes neut. pl. compluria. All other comparatives are declined like altĭor.

Table 5.

PRONOUNS. — I.

PERSONAL, POSSESSIVE, AND DEMONSTRATIVE.

First Person.

SING. *I.*	*My.*			*Of our country.*
N. ego	meus	mea	meum	nostras
G. mei	mei	meæ	mei	nostra'tis
D. mihi	meo	meæ	meo	nostra'ti
A. me	meum	meam	meum	nostra'tem -tras
V. ——	mi	mea	meum	nostras
A. me	meo	mea	meo	nostra'te (i)
PLUR. *We.*				
N. nos	mei	meæ	mea	nostra'tes -tia
G nostrum, -tri	meorum	mearum	meorum	nostra'tium
D. nobis	meis	meis	meis	nostrat'ibus
A. nos	meos	meas	mea	nostra'tes -tia
V. ——	mei	meæ	mea	nostra'tes -tia
A. nobis	meis	meis	meis	nostrat'ibus

Second Person.

SING. *Thou.*	*Your.*			*[Whose.]*
N. tu	vester	vestra	vestrum	cujus -a -um
G. tui	vestri	vestræ	vestri	——
D. tib'i	vestro	vestræ	vestro	——
A. te	vestrum	vestram	vestrum	cujum -am -um
V. tu				——
A. te	vestro	vestra	vestro	cuja
PLUR. *You.*				
N vos	vestri	vestræ	vestra	cujæ
G. vestrum, -tri	vestrorum	vestrarum	vestrorum	——
D. vobis	vestris	vestris	vestris	——
A vos	vestros	vestras	vestra	cujas
V. vos				——
A. vobis	vestris	vestris	vestris	——

Demonstratives.

SING.	*That.*			*Self.*		
N. il'le	il'la	il'lud	ip'se	ip'sa	ip'sum
G. illi'us	illi'us	illi'us	ipsi'us	ipsi'us	ipsi'us
D. il'li	il'li	il'li	ip'si	ip'si	ip'si
A. il'lum	il'lam	il'lud	ip'sum	ip'sam	ip'sum
V. ——			ip'se	ip'sa	ip'sum
A. il'lo	il'la	il'lo	ip'so	ip'sa	ip'so
PLUR.	*Those.*			*Selves.*		
N. il'li	il'læ	il'la	ip'si	ip'sæ	ip'sa
G. illo'rum	illa'rum	illo'rum	ipso'rum	ipsa'rum	ipso'rum
D. il'lis	il'lis	il'lis	ip'sis	ip'sis	ip'sis
A. il'los	il'las	il'la	ip'sos	ip'sas	ip'sa
V. ——			ip'si	ip'sæ	ip'sa
A. il'lis	il'lis	il'lis	ip'sis	ip'sis	ip'sis

The Same.

SING.			PLUR.		
N. i'dem	e'adem	i'dem	ii'dem	eæ'dem	e'adem
G ejus'dem	ejus'dem	ejus'dem	eorun'dem	earun'dem	eorun'dem
D. ei'dem	ei'dem	ei'dem	eis'dem or iis'dem		
A. eun'dem	ean'dem	i'dem	eos'dem	eas'dem	e'adem
A. eo'dem	ea'dem	eo'dem	eis'dem or iis'dem		

Idem is the demonstrative **is, ea, id,** with the affix **-dem,** *same;* which is also added to the ablatives eō, *to that place,* and eā, *by that way.*

Table 6.

PRONOUNS. — II.

RELATIVE, INTERROGATIVE, AND INDEFINITE.

SING.	Who?				Some one.	
N. quis	quæ	quid		al'iquis	al'iqua	al'iquid
G.	cujus				alicu'jus	
D.	cui				al'icui	
A. quem	quam	quid		al'iquem	al'iquam	al'iquid
A. quo	qua	quo		al'iquo	al'iqua	al'iquo
PLUR.						
N. qui	quæ	quæ		al'iqui	al'iquæ	al'iqua
G. quorum	quarum	quorum		aliquo'rum	aliqua'rum	aliquo'rum
D.	quibus				ali'quibus	
A. quos	quas	quæ		al'iquos	al'iquas	al'iqua
A.	quibus				ali'quibus	

Like **alĭquis** are declined the indefinite pronouns **quis, quispiam,** *any.*

SING.	A certain one.			Any at all.	
N. quidam	quæ'dam	quoddam		quisquam	quicquam
G.	cujus'dam			cujus'quam	
D.	cui'dam			cui'quam	
A. quendam	quandam	quoddam		quemquam	quicquam
A. quodam	quadam	quodam		quoquam	
PLUR.				No one.	
N. quidam	quædam	quædam		nemo	
G. quorun'dam	quarun'dam	quorun'dam		(nulli'us)	
D.	quibus'dam			nem'ini	
A. quosdam	quasdam	quædam		nem'inem	
A.	quibus'dam			(nullo)	

Quisque, *every,* and **unusquisque** are thus declined: —

N. unusquis'que	unaquæ'que	unumquid'que (-quodque, -quicquid)
G.	uniuscujus'que	
D.	unicui'que	
A. unumquemque	unamquam'que	unumquid'que
A. unoquo'que	unaqua'que	unoquo'que

Compounds of **quis (qui),** *who,* and **ŭter,** *which of the two,* are: —

quisque,	uterque (utrăque utrumque), *each*
quivis,	utervis,
quilĭbet,	uterlibet, } *whichever you please*
quicumque,	utercumque, *whichever*
[undĭque,]	utrimque (adv.), *on all* (or *both*) *sides*
———	alteruter (-tra, -trum, gen. **trius**), *one or the other*

Quisquam (pron.) and **ullus** (adj.), *any;* **umquam,** *ever;* **usquam,** *anywhere,* are used only in negative, interrogative, and conditional sentences; also after **quam,** *than,* or **sine,** *without.*

The use of these indefinites is seen in the following lines: —

Quis, quispiam, *any,* esse dant   Quivis, quilibet, *any you please,*
Vel ponunt; non determinant: Continebunt cunctas res:
Aliquis, *some one,* denotat   Quisquam, *any at all,* et ullus,
Quempiam, sed non nominat.   Excludunt omnes, sicut nullus.

Donaldson.

With **all** relatives, the enclitic affix **-cumque, -soever,** may be used: as, **qualiscumque,** *of what kind soever.*

Table 7.

FIRST CONJUGATION.

I. ACTIVE VOICE.

INDIC.	SUBJ.

PRESENT, *I love.*

a'mo, *I love*	a'mem
a'mas, *thou lovest*	a'mes
a'mat, *he loves*	a'met
ama'mus, *we love*	ame'mus
ama'tis, *you love*	ame'tis
a'mant, *they love*	a'ment

IMPERFECT, *I loved (used to love).*

ama'bam	ama'rem
ama'bas	ama'res
ama'bat	ama'ret
amaba'mus	amare'mus
amaba'tis	amare'tis
ama'bant	ama'rent

FUTURE, *I shall or will love.*

ama'bo	amatu'rus
ama'bis	sim, &c.
ama'bit	
amab'imus	
amab'itis	
ama'bunt	

PERFECT, *I loved (have loved).*

ama'vi	amav'erim
amavis'ti	amav'eris
ama'vit	amav'erit
amav'imus	amaver'imus
amavis'tis	amaver'itis
amave'runt, -e're	amav'erint

PLUPERFECT, *I had loved.*

amav'eram	amavis'sem
amav'eras	amavis'ses
amav'erat	amavis'set
amavera'mus	amavisse'mus
amavera'tis	amavisse'tis
amav'erant	amavis'sent

FUTURE PERFECT, *I shall have loved.*

amav'ero	amav'erim
amav'eris	&c.
amav'erit	
amaver'imus	
amaver'itis	
amav'erint	

II. PASSIVE VOICE.

INDIC.	SUBJ.

PRESENT, *I am loved.*

a'mor	a'mer
ama'ris (re)	ame'ris (re)
ama'tur	ame'tur
ama'mur	ame'mur
amam'ini	amem'ini
aman'tur	amen'tur

IMPERFECT, *I was loved.*

ama'bar	ama'rer
amaba'ris (re)	amare'ris (re)
amaba'tur	amare'tur
amaba'mur	amare'mur
amabam'ini	amarem'ini
amaban'tur	amaren'tur

FUTURE, *I shall be loved.*

ama'bor	futu'rum sit ut
amab'eris (re)	a'mer, &c.
amab'itur	
amab'imur	
amabim'ini	
amabun'tur	

PERFECT, *I was (have been) loved.*

ama'tus sum	ama'tus sim
ama'tus es	ama'tus sis
ama'tus est	ama'tus sit
ama'ti sumus	ama'ti simus
ama'ti estis	ama'ti sitis
ama'ti sunt	ama'ti sint

PLUPERFECT, *I had been loved.*

ama'tus eram	ama'tus es'sem
ama'tus eras	ama'tus es'ses
ama'tus erat	ama'tus es'set
ama'ti era'mus	ama'ti esse'mus
ama'ti era'tis	ama'ti esse'tis
ama'ti e'rant	ama'ti es'sent

FUTURE PERFECT, *I shall have been loved.*

ama'tus ero	ama'tus sim
ama'tus eris	&c.
ama'tus erit	
ama'ti er'imus	
ama'ti er'itis	
ama'ti e'runt	

IMPERATIVE.

	SING.	PLUR.	SING.	PLUR.
PR.	a'ma, *love thou*	ama'te, *love ye*	ama're	amam'ini
F.	ama'to	amato'te	———	———
	ama'to	aman'to	ama'tor	aman'tor

INFINITIVE.

PR. ama're, *to love* PF. amavis'se, *to* PR. ama'ri PF. ama'tus esse
F. amatu'rus esse[*have loved* F. ama'tum iri (ama'tus fo're)

PARTICIPLES.

PR. a'mans FUT. amatu'rus PERF. ama'tus GER. aman'dus, a, um
  loving   *about to love*   *loved*   *to be loved.*
  GER. aman'dum, *loving*   SUP. ama'tum, ama'tu, *to love*

Table 8.

Second Conjugation.

I. Active Voice.		II. Passive Voice.	
INDIC.	SUBJ.	INDIC.	SUBJ.

PRESENT, *I warn.* / PRESENT, *I am warned.*

mo′neo, *I warn*	mo′neam	mo′neor	mo′near
mo′nes, *you warn*	mo′neas	mone′ris (re)	monea′ris (re)
mo′net, *he warns*	mo′neat	mone′tur	monea′tur
mone′mus [&c.	monea′mus	mone′mur	monea′mur
mone′tis	monea′tis	monem′ini	moneam′ini
mo′nent	mo′neant	monen′tur	monean′tur

IMPERFECT, *I was warning.* / IMPERFECT, *I was warned.*

mone′bam	mone′rem	mone′bar	mone′rer
mone′bas	mone′res	moneba′ris (re)	monere′ris (re)
mone′bat	mone′ret	moneba′tur	monere′tur
moneba′mus	monere′mus	moneba′mur	monere′mur
moneba′tis	monere′tis	monebam′ini	monerem′ini
mone′bant	mone′rent	moneban′tur	moneren′tur

FUTURE, *I shall warn.* / FUTURE, *I shall be warned.*

mone′bo	monitu′rus sim	mone′bor	futu′rum sit ut
mone′bis	monitu′rus sis	moneb′eris (re)	monear,
mone′bit	monitu′rus sit	moneb′itur	-a′ris, &c.
moneb′imus	monitu′ri simus	moneb′imur	
moneb′itis	monitu′ri sitis	monebim′ini	
mone′bunt	monitu′ri sint	monebun′tur	

PERFECT, *I warned (have warned).* / PERFECT, *I was (have been) warned.*

mon′ui	monu′erim	mon′itus sum	mon′itus sim
monuis′ti	monu′eris	mon′itus es	mon′itus sis
mon′uit	monu′erit	mon′itus est	mon′itus sit
monu′imus	monuer′imus	mon′iti sumus	mon′iti simus
monuis′tis	monuer′itis	mon′iti estis	mon′iti sitis
monue′runt (re)	monu′erint	mon′iti sunt	mon′iti sint

PLUPERFECT, *I had warned.* / PLUPERFECT, *I had been warned.*

monu′eram	monuis′sem	mon′itus eram	mon′itus essem
monu′eras	monuis′ses	mon′itus eras	mon′itus esses
monu′erat	monuis′set	mon′itus erat	mon′itus esset
monuera′mus	monuisse′mus	mon′iti era′mus	mon′iti esse′mus
monuera′tis	monuisse′tis	mon′iti era′tis	mon′iti esse′tis
monu′erant	monuis′sent	mon′iti erant	mon′iti essent

FUTURE PERFECT, *I shall have warned.* / FUTURE PERFECT, *I shall have been warned.*

monu′ero	monu′erim	mon′itus ero	mon′itus sim
monu′eris	&c.	mon′itus eris	&c.
monu′erit		mon′itus erit	
monuer′imus		mon′iti er′imus	
monuer′itis		mon′iti er′itis	
monu′erint		mon′iti erunt	

IMPERATIVE.

	SING.	PLUR.		SING.	PLUR.
PR.	mo′ne	mone′te		mone′re	monem′ini
F.	mone′to	moneto′te		——	——
	mone′to	monen′to		mone′tor	monen′tor

INFINITIVE.

PR.	mone′re	PF monuis′se	PR.	mone′ri	PF. mo′nitus esse
F.	monitu′rus esse		F.	mon′itum iri (mon′itus fo′re)	

PARTICIPLES.

mo′nens	monitu′rus	mon′itus	monen′dus

GER. monen′dum, di, &c.   SUP. mon′itum, mon′itu

Table 9.

THIRD CONJUGATION (*Consonant Stem*).

I. ACTIVE VOICE.		II. PASSIVE VOICE.	
INDIC.	SUBJ.	INDIC.	SUBJ.

PRESENT, *I rule.*

		PRESENT, *I am ruled.*	
re′go, *I rule.*	re′gam	re′gor	re′gar
re′gis, *thou rulest.*	re′gas	reg′eris (re)	rega′ris (re)
re′git, *he rules.*	re′gat	reg′itur	rega′tur
reg′imus, *we rule.*	rega′mus	reg′imur	rega′mur
reg′itis, *you rule.*	rega′tis	regim′ini	regam′ini
re′gunt, *they rule.*	re′gant	regun′tur	regan′tur

IMPERFECT, *I was ruling.*

		IMPERFECT, *I was ruled.*	
rege′bam	reg′erem	rege′bar	re′gerer
rege′bas	reg′eres	regeba′ris (re)	regere′ris (re)
rege′bat	reg′eret	regeba′tur	regere′tur
regeba′mus	regere′mus	regeba′mur	regere′mur
regeba′tis	regere′tis	regebam′ini	regerem′ini
rege′bant	reg′erent	regeban′tur	regeren′tur

FUTURE, *I shall rule.*

		FUTURE, *I shall be ruled.*	
re′gam	rectu′rus sim	re′gar	futu′rum sit ut
re′ges	rectu′rus sis	rege′ris (re)	re′gar
re′get	rectu′rus sit	rege′tur	rega′ris, &c.
rege′mus	rectu′ri simus	rege′mur	
rege′tis	rectu′ri sitis	regem′ini	
re′gent	rectu′ri sint	regen′tur	

PERFECT, *I ruled (have ruled).*

		PERFECT, *I was (have been) ruled.*	
rex′i	rex′erim	rec′tus sum	rec′tus sim
rexis′ti	rex′eris	rec′tus es	rec′tus sis
rex′it	rex′erit	rec′tus est	rec′tus sit
rex′imus	rexer′imus	rec′ti sumus	rec′ti simus
rexis′tis	rexer′itis	rec′ti estis	rec′ti sitis
rexe′runt (re)	rex′erint	rec′ti sunt	rec′ti sint

PLUPERFECT, *I had ruled.*

		PLUPERFECT, *I had been ruled.*	
rex′eram	rexis′sem	rec′tus eram	rec′tus essem
rex′eras	rexis′ses	rec′tus eras	rec′tus esses
rex′erat	rexis′set	rec′tus erat	rec′tus esset
rexera′mus	rexisse′mus	rec′ti era′mus	rec′ti esse′mus
rexera′tis	rexisse′tis	rec′ti era′tis	rec′ti esse′tis
rex′erant	rexis′sent	rec′ti erant	rec′ti essent

FUTURE PERFECT, *I shall have ruled.*

		FUTURE PERFECT, *I shall have been ruled.*	
rex′ere	rex′erim	rec′tus ero	rec′tus sim
rex′eris	&c.	rec′tus eris	&c.
rex′erit		rec′tus erit	
rexer′imus		rec′ti er′imus	
rexer′itis		rec′ti er′itis	
rex′erint		rec′ti erunt	

IMPERATIVE.

	SING.	PLUR.	SING.	PLUR.
PR. 2.	re′ge	regi′te	reg′ere	regim′ini
F. 2.	reg′ito	regito′te	—	
8.	reg′ito	regun′to	re′gitor	regun′tor

INFINITIVE.

PR. reg′ere	PF. rexis′se	PR re′gi	PF. rec′tus esse
F. rectu′rus esse		F. rec′tum iri (rec′tus fo′re)	

PARTICIPLES.

re′gens	rectu′rus	rec′tus	regen′dus

GER. regen′dum, di, &c.   SUP. rec′tum, rec′tu

Table 10.

THIRD CONJUGATION (*Vowel Stem*).

I. ACTIVE VOICE.		II. PASSIVE VOICE.	
INDIC.	SUBJ.	INDIC.	SUBJ.

PRESENT, *I take.*

		PRESENT, *I am taken.*	
ca'pio, *I take.*	ca'piam	ca'pior	ca'piar
ca'pis, *thou takest.*	ca'pias	cap'eris (re)	capia'ris (re)
ca'pit, *he takes.*	ca'piat	capi'tur	capia'tur
cap'imus, *we take.*	capia'mus	cap'imur	capia'mur
cap'itis, *you take.*	capia'tis	capim'ini	capiam'ini
ca'piunt, *they take.*	ca'piant	capiun'tur	capian'tur

IMPERFECT, *I was taking.*

		IMPERFECT, *I was taken.*	
capie'bam	cap'erem	capie'bar	cap'erer
capie'bas	cap'eres	capieba'ris (re)	capere'ris (re)
capie'bat	cap'eret	capieba'tur	capere'tur
capieba'mus	capere'mus	capieba'mur	capere'mur
capieba'tis	capere'tis	capiebam'ini	caperem'ini
capie'bant	cap'erent	capieban'tur	caperen'tur

FUTURE, *I shall take.*

		FUTURE, *I shall be taken.*	
ca'piam	captu'rus sim	ca'piar	futu'rum sit ut
ca'pies	captu'rus sis	capie'ris (re)	ca'piar
ca'piet	captu'rus sit	capie'tur	-a'ris, &c.
capie'mus	captu'ri simus	capie'mur	
capie'tis	captu'ri sitis	capiem'ini	
ca'pient	captu'ri sint	capien'tur	

PERFECT, *I took (have taken).*

		PERFECT, *I was (have been) taken.*	
ce'pi	cep'erim	cap'tus sum	cap'tus sim
cepis'ti	cep'eris	cap'tus es	cap'tus sis
ce'pit	cep'erit	cap'tus est	cap'tus sit
cep'imus	ceper'imus	cap'ti sumus	cap'ti simus
cepis'tis	ceper'itis	cap'ti estis	cap'ti sitis
cepe'runt (re)	cep'erint	cap'ti sunt	cap'ti sint

PLUPERFECT, *I had taken.*

		PLUPERFECT, *I had been taken.*	
cep'eram	cepis'sem	cap'tus eram	cap'tus essem
cep'eras	cepis'ses	cap'tus eras	cap'tus esses
cep'erat	cepis'set	cap'tus erat	cap'tus esset
cepera'mus	cepisse'mus	cap'ti era'mus	cap'ti esse'mus
cepera'tis	cepisse'tis	cap'ti era'tis	cap'ti esse'tis
cep'erant	cepis'sent	cap'ti erant	cap'ti essent

FUTURE PERFECT, *I shall have taken.*

		FUTURE PERFECT, *I shall have been taken.*	
cep'ero	cep'erim	cap'tus ero	cap'tus sim
cep'eris	&c.	cap'tus eris	&c.
cep'erit		cap'tus erit	
ceper'imus		cap'ti er'imus	
ceper'itis		cap'ti er'itis	
cep'erint		cap'ti erunt	

IMPERATIVE.

	SING.	PLUR.	SING.	PLUR.
PR. 2.	ca'pe	cap'ite	cap'ere	capim'ini
F. 2.	cap'ito	capito'te	———	
3.	cap'ito	capiun'to	cap'itor	capiun'tor

INFINITIVE.

PR. cap'ere	PF. cepis'se	PR. ca'pi	PF. cap'tus esse
F. captu'rus esse		F. cap'tum iri (cap'tus fo're)	

PARTICIPLES.

ca'piens	captu'rus	cap'tus	capien'dus
GER capien'dum, di, &c.		SUP. cap'tum, cap'tu	

Table 11.

FOURTH CONJUGATION

I. ACTIVE VOICE.		II. PASSIVE VOICE.	
INDIC.	**SUBJ.**	**INDIC.**	**SUBJ.**

PRESENT, *I hear.*   **PRESENT, *I am heard.***

au'dio, *I hear.*	au'diam	au'dior	au'diar
au'dis, *thou hearest.*	au'dias	audi'ris (re)	audia'ris (re)
au'dit, *he hears.*	au'diat	audi'tur	audia'tur
audi'mus, *we hear.*	audia'mus	audi'mur	audia'mur
audi'tis, *you hear.*	audia'tis	audim'ini	audiam'ini
au'diunt, *they hear.*	au'diant	audiun'tur	audian'tur

IMPERFECT, *I was hearing.*   **IMPERFECT, *I was heard.***

audie'bam	audi'rem	audie'bar	audi'rer
audie'bas	audi'res	audieba'ris (re)	audire'ris (re)
audie'bat	audi'ret	audieba'tur	audire'tur
audieba'mus	audire'mus	audieba'mur	audire'mur
audieba'tis	audire'tis	audiebam'ini	audi'rem'ini
audio'bant	audi'rent	audieban'tur	audiren'tur

FUTURE, *I shall hear.*   **FUTURE, *I shall be heard.***

au'diam	auditu'rus sim	au'diar	futu'rum sit ut
au'dies	auditu'rus sis	audie'ris (re)	audi'ar,
au'diet	auditu'rus sit	audie'tur	-a'ris, &c.
audie'mus	auditu'ri simus	audie'mur	
audie'tis	auditu'ri sitis	audiem'ini	
au'dient	auditu'ri sint	audien'tur	

PERFECT, *I heard (have heard).*   **PERFECT, *I was (have been) heard.***

audi'vi	audiv'erim	audi'tus sum	audi'tus sim
audivis'ti	audiv'eris	audi'tus es	audi'tus sis
audi'vit	audiv'erit	audi'tus est	audi'tus sit
audiv'imus	audiver'imus	audi'ti sumus	audi'ti simus
audivis'tis	audiver'itis	audi'ti estis	audi'ti sitis
audive'runt (re)	audiv'erint	audi'ti sunt	audi'ti sint

PLUPERFECT, *I had heard.*   **PLUPERFECT, *I had been heard.***

audiv'eram	audivis'sem	audi'tus eram	audi'tus essem
audiv'eras	audivis'ses	audi'tus eras	audi'tus esses
audiv'erat	audivis'set	audi'tus erat	audi'tus esset
audivera'mus	audivisse'mus	audi'ti era'mus	audi'ti esse'mus
audivera'tis	audivisse'tis	audi'ti era'tis	audi'ti esse'tis
audiv'erant	audivis'sent	audi'ti erant	audi'ti essent

FUTURE PERFECT, *I shall have heard.*   **FUTURE PERFECT, *I shall have been heard.***

audiv'ero	audiv'erim	audi'tus ero	audi'tus sim
audiv'eris	&c.	audi'tus eris	&c.
audiv'erit		audi'tus erit	
audiver'imus		audi'ti er'imus	
audiver'itis		audi'ti er'itis	
audiv'erint		audi'ti erunt	

IMPERATIVE.

	SING.	PLUR.		SING.	PLUR.
PR. 2.	au'di	audi'te		audi're	audim'ini
F. 2.	audi'to	audito'te		——	——
3.	audi'to	audiun'to		audi'tor	audiun'tor

INFINITIVE.

PR. audi're	PF. audivis'se	PR. audi'ri	PF. audi'tus esse	
F. auditu'rus esse		F. audi'tum iri (audi'tus fo're)		

PARTICIPLES.

au'diens	auditu'rus	audi'tus	audien'dus

GER. audien'dum, di, &c.   SUP. audi'tum, audi'tu

Table 12.

Esse, *to be*, AND ITS COMPOUNDS.

INDIC.	SUBJ.	INDIC.	SUBJ.	INDIC.	SUBJ.
		I can	PRESENT.	*I help*	
sum, *I am*	sim	possum	possim	prosum,	prosim
es, *thou art*	sis	potes	possis	prodes	prosis
est, *he is*	sit	potest	possit	prodest	prosit
sumus	simus	pos'sumus	possi'mus	pro'sumus	prosi'mus
estis	sitis	potes'tis	possi'tis	prodestis	prosi'tis
sunt	sint	possunt	possint	prosunt	prosint
		I could	IMPERFECT.	*I helped*	
eram	essem	pot'eram	possem	prod'eram	prodessem
eras	esses	pot'eras	posses	prod'eras	prodesses
erat	esset	pot'erat	posset	prod'erat	prodesset
era'mus	esse'mus	potera'mus	posse'mus	prodera'mus	prodessemus
era'tis	esse'tis	potera'tis	posse'tis	prodera'tis	prodessetis
erant	essent	pot'erant	possent	prod'erant	prodessent

FUTURE.

ero, *I shall be*		pot'ero, *I shall be able,*		prod'ero, *I shall help,*	
eris &c		pot'eris &c.		prod'eris &c.	
erit		pot'erit		prod'erit	
er'imus		poter'imus		proder'imus	
er'itis		poter'itis		proder'itis	
erunt		pot'erunt		prod'erunt	

PERFECT.

I was or *have been*					
fui	fu'erim	potui	potuerim	profui	profu'erim
fuisti	fu'eris	potuisti	potu'eris	profuisti	profu'eris
fuit	fu'erit	potuit	potu'erit	profuit	profu'erit
fu'imus	fuer'imus	potu'imus	potuerimus	profu'imus	profuerimus
fuistis	fuer'itis	potuistis	potuer'itis	profuistis	profue'ritis
fue'runt or fue're	fu'erint	potue'runt or potu're	potu'erint	profue'runt or profue're	profu'erint

PLUPERFECT.

I had been					
fu'eram	fuis'sem	potu'eram	potuis'sem	profu'eram	profuis'sem
fu'eras	fuis'ses	potu'eras	potuis'ses	profu'eras	profuis'ses
fu'erat	fuis'set	potu'erat	potuis'set	profu'erat	profuis'set
fuera'-mus	fuisse'-mus	potuera'-mus	potuisse'-mus	profuera'-mus	profuisse'-mus
fuera'tis	fuisse'tis	potuera'tis	potuisse'tis	profuera'tis	profuissetis
fu'erant	fuis'sent	potu'erant	potuis'sent	profu'erant	profuis'sent

FUTURE PERFECT.

fu'ero, *I shall have been*	potu'ero			profu'ero	
fu'eris	potu'eris			profu'eris	
fu'erit	potu'erit			profu'erit	
fuer'imus	potuer'imus			profuer'imus	
fuer'itis	potue'ritis			profuer'itis	
fu'erint	potu'erint			profu'erint	

IMPERATIVE.

PR. es, *be thou* este, *be ye*

FUT. esto, *thou shalt be* estote, *ye shall be*
sunto, *they shall be*

INFINITIVE.

esse, *to be* fuisse, *to have been* posse potuisse prodesse profuisse
fore or futurus esse, *to be about to be*

PARTICIPLES.

FUT. futurus, *about to be* [potens, *powerful.*] profuturus

Esse is also combined with the prepositions ab, ad, de, in,
inter, ob, prae, sub, super.

Table 13.

Irregular Conjugation. — I.

The following list contains the Stem-endings of all the simple Verbs which form their Perfect and Supine Stems otherwise than by § 30, ii. iii.   Those marked † have also regular forms.

Forms preceded by a hyphen are found only in compounds.

Compounds generally change ă or ĕ of the stem into ĭ

I.

†crepo, ui, it- *resound*.
cubo, ui, it-, *lie down*.
do, dedi, dăt-, *give*.
domo, ui, it-, *subdue*.
frico, cui, †ct-, *rub*.
juvo, juvi, jut-, *help*.
mico, micui, *glitter*.
†neco, necui, ct-, *kill*.
plico, cui, -cit-, *fold*.
†poto, — pot-, *drink*.
seco, cui, ct-, *cut*.
sono, ui, it-, *sound*.
sto, steti, stat-, *stand*.
tono, ui, it-, *thunder*.
veto, ui, it-, *forbid*.

II.

algeo, alsi, *be cold*.
ardeo, arsi, ars-, *burn*.
augeo, xi, ct-, *increase*.
caveo, cavi, caut-, *care*.
censeo, nsui, ns-, *value*.
cieo, civi, cit-, *excite*.
deleo, evi, et-, *destroy*.
doceo, cui, doct-, *teach*.
faveo, vi, faut-, *favor*.
ferveo, vi, bui, *boil*.
fleo, flevi, flet-, *weep*.
foveo, fovi, fot-, *cherish*.
frigeo, frixi, *be cold*.
fulgeo, fulsi, *shine*.
haereo, si, haes-, *stick*.
indulgeo, si, s-, *indulge*.
jubeo, jussi, juss-, *bid*.
langueo, gui, *faint*.
liqueo, liqui (cui), *melt*.
luceo, luxi, *shine*.
lugeo, xi, ct-, *mourn*.
maneo, si, mans-, *wait*.
misceo, scui, st-, (xt-) *mix, mingle*.
mordeo, momordi, mors-, *bite*.
moveo, vi, mot-, *move*.
mulceo, lsi, ls-, *soothe*.
mulgeo, lsi (xi), ls- (lct-), *milk*.
neo, nevi, net-, *spin*.
niveo, †nixi, *wink*.
paveo, pavi, *fear*.
pendeo, pependi, *hang*.
-pleo, plevi, plet-, *fill*.
prandeo, ndi, ns-, *dine*.
rideo, risi, ris-, *laugh*.
sedeo, sedi, sess-, *sit*.
sorbeo, bui (psi), *suck*.
spondeo, spopondi, spons-, *pledge*.

strideo, stridi, *whiz*.
suadeo, suasi, suas-, *persuade*.
teneo, tenui, tent-, *hold*.
tergeo, rsi, ters-, *wipe*.
tondeo, totondi, tons-, *shear*.
torqueo, rsi, rt-, *twist*.
torreo, ui, tost-, *roast*.
turgeo, tursi, *swell*.
urgeo, ursi, *urge*.
video, vidi, vis-, *see*.
voveo, vovi, vot-, *vow*.

III.

abdo, didi, dit-, *hide*.
ago, egi, act-, *drive*.
alo, ui, alt- (it-), *nourish*.
arcesso, ivi, it-, *summon*.
bibo, bibi, bibit-, *drink*.
cado, cecidi, cas-, *fall*.
caedo, cecidi, caes-, *cut*.
cano, cecini, cant-, *sing*.
capesso, sivi, *undertake*.
capio, cepi, capt-, *take*.
cedo, cessi, cess-, *move*.
-cello, -ui, -cels-, *impel*.
-cendo, di, cens-, *kindle*.
cerno-, crevi, cret-, *decree*.
cingo, cinxi, nct-, *gird*.
claudo, si, claus-, *shut*.
colo, colui, cult-, *till*.
compesco, cui, *restrain*.
consulo, lui, lt-, *consult*.
coquo, coxi, coct-, *cook*.
credo, didi, dit-, *trust*.
cresco, evi, et-, *grow*.
cudo, -di, -cus-, *forge*.
-cumbo, -cubui, -cubit-, *lie down*.
cupio, ivi, it-, *desire*.
curro, cucurri, curs-, *run*.
-cutio, -ssi, -ss-, *shake*.
demo, mpsi, mpt-, *take away*.
depso, sui, st-, *knead*.
disco, didici, discituris, *learn*.
divido, visi, vis-, *divide*.
-do, -didi, -dit-, *give*.
edo, edi, es-, *eat* (p.42).
emo, emi, empt-, *buy*.
facesso, si, sit-, *execute*.
facio, feci, fact-, *make*.
fallo, fefelli, fals-, *fail*.
-fendo, -di, -ns-, *ward*.
fero, tuli, lat-, *bear*.

figo, fixi, fix-, *fix*.
findo, fidi, fiss-, *split*.
fingo, nxi, ct-, *fashion*.
flecto, xi, flex-, *bend*.
fluo, fluxi, flux-, *flow*.
fodio, fodi, foss-, *dig*.
frango, fregi, fract-, *break*.
fremo, ui, it-, *roar*.
frendo, -fres- ss-, *gnash*.
fugio, fugi, fugit-, *flee*.
fundo, fudi, fus-, *pour*.
furo, furui, *rage*.
gemo, ui, it-, *groan*.
gero, gessi, gest-, *bear*.
gigno, genui, it-, *beget*.
ico, ici, ict-, *strike*.
incesso, ivi, *attack*.
jacio, jeci, jact-, *throw*.
lacesso, sivi, it-, *provoke*.
laedo, laesi, laes-, *hurt*.
lambo, bi, bit-, *lick*.
†lavo, lavi, lot-, laut-, *wash* (reg. 1st conj).
lego, gi, -xi, ct-, *gather*.
-licio, lexi, lect-, *allure*.
lino, vi (levi), lit-, *smear*.
linquo, -liqui, lict-, *leave*.
ludo, lusi, lus-, *play*.
luo, lui, luit-, *atone*.
mando, di, mans-, *chew*.
mergo, si, mers-, *dip*.
meto, messui, mess-, *reap*.   [*make water*.
mingo, minxi, mict-,
mitto, misi, miss-, *send*.
molo, lui, lit-, *grind*.
necto, xi(ui), nex-, *weave*.
nosco, novi, not-, *learn*.
nubo, psi, pt-, *marry*.
-nuo, nui, nuit-, *nod*.
occulo, lui, lt-, *hide*.
pando, di, pans-, pass-, *open*.
pango, nxi, nct-; pegi pepigi, pact-, *fasten*.
parco, peperci, parsi; parcit-pars-, *spare*.
pario, peperi, parit-, part-, *bring forth*.
pasco, pavi, past-, *feed*.
pecto, pexi, pex -(pectit-), *comb*.
pello, pepuli, puls-, *drive*.   [*weigh*.
pendo, pependi, pens-,
pergo, perrexi, ct-, *go on*.
peto, petivi, petit-, *seek*.

Table 14.

IRREGULAR CONJUGATION. — II.

pingo, nxi, pict-, *paint.*
pinso, nai, ns-, nst-, st-, *bray, bruise.* [*plaud.*
plaudo, si, plaus-, applecto, xi, xui, x-, *twine.*
pluo, plui, pluvi, *rain.*
pono, posui, posit-, *put.*
posco, poposci, *demand.*
prehendo, di, ns-, *seize.*
premo, pressi, ss-, *press.*
promo, mpsi, mpt-, *bring out.* [*prick.*
pungo, pupugi, punct-, quæro, sivi, sit-, *seek.*
quatio, -cussi, quass-, *shake.*
quiesco, evi, et-, *rest.*
rado, rasi, ras-, *scrape.*
rapio, pui, pt-, *snatch.*
rodo, rosi, ros-, *gnaw.*
rudo, rudivi, it-, *bray.*
rumpo, rupi, pt-, *burst.*
ruo, rui, rut-, it-, *fall.*
sapio, ivi, ui, *be wise.*
scabo, scabi, *scratch.*
scando, di, ns-, *climb.*
scindo, idi, sciss-, *tear.*
scisco, ivi, it-, *ordain.*
scribo, psi, pt-, *write.*
sero, sevi, sat-, *sow.*
sero, -serui, sert-, *entwine.*

sido, sidi (-sedi), sess-, *settle.*
sino, sivi, sit-, *permit.*
sisto, stiti, stat-, *stop.*
solvo, lvi, lutum, *pay.*
spargo, rsi, rs-, *spread.*
sperno, sprevi, spret-, *despise.*
-spicio, spexi, spect-, *look.* [*strew.*
sterno, stravi, strat-, sterto, tui, *snore.*
strepo, ui, it-, *sound.*
-stinguo, nxi, nct-, *extinguish.*
stringo, nxi, ct-, *bind.*
struo, struxi, ct-, *build.*
suesco, evi, et-, *bewont.*
surgo, surrexi, ct-, *rise.*
tango, tetigi, tact-, *touch.* [*despise.*
temno, -mpsi, -mpt-, tendo, tetendi, -tendi, tens-, *stretch.*
tergo, tersi, ters-, *wipe.*
tero, trivi, trit-, *rub.*
texo, texui, text-, *weave.* [*raise.*
tollo, sustuli, sublat-, traho, xi, tract-, *draw.*
tremo, mui, *tremble.*
trudo, si, trus-, *thrust.*

tundo, tutudi, tuns-, (tus-), *beat.*
uro, ussi, ust-, *burn.*
vado, -vasi, -vas-, *go.*
veho, xi, ct-, *carry.*
vello, velli (vulsi), vuls-, *pluck.*
vendo, didi, dit-, *sell.*
verro, ri, vers-, *sweep.*
verto, ti, vers-, *turn.*
vinco, vici, vict-, *conquer.*
viso, visi, vis-, *visit.*
vivo, vixi, vict-, *live.*
volvo, lvi, volut-, *roll.*
vomo, vomui, vomit-,
IV. [*comit.*
amicio, xi (cui), *clothe.*
aperio, rui, rt-, *open.*
farcio, rs, rt-, rot-, *stuff.*
fulcio, lsi, lt-, *prop.*
haurio, si, st-, *draw.*
operio, ui, rt-, *cover.*
raucio, si, s-, *be hoarse.*
reperio, ri, rt-, *find.*
salio, ui, ii, salt-, *leap.*
sancio, nxi, ct-, *ratify.*
sarcio, sarsi, sart-, *patch.*
sentio, nsi, ns-, *feel.*
sepelio, ivi, pult-, *bury.*
sepio, psi, pt-, *hedge in.*
venio, veni, nt-, *come.*
vincio, nxi, nct-, *bind.*

DEPONENT VERBS.

IND.	I. *Attempt.* SUBJ.	II. *Fear.*	III. *Fall.*	IV. *Move a mass.*
PRES.	conor -er	vereor -ear	labor -ar	molior -iar
IMP.	conabar -arer	verebar -erer	labebar -erer	moliebar -irer
FUT.	conabor	verebor	labar	moliar
PERF.	conatus sum	veritus sum	lapsus sum	molitus sum
PLUP.	conatus eram	veritus eram	lapsus eram	molitus eram
FUT. P.	conatus ero	veritus ero	lapsus ero	molitus ero
IMP.	conare, -ator	verere, -etor	labere, -itor	molire, -itor
INF.	conari	vereri	labi	moliri
PART.	conans	verens	labens	moliens
	conatus	veritus	lapsus	molitus
	conaturus	veriturus	lapsurus	moliturus
	conandus	verendus		moliendus
GER.	conandum	verendum	labendum	moliendum
SUP.	conatum, -tu	veritum, -tu	lapsum, -su	molitum, -tu

The following list contains all the Irregular Deponents:

II.
fateor, fass-, *acknowledge.*
reor, rat-, *reckon.*
tueor, tuit, tut-, *defend.*
III.
adipiscor, ept-, *obtain.*
amplect, plex-, *embrace.*
expergiscor, rect-, *rouse.*
fruor, fruct-, uit-, *enjoy.*
fungor, funct-, *perform.*
gradior, gress-, *step.*
irascor, irat-, *grow angry.*

labor, laps-, *fall.*
loquor, locut-, *speak.*
-miniscor, ment-, *think.*
morior, mortuus, moriturus, *die.*
nanciscor, nanct-, nact-, *obtain.*
nascor, nat-, *be born.*
nitor, nix-, nis-, *lean on.*
obliviscor, oblit-, *forget.*
orior, ortus-, oriturus, oriri, oreris, *arise.*

paciscor, pact-, *bargain.*
patior, pass-, *suffer.*
proficiscor, fect-, *set out.*
queror, quest-, *complain.*
sequor, secut-, *follow.*
ulciscor, ult-, *avenge.*
utor, us-, *use.*
IV.
experior, expert-, *try.*
metior, mens-, *measure.*
opperior, oppert-, *wait.*
ordior, ors-, *begin.*

Table 15.

IRREGULAR VERBS. — I.

VOLO, *will.*		NOLO, *will not.*		MALO, *prefer.*	
INDIC.	SUBJ.	INDIC.	SUBJ.	INDIC.	SUBJ.
PRESENT.					
volo	velim	nolo	nolim	malo	malim
vis	velis	nonvis	nolis	mavis	malis
vult	velit	nonvult	nolit	mavult	malit
vol'umus	veli'mus	nol'umus	noli'mus	mal'umus	mali'mus
vultis	velitis	nonvultis	nolitis	mavultis	malitis
volunt	velint	nolunt	nolint	malunt	malint
IMPERFECT.					
volebam	vellem	nolebam	nollem	malebam	mallem
volebas	velles	nolebas	nolles	malebas	malles
volebat	vellet	nolebat	nollet	malebat	mallet
volebamus	vellemus	nolebamus	nollemus	malebamus	mallemus
volebatis	velletis	nolebatis	nolletis	malebatis	malletis
volebant	vellent	nolebant	nollent	malebant	mallent
FUTURE.					
volam		nolam †		malam †	
voles		noles		males	
volet		nolet		malet	
volemus		nolemus		malemus	
voletis		noletis		maletis	
volent		nolent		malent	
PERFECT.					
volui	-erim	nolui	-erim	malui	-erim
voluisti	-eris	noluisti	-eris	maluisti	-eris
voluit	-erit	noluit	-erit	maluit	-erit
voluimus	-erimus	noluimus	-erimus	maluimus	-erimus
voluistis	-eritis	noluistis	-eritis	maluistis	-eritis
voluerunt	-erint	noluerunt	-erint	maluerunt	-erint
PLUPERFECT.					
volueram	-issem	nolueram	-issem	malueram	-issem
volueras	-isses	nolueras	-isses	malueras	-isses
voluerat	-isset	noluerat	-isset	maluerat	-isset
volueramus	-issemus	nolueramus	-issemus	malueramus	-issemus
volueratis	-issetis	nolueratis	-issetis	malueratis	-issetis
voluerant	-issent	noluerant	-issent	maluerant	-issent
FUTURE PERFECT.					
voluero	(-erim)	noluero	(-erim)	maluero	(-erim)
volueris		nolueris		malueris	
voluerit		noluerit		maluerit	
voluerimus		noluerimus		maluerimus	
volueritis		nolueritis		malueritis	
voluerint		noluerint		maluerint	

IMPERATIVE.

PR. noli, noli'te, *do not.*
FUT. noli'to, nolito'te, *thou shalt not, ye shall not.*
   noli'to, nolunto, *he shall not, they shall not.*

INFINITIVE.

PRES.	velle,	nolle	malle
PERF.	voluisse,	noluisse	maluisse

PARTICIPLE.

PRESENT, volens, *willing.*   nolens, *unwilling.*
GERUND, volendi, volendo   nolendi   † Rare.

Table 16.

IRREGULAR VERBS. — II.

ACTIVE.   FERO, bear.   PASSIVE.

	INDIC.	SUBJ.		INDIC.	SUBJ.
PRES.	fero	feram		feror	ferar
	fers	feras		ferris	feraris (re)
	fert	ferat		fertur	feratur
	fer'imus	fera'mus		fer'imur	fera'mur
	fertis	feratis		ferimini	feramini
	ferunt	ferant		feruntur	ferantur
IMP.	ferebam	ferrem		ferebar	ferrer
FUT.	feram	laturus sim		ferar	
PERF.	tuli	tulerim		latus sum	latus sim
PLUP.	tuleram	tulissem		latus eram	latus essem
F. PERF	tulero	(tulerim)		latus ero	

	Sing.	Plur.	IMPERATIVE.	Sing.	Plur.
PRES.	fer	ferte		ferre	ferimini
FUT.	ferto	fertote			
	ferto	ferunto		fertor	feruntor

	PRES.	PERF.	INFINITIVE.	PRES.	PERF.
	ferre	tulisse		ferri	latus esse

	PRES.	FUT.	PARTICIPLES.	PERF.	GER.
	ferens	laturus		latus	ferendus

EO, go.   FIO, become.

	INDIC.	SUBJ.	INDIC.	SUBJ.
PRES.	eo, is, it	eam, eas, eat, &c.	fio, fis, fit	fiam, fias, &c.
	imus, itis, eunt.		fimus, fitis, fiunt.	
IMP.	ibam, ibas, &c.	irem	fle'bam, &c.	fi'erem, &c.
FUT.	ibo, ibis, &c.	iturus sim	fiam, es, et, &c.	
PERF.	ivi (ii)	i'verim (ierim)	factus sum	factus sim
PLUP.	i'veram	ivis'sem (iissem)	factus eram	factus essem
F. PER.	i'vero	(iverim)	factus ero	(factus sim)

	Sing.	Plur.	IMPERATIVE.	Sing.	Plur.
PRES.	i	ite		fi	fite
FUT.	ito	itote, eunto		fito	fitote, fiunto

	PRES.	PERF.	INFINITIVE.	PRES.	PERF.
	ire	ivisse		fieri	factus esse

	PRES.	FUT.	PARTICIPLES.	PERF.	GER.
	iens, euntis	iturus		factus	faciendus

QUEO, can.   NEQUEO, cannot.

	INDIC.	SUBJ.	INDIC.	SUBJ.
PRES.	queo, quis, quit	queam	ne'queo, nonquis,	ne'queam, &c.
	quimus, -itis, -eunt		-imus, -itis, -eunt	
IMP.	quibam, quibat	quirem,	nequi'bam, -ibat	nequi'rem
		quibant -ret, -rent	-ibant	
FUT.	quibo, quibunt		nequibunt	
PERF.	quivi, -vit, -erunt	qui'verit	nequi'vi, -isti, -it	nequi'verim
PLUP.		quissent		nequisset
INFIN.	quire, quivisse		nequire, -ivisse	
PRES.	quiens, queuntis		nequiens	

VOCABULARY.

NOTE. — The Conjugation of the Verbs is represented thus : —

amo, 1, signifies . . . **amo, amāre, amāvi, amātum;**
moneo, ui, it-, 2, . . **moneo, monēre, monui, monĭtum;**
duco, xi, ct-, 3, . . . **duco, ducĕre, duxi, ductum;**
audio, 4, ... **audio, audīre, audīvi, audītum.**

Words which are marked ‡ belong to late or modern Latin.

a, ab, by, from.
‡ **abbas,** ātis, M., abbot.
abdo, dĭdi, dĭt-, 3, to hide.
abeo, īre, īvi, ĭt-, to depart.
abies, ĕtis, F., fir-tree.
abjectus (abjicio), despised, cast off.
abnĕgo, 1, deny, refuse.
abs, from.
abscīdo, di, cīs-, 3, to cut off.
absolvo, vi, ūt-, 3, release, acquit.
abstĭneo, tinui, tent-, 2, abstain.
abstersus (tergo), wiped off.
abunde, abundantly.
ac (atque), and, as.
accēdo, cessi, cess-, 3, approach, be added.
accendo, di, cens-, 3, to kindle, inflame.
accĭdo, di, 3, to happen.
accĭpio, cēpi, cept-, 3, to receive, accept.
acer, acris, acre, eager, keen.
acerbus, a, um, harsh, bitter, sour.
acies, ēi, F., edge, line of battle.
actus (ago), driven; **actum,** deed.
ad, to, at, near.
addo, dĭdi, dĭt-, 3, to add, join.
adeo, īre, īvi (ii), ĭt-, go to or near.
adeo, so, to that degree.
adesse (84), to be near.
adhæreo, si, 2, cling, adhere.
adhuc, hitherto, up to this, till now.
adĭtus, ūs, M., approach, passage.
adjăceo, jacui, 2, lie near.
adjungo, nxi, nct-, 3, join, annex.
adlūdo, si, sum, 3, to play near.

admīror, 1, to wonder.
admirātus, a, um, amazed.
admŏdum, very, quite.
admŏneo, ui, ĭt-, 2, admonish.
admŏveo, mōvi, mōt-, 2, bring to.
adnăto, 1, swim near or up to.
adnuo, ui, 3, to nod, consent.
adōro, 1, adore, entreat.
adrŏgo, 1, to claim, assert.
adscendo, di, sum, 3, to ascend, mount.
adsentatio, ōnis, F., consent, flattery.
adspĭcio, spexi, spect-, 3, to view, behold.
adsum (84), to be near.
advĕna, æ, C., stranger, foreigner.
advĕnio, vēni, vent-, 4, come near.
adventus, ūs, M., approach, arrival.
adversus, against.
adverto, ti, sum, 3, notice, perceive.
advesperascit, it grows late.
ædes, ium, F. (pl.), house.
æquālis, e, equal, mate.
æque, equally.
æquipăro, 1, make equal.
æquus, a, um, equal, just.
aër, aëris, M., air, weather.
æs, æris, N., copper, brass, money.
æstas, ātis, F., summer.
æstĭmo, 1, reckon, estimate.
æstuarium, i, N., tide-water stream.
æstus, ūs, M., tide, heat.
ætas, ātis, F., age.
affĕro, afferre, attŭli, allāt-, bring.
afflictus, a, um, afflicted.

agellus, i, M., *little field, yard.*
ager, agri, M., *field.*
agnosco, nōvi, nōt-, 3, *recognize, know.*
agnus, i, M., *lamb.*
ago, egi, act-, 3, *to do, act, render.*
agrestis, e, *rustic.*
agricŏla, æ, M., *farmer.*
aio, ais, ait, aiebam, &c., say.
ala, æ, F., *wing.*
alacris, e, *eager.*
alacrĭtas, ātis, F., *eagerness*
alacriter, *briskly.*
albus, a, um, *white.*
alias, *elsewhere, otherwise.*
alicŭbi, *somewhere.*
aliēnus, a, um, *of another.*
alio, *to another place;* **alius alio,** *in different ways.*
aliqua, *by some way.*
aliquamdiu, *for some time.*
aliquando, *sometimes, at length.*
aliquantum (tulum), *somewhat.*
aliquis, qua, quod (quid), *some one, some.*
aliquot, *some, a few.*
aliter, *otherwise.*
alius, a, ud, *other;* **alius .. alius,** *one . . . another.*
allātus (affero), *brought.*
allocutio, ōnis, F., *address.*
alnus, i, F., *alder.*
alo, alui, alt-, 3, *to feed, nourish.*
alter, era, um, *other, second* **(65).**
alternus, a, um, *alternate.*
altitudo, inis, F., *height, depth.*
altum, i, N., *the deep sea.*
altus, a, um, *high, deep.*
ambo, æ, o, *both* **(117).**
amārus, a, um, *bitter.*
amātor, ōris, M., *lover.*
ambulo, 1, *to walk.*
amīcus, a, um, *friendly, friend.*
amissus (amitto), *lost.*
amnis, is, M., *river.*
amo, 1, *to love.*
amœnus, a, um, *pleasant.*
amor, ōris, M., *love.*
amplexus, a, um, *folding.*
amplexus, ūs, M., *embrace.*
amplius, *more.*

amplus, a, um, *full, ample.*
an, *whether, or.*
anas, ătis, C., *duck.*
ancilla, æ, F., *maid-servant.*
anguis, is, C., *snake.*
angustus, a, um, *narrow.*
anĭma, æ, F., *breath.*
animadverto, ti, sum, 3, *to perceive, proceed against.*
animal, ālis, N., *animal.*
animans, tis, *living-creature.*
animo, 1, *to animate.*
animus, i, M., *mind, temper.*
annulus (anulus), i, M., *ring.*
annus, i, M., *year.*
anser, ĕris, M., *goose.*
ante, *before.*
antecēdo, cessi, cess-, 3, *go before.*
anterior, us, *before, earlier.*
antīquus, a, um, *ancient.*
antrum, i, N., *cave.*
anus, ūs, F., *old woman.*
anxius, a, um, *anxious.*
aper, pri, M., *wild boar.*
apĕrio, ui, ert-, 4, *to open.*
apertus, a, um, *open.*
apis, is, F., *bee.*
apparātus, ūs, M., *preparation, display.*
appāreo, ui, it-, 2, *appear.*
appăro, 1, *to make ready.*
appello, 1, *to call.*
approbo, 1, *to approve.*
appropinquo, 1, *to approach.*
aptus, a, um, *fit.*
apud, *at, near.*
aqua, æ, F., *water.*
aquatĭlis, e, *of the water*
aquĭla, æ, C., *eagle.*
arbor, ŏris, F., *tree.*
arca, æ, F., *ark, chest.*
arcānus, a, um, *secret.*
arceo, ui, 2, *shut, confine.*
arctus, a, um, *close.*
arcus, ūs, M., *bow, arch.*
ardeo, si, ars-, 2, *burn, blaze.*
arēna, æ, F., *sand.*
argenteus, a, um, *of silver.*
argentum, i, N., *silver.*
argumentum, i, N., *proof, argument.*

arĭdus, a, um, *dry*.
aries, ĕtis, M., *ram*.
arma, ōrum, N., *weapons*.
armatus, a, um, *armed*.
aro, I, *to plough*.
arreptus, a, um, *snatched*.
arrīdeo, rīsi, 2, *to laugh at*.
arrĭpio, rĭpui, rept-, 3, *to snatch*.
ars, artis, F., *art, way, skill*.
arsi (ardeo), *blazed*.
arundo, ĭnis, F., *reed*.
arx, arcis, F., *tower, citadel*.
astrictus, a, um, *tight*.
at, *but, but yet*.
ater, atra, atrum, *black*.
atque, *and, as*.
atrium, i, N., *hall*.
atrox, ōcis, *fierce, cruel*.
attendo, di, tum, 3, *to attend*.
attĕro, trivi, trīt-, 3, *wear away*.
attingo, tĭgi, tact-, 3, *to reach*.
attrītus, a, um, *worn, wasted*.
attŭli (affero), *brought*.
audacia, æ, F., *boldness*.
audens, tis, *bold*.
audenter, *boldly*.
audeo, ausus, 2, *to dare*.
audio, 4, *to hear*.
augeo, auxi, auct-, 2, *to increase*.
augustus, a, um, *noble, stately*.
aula, æ, F., *hall, court*.
aura, æ, F., *air, breeze*.
aureus, a, um, *golden*.
aurum, i, N., *gold*.
ausim (audeo), *dare*.
ausus, *having dared*.
aut, *or, either*.
autem, *but*.
autumnālis, e, *autumnal*.
auxilium. i, N., *help*.
avārus, a, um, *greedy, covetous*.
avis, is, F., *bird*.
avius, a, um, *pathless*.
axilla, æ, F., *arm-pit*.

B.

bacca, æ, F., *berry*.
balsămum, i, N., *balsam*.
barba, æ, F., *beard*.

‡baro, ōnis, M., *baron*.
beatus, a, um, *happy*.
bellua, æ, F., *beast*.
bellum, i, N., *war*.
bellus, a, um, *pretty*.
bene, *well*.
benedictus, a, um, *blessed*.
benignus, a, um, *kind, benign*.
bestia, æ, F., *beast, creature*.
betula, æ, F., *birch*.
bibo, 3, *to drink*.
bigæ, arum, F., *span of horses*.
bis, *twice*.
blandus, a, um, *calm, mild*.
bombycĭnus, a, um, *silken*.
bonus, a, um, *good, kind*.
boreālis, e, *northern*.
bos, bovis, C., *ox or cow*.
braccæ, ārum, *breeches*.
brachium, i, N., *arm*.
brevis, e, *short;* brevi, *shortly*.
bruma, æ, F., *frost, winter*.

C.

cado, cecĭdi, cas-, 3, *to fall*.
cæcus, a, um, *blind*.
cædo, cecīdi, cæs-, 3, *to cut*.
cælestis, e, *heavenly*.
cælum, i, N., *heaven, sky*.
cæna, æ, F., *supper*.
cæruleus, a, um, *dark blue*.
calamĭtas, ātis, F., *calamity*.
calceus. i, M., *shoe*.
calfăcio, fēci, fact-, 3, *to heat*.
calĭdus, a, um, *hot*.
callĭdus, a, um, *cunning*.
calor, ōris, M., *heat*.
calx, calcis, M. F., *heel*.
camēlus, i, M., *camel*.
‡campāna, æ, F., *bell* (great bell of the tower).
cancer, cri (ceris), M., *crab*.
candidus, a, um, *white*.
canis, is, M., *dog*.
canistrum, i, N., *basket*.
cano, cecĭni, cant-, 3, *sing, play* (on an instrument), *predict*.
cantillo, I, *to warble*.
canto, I, *to sing, crow*.

cantus, ūs, M., *song or crow.*
caper, pri, M., *goat.*
capio, cepi, capt-, 3, *to take.*
capra, æ, F., *she-goat.*
captus, a, um, *taken.*
caput, ĭtis, N., *head.*
carcer, ĕris, M., *prison.*
cardo, ĭnis, M., *hinge, pivot.*
carĭtas, ātis, F., *dearth, scarcity;*
‡ *divine love, charity.*
carmen, ĭnis, N., *song.*
carnĭfex, icis, M., *executioner.*
carpo, psi, pt-, 3, *to pluck, take.*
carus, a, um, *dear.*
casses, ium, M. (pl)., *snare, trap.*
castellum, i, N., *castle.*
castĭgo, I, *chastise, chide.*
castra, ōrum, N., *camp.*
casŭla, æ, F., *hut.*
catēna (catella, dim.), æ, F., *chain.*
casus, ūs, M., *fall, misfortune.*
cauda, æ, F., *tail.*
causa, æ, F., *cause.*
caute, *carefully.*
cautus, a, um, *careful, cautious.*
cave, *do not.*
caveo, cavi, caut-, 2, *beware.*
cavus, a, um, *hollow.*
cecĭdi (cado), *fell.*
cecīdi (cædo), *cut.*
cedo, cessi, cess-, 3, *to yield, retreat.*
cedrus, i, F., *cedar.*
celĕber, bris, bre, *famous.*
celer, celĕris, celere, *swift.*
celeriter, *swiftly.*
cena, æ, F., *supper, dinner.*
centum, *a hundred.*
cepi (capio), *took.*
certāmen, ĭnis, N., *contest.*
certe (to), *surely.*
certior factus, *informed.*
certo, I, *to contend.*
certus, a, um, *sure, certain.*
cervus, i, M., *stag.*
ceterum, *but.*
ceterus, a, um, *other.*
charta, æ, F., *paper.*
cibus, i, M., *food.*
ciconia. æ. F., *stork* (a bird).
cieo, cīvi, cit-, 2, *call, summon.*

cingo, cinxi, cinct-, 3, *to bind.*
cingŭlum, i, N., *belt, girdle.*
circa, circum, *about, around.*
circumăro, I, *to plough round.*
circumdūco, xi, ct-, 3, *lead about.*
circumeo, īre, īvi, ĭt-, *go round.*
circumfero, ferre, *to carry about.*
circumsisto, stĭti, 3, *stand round.*
circumspecto, I, *look round.*
circumsto, stĕti, stat-, I, *to stand
round.*
circumvagor, I, *wander about.*
circumvĕnio, vēni, vent-, 2, *come
round.*
cirrus, i, M., *curl, tassel.*
cito, I, *to summon.*
civis, is, M., *citizen.*
civĭtas, ātis, F., *city, state.*
clam, *secretly.*
clamo, I, *to cry, shout.*
clamor, ōris, M., *shout.*
clangor, ōris, M., *cry, noise.*
clarus, a, um, *famous.*
classĭcus, i, M., *trumpet.*
claudo, si, sum, 3, *to shut.*
claudus, a, um, *lame.*
clavis, is, F., *key.*
clavus, i, M., *spike, rudder.*
clemens, tis, *kind, merciful.*
coactus (cogo), *compelled.*
cœna (cena), æ, F., *supper.*
coëo, īre, īvi, *go together.*
cœpi, cœpĕram, *began.*
cœtus, ūs, M., *assembly, troop.*
cogitabundus, a, um, *meditating.*
cogĭto, I, *to think, reflect.*
cognosco, nōvi, nĭt-, 3, *find out,
know.*
cogo, coēgi, coact-, 3, *to gather,
compel.*
cohĭbeo, ui, ĭt- (habeo), 2, *restrain.*
colăphus, i, M., *blow, buffet.*
collapsus (labor), *fallen.*
collāris, e, *for the neck.*
collātus (confero), *brought together.*
collectus (collĭgo), *gathered.*
collis, is, M., *hill.*
collŏco, I, *to place, arrange.*
collŏquor, locutus, 3, *to talk with.*
collum, i, N., *neck.*
colo, colui, cult-, 3, *cultivate.*

colonia, æ, F., *colony.*
color, ōris, M., *color.*
columba, æ, F., *dove.*
combūro, ussi, ust-, 3, *to burn up.*
comĕdo, ēdi, ēs-, 3, *to eat.*
comes, ĭtis, C., *companion; ‡ count.*
comĭnus, *close at hand.*
comis, e, *gentle, kind.*
comitium, i, N., *place of meeting.*
commendo, 1, *to commend, commit.*
commigro, 1, *to emigrate, remove.*
commĭnūtus, a, um, *bruised.*
commŏdus, a, um, *convenient.*
commōtus, a, um, *excited, disturbed.*
commŏveo, mōvi, mōt-, 2, *to disturb, remove.*
compāgo, inis, F., *framework.*
compello, 1, *to address.*
compello, pŭli, puls-, 3, *to compel.*
compĕrio, pĕri, pert-, 4, *find out.*
compes, pĕdis, M., *fetter.*
compleo, ēvi, ēt-, 2, *fill, fulfil.*
complures, ia, *many.*
compōno, posui, posĭt-, 3, *put together, arrange, settle.*
conātum, i, N., *effort.*
concēdo, cessi, cess-, 3, *to grant, yield.*
concio, ōnis, F., *speech, meeting.*
conciōnor, 1, *to address, harangue.*
conclāve, is, N., *chamber.*
conclūdo, si, sum (claudo), 3, *to shut up, confine.*
concordia, æ, F., *harmony.*
concors, dis, *harmonious.*
concurro, curri, curs-, 3, *to run together.*
concursus, ūs, M., *running together.*
concŭtio, cussi, cuss- (quatio), 3, *to shatter.*
conditio, ōnis, F., *condition, agreement.*
condo, dĭdi, dĭt-, 3, *lay up, hide.*
condŏleo, ui, 2, *to grieve with.*
condūco, xi, ct-, 3, *guide, hire, conduct.*
confectus, a, um, *worn out.*
confero, ferre, tŭli, collāt-, *compare, bring together.*
confestim, *immediately.*

confĭcio, feci, fect- (facio), 3, *to finish.*
confido, fīsus, 3, *to trust.*
conflīgo, xi, ct-, 3, *to conflict.*
confluo, xi, xum, 3, *flow together.*
confūgio, fūgi, 3, *flee for refuge.*
congelatus, a, um, *chilled, frozen.*
congĕro, gessi, gest-, 3, *contribute.*
congredior, i, gressus, 3 (gradior), *go together.*
congrĕgo, 1, *gather, congregate.*
coniveo, nīvi, 2, *to wink.*
conjectus, ūs, M., *heaping-on.*
conjĭcio, jēci, ject-, 3 (jacio), *throw, cast, conjecture.*
conjux, ŭgis, C., *husband or wife.*
conlūsor, ōris, M., *playmate.*
conor, 1 (dep.), *to try, attempt.*
consalūto, 1, *to salute.*
conscius, a, um (scio), *conscious.*
consensus, ūs, M., *consent, harmony.*
consentio, si, sum, 4, *to consent, agree.*
consĕquor, cūtus, 3, *overtake, obtain.*
consīdo, sēdi, sess-, 3, *to sit, halt.*
consilium, i, N., *counsel, advice.*
consisto, stĭti, stĭt-, 3, *stand firm.*
consistorium, i, N., *gathering, assembly.*
consolatorius, a, um, *comforting.*
conspectus, ūs, M., *sight, view.*
conspĭcio, spexi, spect-, 3, *to view, behold.*
conspicuus, a, um, *conspicuous.*
conspĭcor, 1 (dep.), *to gaze upon.*
constat, *it is evident or agreed.*
consternatus, a, um, *frightened.*
constĭtuo, ui, ūt-, 3, *to establish.*
consuetūdo, ĭnis-, F., *custom.*
consul, ŭlis, M., *consul* (chief magistrate of Rome).
consŭlo, sului, sult-, 3, *to consult, advise.*
consūmo, mps, mpt-, 3, *consume.*
contemplor, 1 (dep.), *contemplate.*
contentio, ōnis, F., *contention, strife.*
contentus, a, um, *content.*
contextus (tego), *woven.*

contĭceo, ui, 2 (taceo), *to keep silent.*

contĭneo, ui, tent-, 2 (teneo), *hold, restrain.*

contingo, tĭgi, tact-, 3 (tango), *to touch.*

continuo, *at once, immediately.*

continuus, a, um, *continual.*

contortus (torqueo), *twisted.*

contra, *against, opposite.*

contrăho, xi, ct-, 3, *draw together.*

contrarius, a, um, *contrary.*

contristor, 1 (dep.), *to sadden, grieve.*

contrītus (tero), *worn, bruised.*

contŭli (confero), *brought.*

contumacia, æ, F., *obstinacy.*

convello, velli, vuls-, 3, *to shatter.*

convĕnio, vēni, vent-, 4, *come together, fit, suit.*

converto, ti, sum, 3, *to turn, change.*

convivium, i, N., *feast, banquet.*

convŏco, 1, *call together.*

coŏrior, īri, ortus, 4, *arise, begin.*

copia, æ, F., *plenty;* pl., *forces.*

coquo, coxi, coct-, 3, *to cook.*

coquus, i, M., *a cook.*

cor, cordis, N., *heart.*

coram, *in the presence of.*

cor-nix, īcis, F., *raven (see p. 85).*

cornu, ūs (u), N., *horn, wing (of army).*

corōna, æ, F., *crown, prize.*

corpus, ŏris, N., *body.*

corrĭgo, rexi, rect-, 3 (con, rego), *to correct.*

corrumpo, rūpi, rupt-, 3, *corrupt, spoil, destroy.*

corruo, ĕre, ui, 3, *to fall together, perish.*

cortex, ĭcis, M., *bark, rind.*

corvus, i, M., *raven, crow.*

cos, cotis, F., *whetstone.*

costa, æ, F., *rib.*

cras, *to-morrow.*

crassus, a, um, *thick.*

creatura, æ, F., *creature.*

creber, bra, um, *thick, close.*

credo, dĭdi, dĭt-, 3, *believe, trust.*

cremo, 1 *to burn.*

creo, 1, *to create.*

crepĭtus, ūs, M., *noise, crackling.*

cresco, crevi, crēt-, 3, *to grow, increase.*

crimen, ĭnis, N., *crime, charge.*

crinis, is, M., *hair.*

croceus, a, um, *yellow, saffron.*

crocus, i, M., *saffron.*

crotălus, i, M., *a rattle.*

crucifixus, i, M., *crucified.*

crudēlis, e, *cruel.*

crudelĭtas, ātis, F., *cruelty.*

crudelĭter, *cruelly.*

crus, cruris, N., *leg.*

crux, crucis, F., *cross, torment.*

cubicularius, i, M., *chamberlain.*

cubicŭlum, i, N., *bed-chamber.*

cui, cujus, *dat. and gen. of* qui, *who.*

culter, tri, M., *knife.*

cum, *with.*

cum (or quum), *when, since.*

cumulus, i, M., *heap.*

cuncti, æ, a, *all.*

cunctor, 1, *to delay.*

cuniculus, i, M., *rabbit.*

cupīdo, ĭnis, M., *eager desire.*

cupĭdus, a, um, *eager, ambitious.*

cupio, ĭvi, ĭt, 3, *to desire.*

cur, *why.*

cura, æ, F., *care.*

curiōsus, a, um, *curious.*

curo, 1, *to care for, manage.*

currus, ūs, M., *car, chariot.*

cutis, is, F., *skin.*

custos, ōdis, C., *guard.*

cyaneŏla, æ, F., *bluebird.*

cymba, æ, F., *boat, skiff.*

D.

dama, æ, C., *fallow-deer.*

damnatio, ōnis, F., *condemnation.*

damnum, i, N., *loss, damage.*

datus, a, um (do), *put, given.*

de, *from, down from.*

dea, æ, F., *goddess.*

deambŭlo, 1, *to walk about, stroll.*

debeo, ui, ĭt-, 2, *to owe, ought.*

debĭtum, i, N., *debt.*

debĭtus, a, um (debeo), *due.*

decem, *ten.*

decerno, crēvi, crēt-, 3, *to decide, determine.*

decet, uit, 2, *it is fit.*

decĭdo, cĭdi, 3 (cado), *to fall down.*

decīdo, cīdi, cīs-, 3 (cædo), *to cut down, decide.*

decĭmus, a, um, *tenth.*

decor, ōris, M., *grace, beauty.*

decus, ōris, N., *ornament, glory.*

dedi (do), *gave.*

dedignor, 1, *to disdain.*

dedo, dedĭdi, dedĭt-, 3, *to give up, surrender.*

dedūco, xi, ct-, 3, *to lead out or down.*

defatigatus, a, um, *tired out.*

defendo, di, sum, 3, *to ward off, defend.*

defĕro, ferre, tŭli, lāt-, *bring down.*

deficio, fēci, fect-, 3 (facio), *to fail, desert.*

defixus (figo), *fastened, driven in.*

deflexus (flecto), *bent down.*

defungor, functus, 3, *to discharge, fulfil.*

dehinc, *hereupon, henceforth.*

deinde, *then, next.*

dejĭcio, jeci, ject-, 3 (jacio), *cast down.*

delibĕro, 1, *to ponder, deliberate.*

delphīnus, i, M., *dolphin.*

dēmigro, 1, *emigrate, remove.*

demissus, a, um, *downcast.*

demitto, mīsi, miss-, 3, *send away or down, let go.*

demo, mpsi, mpt-, 3, *take away.*

demum, *at length, finally.*

densus, a, um, *thick, close.*

denuo, *again, a second time.*

deorsum, *downward.* [*pack away.*

depōno, posui, posit-, 3, *lay down,*

deposco, poposci, poscĭt-, 3, *demand.*

posĭtus, a, um, *laid* or *put down.*

deprĕcor, 1, *entreat* (not to do).

descendo, di, sum, 3 (scando), *to go down, descend.*

desertus (desĕro), *deserted.*

desidero, 1, *to wish, need.*

desĭlio, silui, sult-, 4, *leap down.*

desisto, stĭti, stĭt-, 3, *to leave off.*

desolātus, a, um, *desolate.*

despĭcio, spexi, spect-, 3, *despise.*

destĭno, 1, *to destine, design.*

desum, esse, fui, *to be wanting.*

desŭper, *from above.*

deterreo, ui, it-, 2, *to deter, alarm.*

detrăho, xi, ct-, 3, *to draw off.*

detrūdo, si, sum, 3, *to thrust off.*

deturbo, 1, *to push away.*

deus, i, M., *a god.*

devolvo, vi, volut-, 3, *roll down.*

devōro, 1, *to devour.*

devŏveo, vōvi, vōt-, 2, *to devote.*

dextra, æ, F., *right hand.*

dic (imperat.), *say.*

dico, 1, *to dedicate.*

dico, xi, ct-, 3, *to say, call.*

dictum, i, N., *a word.*

didĭci (disco), *learned.*

dies, ēi, M., *day.*

digĭtus, i, M., *finger, toe, claw.*

dignĭtas, ātis, F., *dignity.*

dignor, 1 (dep.), *deem worthy.*

dignus, a, um, *worthy, fit.*

dilĭgo, lexi, lect-, 3, *love, esteem.*

diluvium, i, N., *flood.*

dĭmitto mīsi, miss-, 3, *dismiss.*

dirĭgo, rexi, ct-, 3 (rego), *direct.*

dirus, a, um, *fierce, dreadful.*

discēdo, cessi, cess-, 3, *depart.*

discessus, ūs, M., *departure.*

disco, didĭci, 3, *to learn.* [*quarrel.*

discordia, æ, F., *discord ;-do* 1, *to*

discus, i, M., *quoit ; ‡ dish, plate.*

discŭtio, cussi, cuss-, 3 (quatio), *to shake to pieces.*

dispendium, i. N., *expense, cost.*

dissĕco, cui, ct-, 1, *cut open.*

dissidium, i, N., *discord.*

dissimĭlis, e, *unlike.*

distribuo, ui, ūt-, 3, *to divide, distribute.*

ditior, ditissimus, *richer, richest.*

diu, diutius, *long, longer.*

diuturnus, a, um, *long-continued.*

diversus, a, um, *diverse, various.*

dives, divĭtis, *rich.*

divĭdo, di, sum, 3, *to divide.*

divinitus, *providentially.*

do, dedi, dat-, 1, *to give, put.*
doceo, ui, ct-, 2, *teach, tell.*
doleo, ui, 2, *to grieve, hurt, suffer.*
dolor, ōris, M., *pain, grief.*
dolorōsus, a, um, *full of sorrow.*
dolus, i, M., *deceit, craft, trick.*
domi, *at home* (74).
dominus, i, M., *master, lord.*
domus, ūs, F., *house, home.*
donec, *until, while.*
dono, 1, *to give, present.*
donum, i, N., *gift.*
dormio, 4, *to sleep.*
dubie, *doubtfully.*
dubito, 1, *to doubt, hesitate.*
dubius, a, um, *doubtful.*
duco, xi, ct-, 3, *to lead, guide.*
dulcis, e, *sweet.*
dum, *while, until.*
dumētum, i, N., *thicket.*
dumus, i, M., *brushwood.*
duo, duae, duo, *two* (117).
duodĕcim, *twelve.*
duodecimus, a, um, *twelfth.*
durus, a, um, *hard, stern, cruel.*
dux, ducis, C., *leader, guide;* ‡ *duke.*

E

e (ex), *out of, from.*
ebur, ŏris, N., *ivory.*
ecce, *lo! behold!*
edax, ācis, *greedy.*
edīco, xi, ct-, 3, *to order, declare.*
edĭtus, a, um, *lofty.*
edo, Idi, It-, 3, *give out, utter.*
edo (esse) ōdi, ēs-, 3, *to eat.*
edūco, xi, ct-, 3, *lead forth.*
effectus, ūs, M., *effect.* [*out, effect.*
efficio, fēci, fect-, 3 (facio), *to work*
effūgo, 1, *put to flight.*
effūgio, fūgi, fugit-, 3, *to escape.*
effundo, fūdi, fūs-, 3, *pour forth.*
egeo, ui, 2, *to need.*
egi, egeram, &c. (ago), *did.*
ego, mei, mihi, me, *I.*
egredior, gressus, 3, *go forth.*
egregius, a, um, *excellent, distinguished.*

ejīcio, jēci, ject-, 3 (jacio), *to cast out, throw away.*
elĕvo, 1, *to raise, elevate.*
emergo, si, sum, 3, *to emerge.*
eminus, *from a distance.*
emitto, mīsi, miss-, 3, *send forth.*
emo, ēmi, empt-, 3, *to buy.*
emptor, ōris, M., *buyer.*
en, *behold!*
enim, *for.*
eo. ire, ivi, it- (Tab. 16), *to go.*
eo (is, ea, id), *by so much.*
eō, *thither, to that place.*
eōdem, *to the same place.*
‡ episcŏpus, i, M., *bishop.*
epistŏla, æ, F., *letter.*
eques, itis, M., *horseman;* ‡ *knight.*
equĭto, 1, *to ride.*
equus, i, M., *horse.*
ergo, *therefore;* erga, *towards.*
erro, 1, *to wander, stray.*
error, ōris, M., *wandering, mistake.*
eruo, rui, rūt-, 3, *to tear away.*
esca, æ, F., *food, provision, bait.*
esse, *to be.*
et, *and, also, even;* et ... et, *both ... and.*
etiam, *also, even.*
etsi, *even if, though.*
eundum (gerund), *must go.*
evādo, si, sum, 3, *go forth, turn out.*
evĕnio, vēni, vent-, 4, *to happen, turn out.*
everto, ti, sum, 3, *overturn.*
ex (e), *from, out of, according to.*
exanĭmis, e, *breathless, lifeless.*
excelsus, a, um, *high.*
excĭpio, cēpi, cept-, 3 (capio), *take up* or *out, overtake, receive.*
excĭto, 1, *to rouse, excite.*
excĭtus, a, um, *roused.*
excludo, si, sum, 3, *to shut out.*
excūso, 1, *to excuse.*
exeo, ire, ivi (ii), it-, *to go out.*
exercĭtus, ūs, M., *army.*
exĭlis, e, *lean.*
exiguus, a, um, *little.*
existĭmo, 1, *to think, suppose.*
exitium, i, N., *destruction.*
exĭtus, ūs, M., *end, event, death.*

exordior, īri, orsus, 4, *to begin.*
exornatus, a, um, *arrayed.*
exōsus, a, um, *hated, scorned.*
expĕdio, 4, *to hasten.*
experimentum, i, N., *experience, trial, experiment.*
experior, īri, pertus, 4, *to try, experience.*
expleo, plevi, plēt-, 4, *to fill up.*
expōno, posui, posĭt-, 3, *set forth.*
exsĭlio, ui, sult-, 4, *to leap forth.*
exstinguo, stinxi, stinct-, 3, *to extinguish.*
exsūdo, 1, *exude.*
exsul, ŭlis, C., *exile.*
exsurgo, surrexi, 3, *rise up* or *out.*
exsupĕro, 1, *to surpass, vanquish.*
extra, *outside of.*
extrăho, xi, ct-, 3, *to draw off.*
extrēmus, a, um, *last, furthest.*
exuo, ui, ūt-, 3, *to put off* or *out, get clear.*

F.

faber, bri, M., *smith, workman.*
fabŭla, æ, F., *story.*
facētus, a, um, *elegant, fine, funny.*
facies, ēi, F., *face, aspect.*
facĭlis, e, *easy.*
facĭnus, ŏris, N., *deed, crime.*
facio, fēci, fact-, 3, *to do, make.*
factum, i, N., *deed.*
factus, a, um (fio), *done.*
fallo, fefelli, fals-, 3, *to deceive.*
falx, falcis, F., *scythe, sickle.*
fama, æ, F., *fame, report.*
fames, is, F., *hunger, famine.*
famŭla, æ, F., *maid-servant.*
familia, æ, F., *family.*
famŭlus, i, M., *man-servant.*
far, farris, N., *wheat, grain.*
fas, N., *right.*
fascis, is, M., *bundle, fagot.*
fastidiōse, *disdainfully.*
fastidiōsus, a, um, *disdainful.*
fatum, i, N. (for), *fate.*
faucis (gen. sing.), F., *jaw* (generally plural).
faveo, favi, faut-, 2, *to favor.*
favilla, æ, F., *ashes, embers.*

fax, facis, F., *torch.*
fefelli (fallo), *deceived.*
fel, fellis, N., *gall.*
feles, is, F., *a cat.*
felicĭtas, ātis, F., *happiness, fortune, felicity.*
felix, īcis, *happy, fortunate.*
femĭna, æ, F., *woman.*
fenestra, æ, F., *window.*
fer (imperative), *carry.*
fera, æ, F., *wild beast.*
fercŭlum, i, N., *litter, dish.*
fere, *almost.*
ferio, 4, *to strike.*
fero, ferre, tŭli, lāt-, *to bear, carry, tell* (see Table 16).
ferox, ōcis, *fierce.*
ferreus, a, um, *of iron, hard, stern.*
ferrum, i, N., *iron, steel.*
ferus, a, um, *wild, fierce.*
ferveo, bui, 2, *to boil.*
festīno, 1, *to hasten.*
festus, a, um, *festival.*
fiber, bri, M., *beaver.*
fictus (fingo), *feigned, fashioned.*
fidēlis, e, *faithful.*
fidelĭter, *faithfully.*
fides, ĕi, F., *faith, trust, belief.*
fiducia, æ, F., *confidence.*
fiduciālis, e, *confident.*
fidus, a, um, *faithful.*
figo, fixi, fixum, 3, *to fix, fasten.*
filia, æ, F., *daughter.*
filius, i, M., *son.*
fimus, i, M., *dunghill, manure.*
fingo, finxi, fict-, 3, *to fashion, pretend.*
finis, is, M., *end.*
fio, fiĕri, factus (T. 16), *be made, become* (pass. of facio).
firmus, a, um, *firm, strong.*
fiscīna (fiscella), æ, F., *basket.*
flagellum, i, N., *whip, scourge.*
flagĭto, 1, *to ask, urge.*
flamma, æ, F., *flame.*
flatus, ūs, M., *blast.*
flavus, a, um, *yellow.*
flebĭlis, e, *tearful, mournful.*
flecto, xi, xum, 3, *to bend, turn.*
fleo, flēvi, 2, *to weep.*

fletus, ūs, M., *weeping.*
floreo, ui, 2, *to flourish.*
flos, floris, M., *flower.*
flumen, ĭnis, N., *river, stream.*
fluviālis, e, *of a river.*
fodio, fodi, foss-, 3, *to dig.*
fœdus, ĕris, N., *league, covenant.*
fœdus, a, um, *foul, ugly.*
folium, i, N., *leaf.*
for, fari, fatus, I, *to speak.*
foras and foris, *out of doors, abroad.*
fore (fut. infin. of esse), *will be;* forem, *would be.*
forma, æ, F., *shape, beauty.*
formīca, æ, F., *ant.*
formīdo, ĭnis, F., *fear, dread.*
formīdo, I, *to fear.*
formōsus, a, um, *beautiful.*
fors, fortis, F., *fortune.*
forte, *by chance, perhaps.*
fortis, e, *strong, brave.*
fortĭter, *bravely.*
forum, i, N., *public square.*
fossa, æ, F., *ditch, trench.*
fovea, æ, F., *hole, pit.*
fractus (frango), *broken.*
fræno, I, *to curb, bridle.*
fragĭlis, e (frango), *frail.*
fragor, ōris, M., *crash.*
frango, frēgi, fract-, 3, *to break.*
frater, tris, M., *brother.*
fraus, fraudis, F., *fraud, deceit.*
fraxĭnus, i, F., *ash-tree.*
frendo. di, 3, *to gnash, grit.*
frequenter, *constantly.*
frequentia, æ, F., *crowd, great number.*
frigĭdus, a, um, *cold.*
frigus, ōris, N., *cold.*
frons, dis, F., *leaf.*
frons, tis, F., *forehead.*
fructus, ūs, M., *fruit.*
fruges, um, F., *fruits, crops.*
frumentum, i, N., *corn.*
frugi, *good, useful.*
frustra, *in vain.*
fuga, æ, F., *flight.*   [I, *drive.*
fŭgio, fūgi, fugĭt-, 3, *to flee;* fugo,
fulgur, ŭris, N., *lightning.*
fundĭtus, *from the bottom, utterly.*

fundo, fudi, fūs-, 3, *to pour, put to flight.*
fundus, i, M., *farm, estate.*
fungor, functus, 3, *to fulfil.*
fur, furis, M., *thief, knave.*
furo, ui, 3, *to rage.*
furtum, i, N., *theft.*
fusus (fundo), *melted, put to flight.*

G.

galea, æ, F., *helmet.*
gallīna, æ, F., *hen.*
gallus, i, M., *cock.*
garrio, 4, *to chatter.*
gaudenter, *gladly, joyfully.*
gaudeo, gavīsus, 2, *to be glad.*
gavīsus (gaudeo), *glad.*
gelu, N., *frost, cold.*
gemma, æ, F., *bud, gem, jewel.*
gemo, ui, 3, *to groan, sigh.*
gena, æ, F., *cheek.*
generōsus, a, um, *high-born, noble.*
genĭtus (gigno), *born, descended.*
gens, gentis, F., *race, family, nation.*
genu, ūs, N., *knee.*
gestus (gero), *borne, done.*
genus, ĕris, N., *birth, race, kind.*
gero, gessi, gest-, 3, *bear, carry, do, wage* (war).
gestātor, ōris, M., *bearer, carrier.*
gigno, genui, genĭt-, 3, *to produce.*
giro, I, *to turn, roll.*
glaciālis, e, *icy.*
glacies, ēi, F., *frost, ice.*
gladius, i, M., *sword.*
glans, dis, F., *nut, acorn.*
gloria, æ, F., *glory.*
gloriōsus, a, um, *boastful;* ‡ *glorious.*
gnavus, a, um, *skilled.*
gracĭlis, e, *slender.*
gradior, gressus, 3, *to go, step.*
gradus, ūs, M., *step, rank.*
gramen, ĭnis, N., *grass.*
granarium, i, N., *barn, granary.*
gratia, æ, F., *favor;* pl. *thanks.*
gratis, *freely, without reward.*

gratulor, I, *congratulate.*
grator, I (dep.), *to thank.*
gratus, a, um, *grateful.*
gravis, e, *heavy, weighty, important.*
gremium, i, N., *lap, bosom.*
grex, gregis, M., *flock.*
grus, gruis, C., *crane.*
guberno, I, *to govern.*
gusto, I, *to taste.*
guttur, ŭris, N., *throat.*

H.

habeo, ui, ĭt-, 2, *to have, hold.*
habĭto, I, *to dwell, live.*
hac, *this way.*
hactenus, *hitherto.*
hædus, i, M., *kid.*
hamus, i, M., *hook.*
hasta, æ, F., *spear.*
hastīle, is, N., *spear-shaft, pole.*
hau, haud, *not.*
haurio, si, st-, 4, *to drain.*
hebes, ĕtis, *blunt.*
herba, æ, F., *grass.*
heredium, i, N., *inheritance.*
heres, ēdis, C., *heir.*
heri, *yesterday.*
herus, i, M., *master.*
hesternus, a, um, *yesterday's.*
hic, hæc, hoc, *this.*
hic, *here.*
hiems, is, M., *winter.*
hilăris, e, *cheerful.*
hinc, *hence.*
hiātus, ūs, M., *chasm.*
historia, æ, F., *story, history.*
hodie, *to-day.*
homo, ĭnis, C., *man.*
honestas, a, um, *honorable.*
honor, ōris, M., *honor.*
honorifĭcus, a, um, *giving honor.*
honōro, I, *to honor.*
hora, æ, F., *hour, season.*
horrendus, a, um, *awful.*
hortor, I (dep.), *to exhort, urge.*
hospes, ĭtis, C., *host, guest.*
hospitium, i, N., *hospitality.*
hostia, æ, F., *victim.*

hostīlis, e, *of an enemy.*
hostis, is, C., *an enemy.*
huc, *hither.*
humānus, a, um, *human, kind.*
humĕrus, i, M., *shoulder.*
humi (74), *on the ground.*
humĭlis, e, *humble, lowly.*
humilĭter, *humbly.*
humus, i, F., *ground.*
hyacinthus, i, N., *hyacinth.*

I

ĭbi, *there.*
ictus, a, um, *struck.*
ictus, ūs, M., *a blow.*
idcirco, *on that account.*
idem, eădem, idem, *the same.*
igĭtur, *therefore, then.*
ignārus, a, um, *ignorant.*
ignāvus, a, um, *slothful.*
ignis, is, M., *fire.*
illātus (infero), *brought.*
ille, illa, illud, *that.*
illic, *there.*
illīdo, si, sum, 3 (lædo), *to dash against.*
illinc, *thence.*
illuc, *thither.*
imāgo, ĭnis, F., *image.*
imbecillis, e, *feeble.*
imber, bris, M., *rain-storm, shower.*
immĕmor, ŏris, *forgetful.*
immensus, a, um, *immense.*
immergo, si, sum, 3, *to plunge in.*
immerĭtus, a, ŭm, *blameless.*
immersus, a, um, *plunged in.*
immĭnens, tis, *imminent, threatening.*
immītis, e, *harsh, cruel.*
immitto, mīsi, miss-, 3, *to send upon.*
immo (imo), *nay, indeed, yes.*
immōtus, a, um (moveo), *still.*
immortālis, e, *immortal.*
impello, pŭli, puls-, 3, *to impel, push.*
imperātor, ōris, M., *commander, emperor.*

imperium, i, N., *authority, command.*

impĕro, 1, *to command.*

impetro, 1, *to obtain* (by entreaty).

impetus, ūs, M., *attack.*

impius, a, um, *wicked.*

impleo, plēvi, plēt-, 2, *to fill.*

implicito, 1, *entangle, wind about.*

impluvium, i, N., *rain-tank, cistern.*

impōno, posui, posĭt-, 3, *to put upon, impose.*

impŏtens, tis, *weak, ungovernable.*

imprŏbus, a, um, *wicked.*

impŭdens, tis, *shameless.*

impudenter, *impudently.*

impūrus, a, um, *unclean.*

imus, a, um, *lowest, bottom of.*

in, *into, against ; in, on, among.*

inānis, e, *empty, vain.*

incalesco, calui, 3, *to grow hot.*

incēdo, cessi, 3, *to advance, step.*

incendo, di, sum, 3, *to burn, kindle.*

incertus, a, um, *uncertain.*

‡incessanter, *incessantly.*

incĭdo, di, 3 (cado), *to fall upon, happen.*

incĭdo, di, sum, 3 (cædo), *to cut.*

incĭpio, cēpi, cept-, 3 (capio), *to begin.*

inclĭtus, a, um, *glorious.*

incŏla, æ, C., *inhabitant.*

incolŭmis, e, *safe.*

‡incomparabilis, e, *incomparable.*

incredĭbĭlis, e, *incredible.*

incrĕpo, ui, ĭt-, 1, *chide, reproach.*

incumbo, cubui, cubĭt-, 3, *to lie upon, insist.*

incursio, ōnis, F., *advance, attack.*

inde, *thence, thereupon.*

indecōrus, a, um, *unbecoming.*

indefessus, a, um, *unwearied, dauntless.*

indigĕna, æ, C., *native.*

indigne, *unworthily.*

indignus, a, um, *unworthy.*

induo, i, ut-, 3, *to put in or on.*

inedia, æ, F., *starvation.*

iners, tis, *inert, sluggish.*

inesse (84), *to be in or among.*

infans, tis, C. (for), *child.*

inferior, us, *lower, inferior.*

infero, ferre, tŭli, illāt-, *to bring in or on.*

infestus, a, um, *hostile.*

infĭmus, a, um, *lowest.*

infixus, a, um, *fixed, fastened.*

infra, *below.*

infrendo, di, 3, *to gnash, chafe.*

infŭla, æ, F., *fillet.*

infusus, a, um (fundo), *poured in or on, stained.*

ingemisco, gemui, 3, *to sigh.*

ingenium, i, N., *talent, mind.*

ingens, tis, *great, vast.*

ingruo, i, 3, *to shed or pour.*

inhæreo, si, 2, *to cling.*

inhonorātus, a, um, *dishonored.*

inimīcus, a, um, *hostile.*

inĭquus, a, um, *unjust.*

initium, i, N., *beginning.*

injĭcio, jēci, ject-, 3 (jacio), *to throw against or upon.*

injuriæ, æ, F., *wrong.*

injustus, a, um, *unjust.*

innăto, 1, *to swim, float.*

innīsus (xus), a, um, *leaning on.*

innoxĭus, a, um, *harmless.*

innutrītus, a, um, *bred to.*

inopia, æ, F., *poverty.*

inquam, inquit (def.), *say, said.*

insĕquor, secutus, 3, *to pursue.*

insĭdeo, sēdi, sess-, 2, *to sit upon.*

insĭdo, sēdi, 3, *to sit, settle, rest.*

insignis, e, *conspicuous.*

insĭlio, silui, sult-, 4, *to leap upon.*

insisto, stĭti, 3, *to insist, stand upon.*

instanter, *urgently.*

instar, *like.*

instituo, ui, ūt-, 3, *to establish, resolve.*

insto, stĭti, 1, *to stand upon.*

insŭper, *over and above.*

intĕger, gra, um, *whole.*

intellĭgo (lego), lexi, lect-, 3, *to understand.*

intentus (intendo), *busy, intent.*

inter, *between, among.*

interdiu, *in the day-time.*

interdum, *at times.*

interea, *in the mean time.*
intereo, Ire, Ii, It-, *to perish.*
interesse, *to be present.* [cerns.
interest, *there is difference; it con-*
interficio, fēci, fect-, 3 (facio), *to kill.*
interim, *in the mean time.*
interior, us, *inner.*
interpello, I, *to interrupt.*
interpres, prĕtis, C., *interpreter.*
interpretatio, ōnis, F., *meaning.*
interprĕtor, I (dep.), *to explain.*
interrŏgo, I, *to ask.*
interrumpo, rūpi, rupt-, 3, *break down, interrupt.*
interstinguo, stinxi, stinct-, 3, *to mark here and there.*
intorqueo, torsi, tort-, 2, *to twist, bend in.*
intro, I, *to enter.*
intro, *inward.*
introdūco, xi, ct-, 3, *to bring in.*
intueor, ēri, Itus, 2, *to look upon.*
intus, *within.*
inultus, a, um (ulciscor), *unpunished, unavenged.*
inutilis, e, *useless.*
invĕnio, vēni, vent-, 4, *to come upon, find.*
invĭcem, *by turns.*
invidia, æ, F., *envy, malice.*
invīsus, a, um, *hated.*
invīto, I, *to invite.*
invītus, a, um, *unwillingly.*
invius, a, um, *pathless.*
invŏco, I, *to call upon.*
ipse, ipsa, ipsum, *self* (56).
ira, æ, F., *anger, passion.*
iracundia, æ, F., *wrath.*
irascor, i, irātus, 3, *to be angry.*
irātus, a, um, *angry.*
ire (eo), *to go.*
irrumpo, rūpi, rupt-, 3, *to burst in.*
is, ea, id, *he, she, it, that.*
iste, ista, istud, *that* (yonder).
ita, *so, thus.*
ităque, *therefore.*
iter, itinĕris, N., *journey, passage.*
itĕro, I, *to repeat.*
itĕrum, *again.*
ivi (eo), *went.*

J.

jacio, jeci, jact-, 3, *to throw.*
jactator, ōris, M., *boaster.*
jactūra, æ, F., *throwing-away, loss.*
jam, *now, already.*
jamdīu, *now, long ago.*
jejunium, i, N., *fast.*
jocus, i, M., *joke, jest, fun.*
jubeo, jussi, juss-, 2, *to order.*
jucundus, a, um, *pleasant, cheerful.*
judex, Icis, C., *judge.*
juger, ĕris, N., *acre.*
jugum, i, N., *yoke, ridge* (of hill).
jungo, junxi, junct-, 3, *to join.*
juro, I, *to swear.*
jussi (jubeo), *ordered.*
jussu, *by command.*
justus, a, um, *just.*
juvenca, æ, F., *heifer.*
juvo, juvi, jut-, I, *to help.*
juvĕnis, is, C., *a youth.*
juxta, *near.*

L.

labor, ōris, M., *task, toil.*
labor, i, lapsus, 3, *to fall, glide.*
lac, lactis, N., *milk.*
lacrĭma, æ, F., *tear.*
lacrĭmo, I, *to weep.*
lacrĭmōsus, a, um, *tearful.*
lacus, ūs, M., *lake.*
læva, æ, F., *left hand.*
lætus, a, um, *glad.*
lævus, a, um, *left.*
lamentor, I (dep.), *to lament.*
lamentum, i, N., *lamentation.*
lana, æ, F., *wool.*
languĭdus, a, um, *weak, languid.*
lanio, I, *to tear, mangle.*
lapideus, a, um, *of stone.*
lapillus, i, M., *pebble.*
lapis, Idis, M., *stone.*
lapsus, a, um (labor), *fallen.*
laqueus, i, M., *noose, halter.*
larix, Icis, F., *larch.*
lascivia, æ, F., *playfulness.*
latebra, æ, F., *hiding-place, refuge.*

lateo, ui, ĭt-, 2, *to be hidden.*
latro, ōnis, M., *robber.*
latūrus (fero), *about to bear.*
latus, ĕris, N., *side.*
latus (fero), *borne.*
latus, a, um, *broad, wide.*
laudo, I, *to praise.*
laus, laudis, F., *praise, glory.*
lautus, a, um, *sumptuous.*
lavo, lavi, laut (lot-), I, *to wash.*
legātus, i, M., *deputy, messenger.*
legatorius, i, M., *ambassador.*
lenis, e, *smooth, gentle.*
lenĭter, *gently.*
lentitūdo, ĭnis, F., *toughness.*
lentus, a, um, *tough, slow, supple.*
lepĭdus, a, um, *pleasant.*
leo, ōnis, M., *lion.*
levis, e, *light.*
levĭtas, ātis, F., *lightness.*
lex, legis, F., *law.*
libenter, *gladly.*
liber, libri, M., *book.*
liber, era, um, *free.*
liberi, ōrum, M., *children.*
libĕro, I, *to set free.*
libet (lubet), libuit, 2, *it pleases.*
libertas, ātis, F., *freedom.*
libum, i, N., *cake.*
licet, ebat, uit, 2, *it is allowed.*
lignum, i, N., *wood, stick.*
lilium, i, N., *lily.*
lima, æ, F., *file.*
limes, ĭtis, M., *path, boundary.*
linum, i, N., *linen.*
littus (litus), ŏris, N., *shore.*
locuples, ētis, *wealthy.*
locus, i, M. (pl. loca, N.), *place.*
locūtus (loquor), *having spoken.*
longævus, a, um, *old, ancient.*
longe, longius, longissĭme, *far.*
longitūdo, ĭnis, F., *length.*
longus, a, um, *long, far.*
loquor, locūtus, 3, *to speak.*
lucĭdus, a, um, *bright, clear.*
luctor, I, *to wrestle, struggle.*
luctuosus, a, um, *mournful.*
lucus, ūs, M., *grove.*
ludo, si, sum, 3, *to play.*
ludus, i, M., *game.*
lumen, ĭnis, M., *light.*

lupus, i, M., *wolf.*
lusus, ūs, M., *play, sport.*
luteus, a, um, *muddy; yellow.*
lux, lucis, F., *light.*

M.

macer, cra, um, *lean.*
macilentus, a, um, *lean.*
maculentus, a, um, *speckled.*
madeo, 2, *to be wet.*
mæreo, 2, *to grieve, mourn.*
mæstus, a, um, *sad, distressed.*
magĭcus, a, um, *magical.*
magis, *more, rather.*
magistrātus, ūs, M., *magistrate.*
magnifĭce, *famously, splendidly.*
magnopere, *greatly.*
magnus, a, um, *great.*
major, us, *greater.*
majōres, um, *ancestors.*
malo, malle, malui (T.15), *choose, wish rather.*
mălum, i, N., *evil, misfortune.*
mălum, i, N., *apple.*
malus, i, F., *mast, apple-tree.*
malus, a, um, *evil, bad.*
mamma, æ, F., *breast.*
mandātum, i, N., *command.*
mando, I, *to command, commit.*
mandūco, I, *to eat, chew.*
mane, is, N., *morning.*
maneo, mansi, mans-, 2, *to stay, wait.*
mansuetudo, ĭnis, F., *gentleness.*
manus, ūs, F., *hand.*
mare, is, N., *sea.*
mater, tris, F., *mother.*
materia, æ, F., *matter, material.*
matūrus, a, um, *ripe, early.*
matutīnus, a, um, *of the morning.*
maxime, *especially, by all means.*
maximus, a, um (magnus), *greatest, chief.*
me, mei, mihi (ego), *me.*
medius, a, um, *middle of.*
mel, mellis, N., *honey.*
melior, us (bonus), *better.*
membrum, i, N., *limb.*
memini, eram, &c., *remember.*

memor, ŏris, *mindful.*
memoria, æ, F., *memory.*
mendax, ācis, *lying, false.* ·
mendīco, 1, *to beg.*
mens, mentis, F., *mind.*
mensa, æ, F., *table.*
mensis, is, M., *month.*
mensus (metior), *measured.*
mentior, 4, *to speak falsely.*
mercātor, ŏris, M., *merchant.*
merces, ēdis, F., *pay.*
mereo, ui, ĭt-; mereor, eri, ĭtus, 2, *to deserve.*
mergo, si, sum, 3, *to plunge, dive.*
mergus, ĭ, C., *gull, diver* (a bird).
merĭtum, i, N., *desert, merit.*
merĭtus, a, um, *deserving.*
merus, a, um, *mere, only.*
metuo, 3, *to fear.*
metus, ūs, M., *fear.*
meus, a, um, *my, mine.*
mico, 1, *to sparkle, glitter, flutter.*
migro, 1, *to remove, emigrate.*
miles, ĭtis, M., *soldier.*
militāris, e, *military.*
militia, æ, F., *military service, soldiery.*
mille, millia (milia), *thousand.*
minaciter, *threateningly.*
minæ, arum, F., *threats.*
minĭme, *least, by no means, no.*
minĭmus (parvus), *least.*
minister, tri, M., *servant, attendant.*
ministerium, i, N., *service.*
minor, minus (parvus), *less.*
miracŭlum, i, N., *marvel, prodigy.*
mire, *strangely.*
miror, 1 (dep.), *to gaze at, admire, wonder.*
mirus, a, um, *strange, wonderful.*
misceo, miscui, mixt- (mist-), 2, *to mix, mingle.*
miser, era, um, *wretched.*
miserātio, ōnis, F., *compassion.*
misereor, ĭtus (tus), 2, *to pity.*
miseret, uit, 2, *it causes pity.*
misericordia, æ, F., *mercy.*
miseror, 1 (dep.), *to have pity on.*
missĭlis, e, *missile* (for throwing).
missus (mitto), *sent;* ‡ *an envoy.*
mitĭgo, 1, *to soften, soothe.*

mitto, misi, miss-, 3, *to send.*
mixtus (misceo), *mixed.*
modo, *only, just now.*
modus, i, M., *manner, degree.*
mœnia, ium, N., *walls, defences.*
mollis, e, *soft, smooth.*
moneo, ui, ĭt-, 2, *to warn, advise.*
monīle, is, N., *necklace.*
monĭtus, ūs, M., *warning.*
mons, montis, M., *mountain.*
monstro, 1, *to show.*
moribundus, *dying.*
morior, i, mortuus, 3, *to die.*
moriturus, a, um, *about to die.*
moror, 1 (dep.), *to delay.*
mors, mortis, F., *death.*
mortālis, e, *mortal.*
‡ mortifĭco, 1, *to mortify* (by penance or fasting).
mos, moris, M., *manner, custom.*
motio, ōnis, F., *motion.*
motus, ūs, M., *movement.*
motus (moveo), *excited.*
mox, *soon, presently.*
moveo, movi, mot-, 2, *to move.*
mulier, ĕris, F., *woman.*
multi, æ, a, *many.*
multitudo, ĭnis, F., *multitude.*
multo, *by much.*
multum, *much.*
mundus, i, M., *world.*
munus, ĕris, N., *gift, office.*
mus, muris, C., *mouse.*
mussĭto, 1, *to murmur.*
mutus, a, um, *dumb, silent.*
mutuus, a, um, *mutual;* N., *a loan.*

N.

næ (ne), *nay, indeed.*
nam, *for.*
nares, ium, F., *nostrils.*
narro, 1, *to relate, tell.*
nascor, i, natus, 3, *to be born, spring up.*
nasus, i, M., *nose.*
nates, ium, M., *back, hips.*
natio, ōnis, F., *nation.*
nato, 1, *to swim.*
natūra, æ, F., *nature.*

natu, *by birth.*
natus, a, um, *born ; a son.*
navāle, is, N., *dockyard.*
navigabilis, e, *navigable.*
navĭgor, I, *to sail, go to sea.*
navis, is, F., *ship.*
ne, *lest, not* (114).
ne ... quidem, *not even.*
nec, *neither, nor, and not.*
necdum, *and not yet.*
necne, *or not* (in questions).
necnon, *also.*
necto, xi, xum, 3, *bind, fasten.*
nedum, *much less.*
neco (necui), I, *to kill.*
nefandus, a, um, *shocking.*
nego, I, *to deny.*
nemo, ĭnis (nullius), C., *no one.*
nempe, *surely, forsooth.*
nemus, ŏris, N., *wood, grove.*
nequam, *worthless.*
nequāquam, *by no means.*
neque (nec), *neither, nor.*
nequeo, ivi (Tab. **16**), *cannot.*
nequidquam, *in vain.*
nequis, qua, quid, *lest any.*
nervus, i, M., *string, sinew.*
nescio, 4, *not to know.*
neuter, tra, um (trius), *neither.*
neve, *nor* (with imperat.).
nexo, nexui, 3, *bind, fasten.*
nexus (necto), *fastened.*
ni, *unless.*
nictus, ūs, M., *winking.*
nidus, i, M., *nest.*
niger, gra, um, *black.*
nihil, (nil, nihilum, i,), *nothing.*
nihilomĭnus, *nevertheless.*
nimbus, i, M., *cloud.*
nimis, *too, too much.*
nimius, a, um, *too much.*
nisi, *unless.*
nisus, ūs, M., *effort.*
nitor, ŏris, M., *gleam, glitter.*
nitor, nisus, 3, *to strive, rely.*
nivālis, e, *snowy.*
niveo, 2, *to wink.*
nix, nivis, F., *snow.*
nobĭlis, e, *noble.*
nobilĭtas, ātis, F., *nobility.*
noctu, *by night.*

nocturnus, a, um, *nightly.*
noli, *do not.*
nolo, nolle, nolui (nonvolo, Tab. **15),** *will not.*
nomen, ĭnis, N., *name.*
non, *not, no.*
nondum, *not yet.*
nonne, *not* (interrogat., **55**).
noscĭto, I, *to find out.*
nosco, novi, nōt-, 3, *to learn, know.*
noster, tra, um, *our.*
nota, æ, F., *mark.*
novi, noveram (nosco), *know.*
novĭtas, ātis, F., *newness, strangeness.*
novus, a, um, *new.*
nox, noctis, F., *night.*
noxa, æ, F., *harm, mischief.*
noxius, a, um, *harmful.*
nubes, is, F., *cloud.*
nubo, nupsi, nupt-, 3, *to marry.*
nudo, I, *to strip, make bare.*
nudus, a, um, *bare, naked.*
nullus, a, um (ius), *none, no.*
num, *whether.*
numen, ĭnis, N., *divinity, providence.*
numĕrus, i, M., *number.*
nummus, i, M., *money, coin.*
numquam (nunquam), *never.*
nunc, *now.*
nuntio, I, *to tell, announce.*
nuntius, i, M., *messenger, message.*
nusquam, *nowhere.*
nutrio, 4, *to nourish.*
nutus, ūs, M., *nod.*
nux, nucis, M., *nut.*

O.

ob, *on account of.*
obeo, ire, ii, *to meet ; die.*
objĭcio, jēci, ject-, 3 **(jacio),** *throw in the way, cast against.*
oblītus, a, um, *forgetful.*
oblĭtus, a, um (lino), *besmeared.*
obliviscor, oblītus, 3, *to forget.*
obruo, rui, rūt-, 3, *overwhelm.*
obscūro, I, *to darken, hide.*

obscurus — parum.

obscŭrus, a, um, *dark, obscure.*
obsecro, 1, *to beseech, entreat.*
obses, ĭdis, C., *hostage.*
obsĭdeo, sēdi, sess-, 2, *to besiege, beset.*
obsisto, stĭti, 1, *to stand in the way, resist.*
obstinātus, a, um, *obstinate.*
obstupefacio, fēci, fact-, 3, *to amaze.*
obstupefactus, a, um, *amazed.*
obstŭpeo, ui, 2, *to be amazed.*
obtestor, 1, *to adjure, appeal to.*
obtĭneo, tinui, tent-, 2 (teneo), *to hold fast.*
obtingo, tĭgi, 3, *to happen, befall.*
obtŭli (offero), *offered.*
obviam, *in the way of, to meet.*
occasio, ōnis, F., *opportunity.*
occĭdo, di, cāsum (cado), 3, *to fall, die.*
occĭdo, di, sum, 3 (cædo), *to cut down, kill.*
occulte, *secretly.*
occulto, 1, *to hide.*
occultus, a, um, *hidden.*
occŭpo, 1, *to seize.*
occurro, curri, cursum, 3, *to run to meet.*
ocior, ocius, *swifter, quickly.*
ocŭlus (ocellus), i, M., *eye.*
odi, oderam, osus, *to hate.*
odor, ōris, M., *smell.*
offero, ferre, obtŭli, oblāt-, *to offer.*
olens, tis, *fragrant.*
olim, *once, formerly.*
olīva, æ, F., *olive.*
ominatus, a, um, *betokening.*
omitto, mīsi, miss-, 3, *to neglect, let go.*
omnīno, *wholly, at all.*
omnis, e, *all.*
opācus, a, um, *shady, dark.*
opera, æ, F., *work, means.*
operōse, *laboriously, urgently.*
opertus (operio), *hidden.*
opes (pl.), F., *wealth, goods.*
oportet, uit, 2 (108), *it must be.*
oppidānus, i, M., *townsman, citizen.*
oppugno, 1, *to attack.*
optimus, a, um, *best.*
opus, ĕris, N., *work, need.*
ora, æ, F., *shore.*
oratio, ōnis, F., *speech, prayer.*
orbis, is, M., *circle.*
ordo, ĭnis, M., *rank, order.*
oriens, tis, M., *east; rising.*
orīgo, ĭnis, F., *origin.*
orior, ortus, 4, *to rise.*
ornatus, a, um, *adorned, equipped.*
orno, 1, *to adorn, equip.*
ornus, i, F., *mountain-ash.*
oro, 1, *to pray, entreat.*
ortus (orior), *risen, descended.*
ortus, ūs, M., *rising, beginning.*
os, oris, N., *mouth.*
os, ossis, N., *bone.*
osculor, 1 (dep.), *to kiss.*
ostendo, di, sum, 3, *to show.*
ostento, 1, *to display, exhibit.*
otium, i, N., *ease, leisure, peace.*
ovis, is, F., *sheep.*
ovum, i, N., *egg.*

P.

pactum, i, N., *bargain, means.*
pæne, *almost.*
pala, æ, F., *spade.*
palam, *openly.*
palatium, i, N., *palace.*
palus, ūdis, F., *marsh.*
pando, di, sum, 3, *to spread.*
panis, is, M., *bread.*
par, paris, *equal; a pair.*
parātus, a, um, *ready.*
parco, peperci, parcit-, 3, *to spare.*
parcus, a, um, *sparing.*
parens, tis, C., *parent.*
pareo, ui, it-, *to obey, appear.*
pario, pepĕri, part-, 3, *to produce, lay* (an egg).
parĭter, *equally.*
paro, 1, *to prepare, provide.*
pars, partis, F., *part.*
partĭceps, cĭpis, C., *sharer.*
partus, ūs, M., *birth.*
parum, *not enough, ill.*

parumper, *for a little while.*

parvus, a, um (minor, minimus), *small.*

pasco, pavi, past-, 3, *to feed.*

passer, ŏris, M., *sparrow.*

passim, *here and there, scattered.*

passus (**patior**), *having suffered.*

patens, tis, *open, wide.*

pater, patris, M., *father.*

patior, passus, 3, *to suffer, permit.*

patria, æ, F., *native country.*

patro, 1, *to commit.*

patrōnus, i, M., *patron, protector.*

pauci, æ, a, *few.*

paulatim, *little by little.*

paulisper, *for a little while.*

paulus, a, um, *little.*

pauper, pĕris, *poor.*

pavefactus, a, um, *frightened.*

pavĭdus, a, um, *fearful.*

pavimentum, i, N., *pavement.*

pavor, ōris, M., *fear.*

pax, pacis, F., *peace, good-will.*

peccātum, i, N., *sin, fault.*

pectus, ŏris, N., *breast.*

pecunia, æ, F., *money.*

pecus, ŭdis, F., *one of the flock.*

pecus, ŏris, N., *flock, herd.*

pejor, pejus (**malus**), *worse.*

pellis, is, F., *skin.*

pello, pepŭli, puls-, 3, *drive.*

pelvis, is, F., *basin.*

pendeo, pependi, 2, *to hang.*

pendo, pependi, pens-, 3, *to weigh, pay.*

penĭtus, *inwardly, utterly.*

penniger, era, um, *feathered.*

penuria, æ, F., *poverty.*

peperci (**parco**), *spared.*

pepĕri (**pario**), *produced.*

per, *through;* in compos., *very.*

perăgo, ēgi, act-, 3, *to carry through.*

percunctor, 1 (dep.), *inquire.*

perdo, dĭdi, dĭt-, 3, *to destroy.*

perdūco, xi, ct-, 3, *to lead through.*

peregre, *in foreign lands.*

peregrīnor, 1 (dep.), *to travel.*

pereo, ĭre, ii, *to perish.*

perfectus (**perficio**), *perfect.*

perfĕro, ferre, tŭli, lāt-, *to endure.*

perfĭcio, fēci, fect-, 3, *to finish.*

perfringo, frēgi, fract-, 3, *to break through.*

pergo, perrexi, perrect-, 3, *to advance.*

pericŭlum, i, N., *danger.*

perlĕgo, 3, *to read through.*

perlibenter, *very gladly.*

perpĕram, *wrong.*

perpetuus, a, um, *perpetual.*

Persis, ĭdis (acc. ĭda), F., *Persia.*

pertĭca, æ, F., *perch, roost.*

pertĭneo, ui, tent-, 2 (**teneo**), *to belong, extend.*

pertranseo, ire, ivi, 3, *pass* or *pierce through.*

pertrecto, 1, *to handle.*

pervĕnio, vēni, vent-, 4, *to arrive.*

pes, pedis, M., *foot.*

pestĭfer, fera, ferum, *pestilential, fatal.*

petitio, ōnis, F., *petition.*

peto, petīvi, petīt-, 3, *to seek, ask, aim at, attack.*

pietas, ātis, F., *piety.*

pigmentum, i, N., *pigment, color.*

pinguis, e, *fat.*

piscis, is, M., *fish.*

piscor, 1 (dep.), *to fish.*

pius, a, um, *pious, tender.*

placeo, ui, ĭt-, 2, *to please;* **placet,** *it is resolved.*

placĭde, *calmly.*

placĭdus, a, um, *calm.*

plaga, æ, F., *blow, plague.*

planctus, ūs, M., *mourning.*

plane, *plainly, fully.*

plango, 3, *to lament.*

planus, a, um, *level, even.*

plaustrum, i, N., *waggon.*

plenus, a, um, *full.*

ploro, 1, *to lament.*

plumeus, a, um, *feathery.*

pluries, *several times.*

plurimus, a, um, *most.*

plus, pluris (**multum**), *more.*

pocŭlum, i, N., *cup.*

pœna, æ, F., *punishment, penalty.*

pœnitentia, æ, F., *penitence, penance.*

pœnitet (**108**), *it grieves, repents.*

pollex, ĭcis, M., *thumb.*
pondus, ĕris, N., *weight.*
pono, posui, posĭt-, 3, *to put, place.*
pons, pontis, M., *bridge.*
pontĭfex, fĭcis, M., *priest.*
poposci (posco), *demanded.*
popŭlus, i, M., *people.*
porcus, i, M., *hog.*
porrĭgo, rexi, rect-, 3, *extend.*
porro, *further, again, no doubt.*
posco, poposci, poscĭt-, 3, *to demand.*
posĭtus (pono), *put, placed.*
‡possibĭlis, e, *possible.*
possum, posse, potui, *can* (84).
post, *after, behind.*
postea, *afterwards.*
postĕri, ōrum, M., *posterity.*
postquam, *after* (that), *when.*
postrēmo, *lastly.*
postrēmus, a, um, *last.*
postridie, *the next day.*
postŭlo, I, *to demand, require.*
potius, *rather.*
potus, ūs, M., *drinking.*
præ, *before, considering, through.*
præbeo, præbui, præbĭt-, 3, *to furnish, present.*
præcēdo, cessi, cess-, 3, *to go before, precede.*
præcellens, tis, *excellent.*
præceps, cipĭtis, *headlong.*
præceptum, i, N., *precept, moral.*
præcordium, i, N., *heart, breast.*
præda, æ, F., *prize, booty.*
prædĭco, xi, ct-, 3, *to predict.*
prædĭco, I, *to say, assert.*
prædor, I, *to plunder.*
‡præfātus, a, um, *aforesaid.*
præfectus, i, M., *governor.*
præscrĭbo, psi, pt-, 3, *to prescribe.*
præsens, tis, *present.*
‡præsento, I, *to present.*
præsertim, *especially.*
præses, ĭdis, M., *chief.*
præsidium, i, N., *guard, defence.*
præstans, tis, *excellent.*
præstantia, æ, F., *excellence.*
præstat, *it is better.*
præsto, stĭti, stĭt-, I, *to excel, furnish.*

præter, præterquam, *besides, except.*
prando, di, sum, 3, *to dine.*
prasĭnus, a, um, *leek-green.*
pratum, i, N., *meadow.*
pravus, a, um, *wicked, bad.*
precātio, ōnis, F., *entreaty.*
precis (gen.), F., *prayer.*
precor, I (dep.), *to pray, supplicate.*
premo, pressi, press-, 3, *to press.*
pretium, i, N., *price, value.*
primo, *at first.*
primus, a, um, *first.*
princeps, ĭpis, M., *chief, prince.*
prior, prius, *former, first.*
pristĭnus, a, um, *former, previous.*
prius ... quam, *before* (that), *till.*
privatus, a, um, *private.*
privo, I, *to deprive.*
pro, *before, for, in behalf of.*
procēdo, cessi, cess-, 3, *proceed.*
procella, æ, F., *storm, tempest.*
procĕres, um, C., *chiefs, nobles.*
procērus, a, um, *tall.*
procul, *far away.*
procumbo, cubui, cubĭt-, 3, *to fall down.*
prœlium, i, N., *battle.*
profecto, *surely.*
profectus (proficiscor), *having gone.*
profĕro, ferre, tŭli, lāt-, *to bring forward.*
profĭcio, 3, *go forward, effect.*
proficiscor, profect-, 3 (dep.), *to go, advance.*
progredior, gressus, 3 (gradior), *to advance.*
proh, *oh!*
projĭcio, jēci, ject-, 3 (jacio), *to throw forward, cast away.*
prolapsus (labor), *fallen forward.*
‡promissio, ōnis, F., *promise.*
promitto, mīsi, miss-, 3, *to promise.*
pronuntio, I, *to announce, proclaim.*
pronus, a, um, *fallen forward.*
prope, *near.*

propello, pŭli, puls-, 3, *to push forward.*
propĕre, *hastily.*
propinquus, a, um, *near, kindred.*
propior, us, *nearer.*
propitius, a, um, *favorable.*
propōno, posui, posĭt-, 3, *to put forward, propose.*
propter, *near, on account of.*
prora, æ, F., *prow.*
prorsus, *altogether, completely.*
prorumpo, rūpi, rupt-, 3, *burst forth.*
prospecto, I, *to look out.*
prosterno, strāvi, strāt-, 3, *throw down, destroy.*
prostrātus, a, um, *prostrate.*
protĭnus, *forth, right on.*
protractus (traho), *long-drawn, delayed.*
proturbo, I, *drive forth.*
prout, *according as.*
provĕhor, vectus, 3, *to ride forward.*
provĭdus, a, um, *prudent.*
provŏco, I, *to challenge.*
proximus, a, um, *nearest, next.*
pruīna, æ, F., *frost.*
pruna, æ, F., *live coal.*
publĭce, *publicly.*
pudor, ōris, M., *shame.*
puella, æ, F., *girl.*
puer, puĕri, M., *boy.*
pugna, æ, F., *battle.*
pugno, I, *to fight.*
pugnus, i, M., *fist.*
pulcher, chra, um, *beautiful.*
pulchritūdo, ĭnis, F., *beauty.*
pullus, i, M., *chicken.*
pulvis, ĕris, M., *dust.*
pungo, pupŭgi, punct-, 3, *to sting, prick.*
purus, a, um, *pure, clean.*
puteus, i, M., *well, pit.*
puto, I, *to think, suppose; prune.*

Q.

qua, *whereby, what way.*
quadraginta, *forty.*

quæro, sīvi, sīt-, 3, *to seek, ask.*
quæso, I, *to seek urgently.*
quæstio, ōnis, F., *question, search.*
qualis, e, *of what sort, as.*
quam, *as, than, how* (See **82**).
quamvis, *however much.*
quando, *when.*
quantum, *how much, as much as.*
quantus, a, um, *how great.*
quapropter, *on which account.*
quare, *wherefore, why.*
quasi, *as if.*
quartārius, i, M., *gill-measure.*
quartus, a, um, *fourth.*
quaternus, *how far, by what way.*
quatuor (quattuor), *four.*
-que, *and.*
queo (Table **16**), *can.*
quercus, ūs, F., *oak.*
querēla, æ, F., *complaint.*
queror, questus, 3, *to complain.*
qui, quæ, quod, *who, which.*
qui, *how.*
quia, *because.*
quicquam (quidquam), *any thing.*
quicumque, quæcumque, &c., *whoever.*
quid, *what?*
quidam, quædam, &c., *a-certain.*
quidem, *indeed;* ne ... **quidem,** *not even.*
quidquam, *any thing.*
quies, ētis, F., *rest, quiet.*
quin, *but that, why not, nay.*
quinquaginta, *fifty.*
quinquagesĭmus, a, um, *fiftieth.*
quinque, *five.*
quini, æ, a, *by fives.*
quintus, a, um, *fifth.*
quippe, *since.*
quis, quæ, quid, *who? what?*
quisnam, quænam, &c., *who?*
quisquam, quæquam, &c., *any.*
quo, *whither;* (abl.), *by which.*
quod, *that, because.*
quomŏdo, *how.*
quoniam, *since.*
quoque, *also.*
quotannis, *yearly.*
quotidiānus, a, um, *daily.*
quum (cum), *when, though, since.*

R.

radior, I (dep.), *to radiate.*
radius, i, M., *ray.*
radix, īcis, F., *root, foot* (of hill).
rado, rasi, rasum, 3, *to scrape.*
ramus, i, M., *branch.*
rana, æ, F., *frog.*
rapĭdus, a, um, *swift.*
rapio, rapui, rapt-, 3, *to snatch.*
rarus, a, um, *rare.*
ratio, ōnis, F., *reason, method.*
ratus (reor), *supposing.*
recalefăcio, 3, *to warm again.*
recēdo, cessi, cess-, 3, *retreat.*
recens, tis, *recent, fresh.*
recreo, I, *to recreate, revive.*
recte, *rightly.*
rectus (rego), *straight, right.*
recūso, I, *to refuse.*
reddo, reddĭdi, reddĭt-, 3, *to restore, render.*
redeo, īre, ii, ĭt-, *to return.*
redūco, xi, ct-, 3, *to draw back.*
refĕro, ferre, tŭli, lāt-, *to return, reply.*
refŭgio, fūgi, 3, *to flee back.*
regia, æ, F., *palace.*
regīna, æ, F., *queen, empress.*
regio, ōnis, F., *region.*
regius, a, um, *royal.*
regnum, i, N., *kingdom.*
rego, rexi, rect-, 3, *to guide, rule.*
rejĭcio, jēci, ject-, 3 (jacio), *to reject.*
relevātus, a, um, *relieved.*
relictus (relinquo), *left.*
religio, ōnis, F., *religion, superstition.*
relinquo, līqui, lict-, 3, *to leave.*
relĭquus, a, um, *remaining, rest of.*
remăneo, mansi, 2, *to stay behind.*
remex, ĭgis, M., *rower.*
remus, i, M., *oar.*
reor, ratus, 2, *to suppose.*
repello, repŭli, repuls-, 3, *to drive back.*
repente, *suddenly.*
reperio, repĕri, repert-, 4, *to find.*

repĕto, petīvi, petĭt-, 3, *to seek, claim, resume.*
reposĭtus, a, um, *put back.*
reprehenso, 1, *to check, chide.*
reprĭmo, pressi, press-, 3, *to repress.*
repulsus (repello), *driven back.*
repŭto, I, *to think, reflect.*
requies, ētis, F., *rest.*
res, rei, F., *thing, property.*
resīna, æ, F., *gum-resin.*
res-publica, F., *republic.*
resŏnans, tis, *loud, resounding.*
respĭcio, spexi, spect-, 3, *to look back, consider.*
respondeo, di, sum, 2, *to answer.*
restinguo, stinxi, stinct-, 3, *to extinguish.*
resurgo, surrexi, surrect-, 3, *to rise again.*
retĭceo, cui, 2 (taceo), *to be silent.*
retĭneo, tinui, tent-, 2 (teneo), *to hold back, keep in memory.*
retrăho, xi, ct-, 3, *to draw back.*
retro, *back, backward.*
reus, a, um, *accused, arraigned.*
revertor, reversus, 3, *to return.*
revŏco, I, *to call back.*
revolvo, volvi, volūt-, 3, *to revolve, reflect.*
rex, regis, M., *king, emperor.*
rideo, risi, 2, *to laugh, laugh at.*
ridicŭlus, a, um, *ridiculous.*
rigens, tis, *stiff.*
rīgeo, rigui, 2, *to be stiff.*
rima, æ, F., *crack, chink.*
rimor, I, *to scratch.*
ripa, æ, F., *river-bank.*
risus, ūs, M., *laughter.*
rivus, i, M., *stream.*
robur, ŏris, N., *strength, stoutness.*
rodo, rosi, rosum, 3, *to gnaw.*
rogo, I, *to ask, claim.*
rogus, i, M., *funeral-pile.*
rosa, æ, F., *rose.*
rostrum, i, N., *beak.*
rosus (rodo), *gnawn.*
rubecŭla (rubicilla), æ, F., *robin.*
rubeo, rubui, 2, *to be red.*
ruber, rubra, rubrum, *red.*
ruīna, æ, F., *ruin, downfall.*

rumpo, rupi, rupt-, 3, *to break, burst.*
rursum (rursus), *again.*
rus, ruris, N., *the country.*
rusticus, a, um, *rude, rustic.*

S.

saccus, i, N., *bag.*
sacer, sacra, sacrum, *sacred.*
sacerdos, ōtis, C., *priest.*
sacramentum, i, N., *oath.*
sacrificium, i, N., *sacrifice.*
saeclum (seculum), i, N., *an age* or *century, the world.*
saepe, *often.*
saeviter, *cruelly.*
saevitia, ae, F., *cruelty.*
sagax, ācis, *sagacious.*
sagitta, ae, F., *arrow.*
sal, salis, M., *salt.*
salio, salui, salt-, 4, *to leap.*
salix, īcis, F., *willow.*
saltem, *at least.*
saltus, ūs, M., *a leap; grove or shade.*
salus, salūtis, F., *safety, health.*
salutāris, e, *saving, wholesome.*
salve, *hail!*
salvo, I, *to save.*
salvus, a, um, *safe.*
sancte, *religiously.*
sanctitas, ātis, F., *holiness.*
sanctus, a, um, *holy, sacred.*
sane, *no doubt, to be sure.*
sanguis, inis, M., *blood.*
sanus, a, um, *sound, sane.*
sapiens, tis, *wise.*
sapientia, ae, F., *wisdom.*
sapo, ōnis, M., *soap.*
sat, satis, *enough.*
satius, *better, preferable.*
satus (sero), *sown.*
saxum, i, N., *rock, crag.*
scaevus, a, um, *awkward.*
scalpturio, 4, *to scratch.*
scalptus, ūs, M., *scraping.*
scapha, ae, F., *boat.*
scatebra, ae, F., *gush, fountain.*
scelus, ĕris, N., *crime, guilt.*

scientia, ae, F., *knowledge.*
scilicet, *no doubt, to be sure.*
scindo, scidi, sciss-, 3, *to rend.*
scintilla, ae, F., *spark.*
scio, 4, *to know.*
scirpus, i, M., *bulrush.*
sciscitor, I (dep.), *to inquire.*
scissus (scindo), *split.*
sciūrus, i, M., *squirrel.*
scrībo, scripsi, script-, 3, *write.*
scrutor, I, *to search.*
scutum, i, N., *shield.*
se, sui, sibi (57), *self.*
secerno, crēvi, crēt-, 3, *separate.*
seco, secui, sect-, I, *cut.*
secrētum, i, N., *privacy.*
secrētus, a, um, *secret.*
secum, *with him* or *them.*
secundum, *according to.*
secundus, a, um, *second.*
secūris, is, F., *axe.*
secūrus, a, um, *secure, without fear.*
sed, *but.*
sedĕcim, *sixteen.*
sedeo, sēdi, sess-, 2, *to sit.*
sedes, is, F., *seat.*
sēdo, I, *to settle.*
seges, ĕtis, F., *crop.*
selibra, ae, F., *half-pound.*
semel, *once.*
semen, inis, N., *seed.*
semis, *half.*
semita, ae, F., *path.*
semper, *always.*
senātus, ūs (i), M., *senate.*
senex, senis, M., *old, old man.*
seni, ae, a, *by sixes.*
sentio, si, sum, 4, *to feel, think.*
sentis, is, M., *thorn, brier.*
separo, I, *to divide.*
sepĕlio, ii, sepult-, 4, *bury.*
sepes, is, F., *hedge.*
septem, *seven.*
septemtrio, ōnis, M., *north.*
sepulorum, i, N., *tomb.*
sepultus (sepelio), *buried.*
sequor, secūtus, 3, *to follow.*
serēnus, a, um, *calm, fair.*
sermo, ōnis, M., *speech, talk.*
sero, sevi, sat-, 3, *to sow.*

sero, serui, sert-, 3, *to weave.*
serpens, tis, C., *winding, serpent.*
serpo, psi, pt-, 3, *to creep, wind.*
serra, æ, F., *saw.*
sertum, i, N., *a garland, flower-border.*
servitium, i, N., *herd of slaves.*
servo, I, *to save, preserve.*
servus, i, M., *servant, slave.*
set (sed), *but.*   sese = se.
seu, *or if, whether.*
sex, *six.*
sexcenti. æ, a, *six hundred.*
sextus, a, um. *sixth.*
si, *if.*   sibi, *for himself, &c.*
sic, *so, thus.*
sicco, I, *to dry.*
siccus, a, um, *dry.*
sicut, *as, just as.*
sidereus, a, um, *starry.*
sidus, ĕris, N., *star, constellation.*
significo, I, *to signify.*
signo, I, *to mark.*
signum, i, N., *sign, standard.*
silentium, i, N., *silence.*
sileo, silui, 2, *to be silent.*
silex, Icis, M., *flint.*
silva, æ, F., *wood, forest.*
silvestris, e, *of the wood.*
simia, æ, F., *ape.*
similis, e, *like.*
simplex, Icis, *simple.*
simplicitas, ātis, F., *simplicity.*
simul, *at the same time, as soon as.*
simulacrum, i, N., *image.*
sin, *but if.*
sine, *without.*
singuli, æ, a, *single, one by one.*
sinister, tra, um, *on the left.*
sino, sivi, 3, *to permit.*
siquis, siqua, &c., *if any.*
sitis, is, F., *thirst.*
sitŭla, æ, F., *bucket.*
situs, ūs, M., *rust, dust.*
sive (seu), *if, whether.*
sociĕtas, ātis, F., *society, alliance.*
socio, I, *to associate.*
socius, i, M., *companion.*
sol, solis, M., *the sun.*
soleo, solĭtus, 2, *to be accustomed.*

sollicĭtus, a, um, *anxious, watchful;* sollicito, *anxiously.*
solus, a, um (īus), *alone, only.*
solvo, solvi, solūt-, 3, *to dissolve.*
somnium, i, N., *dream.*
somnus, i, M., *sleep.*
sonĭtus, ūs, M., *sound, noise*
sono, I, *to sound.*
sons, sontis, *guilty.*
sonus, i, M., *sound.*
sopor, ōris, M., *sleep.*
sordĭdus, a, um, *dirty.*
soror, ōris, F., *sister.*
spargo, sparsi, sparsum, 3, *to strow, scatter.*
spatior, I (dep.), *to march, stride.*
spatium, i, N., *space.*
spectacŭlum, i, N., *spectacle.*
spectātor, ōris, M., *spectator.*
specto, I, *to look.*
specŭlor, I (dep.), *to gaze at.*
specŭlum, i, N., *mirror.*
specus, ūs, M., *cave, den.*
sperno, sprevi, sprēt-, 3, *to despise, scorn.*
spero, I, *to hope.*
spes, spei, F., *hope.*
spica, æ, F., *ear of corn.*
spina, æ, F., *thorn, quill.*
spirĭtus, i, M., *breath, spirit.*
splendeo, 2, *to shine.*
splendĭdus, a, um, *brilliant.*
sponsio, ōnis, F., *promise.*
spretus (sperno), *scorned.*
stabĭlis, e, *firm, stable.*
stabŭlum, i, N., *stable, stall.*
stadium, i, N., *furlong, race-course.*
stagnum, i, N., *lake, pond.*
statim, *at once, immediately.*
statio, ōnis, F., *station, post.*
statua, æ, F., *statue.*
statuo, statui, statūt-, 3, *to resolve, determine.*
stella, æ, F., *star.*
sterno, stravi, strāt-, 3, *to strow, throw.*
stipor, I, *to wait upon.*
stirps, stirpis. F., *stock, stem.*
sto, stĕti, stat-, I, *to stand.*
stolĭdus, a, um, *stupid.*
strages, is, F., *defeat, destruction.*

strepĭtus, us, M., *noise.*
stricte, *strictly, briefly.*
strictus (stringo), *drawn, strained.*
strīdeo, 2, *to whistle, whizz.*
stringo, nxi, strict-, 3, *draw close.*
struo, xi, ct-, 3, *to pile, build.*
studeo, studui, 2, *to study, strive.*
studium, i, N., *study, zeal.*
stultus, a, um, *foolish.*
stupefactus, a, um, *amazed.*
stupeo, ui, 2, *to be amazed, stunned.*
suadeo, suasi, suas-, 2, *to advise, urge.*
suavis, e, *sweet, mild.*
sub, *under.*
subdo, dĭdi, dĭt-, 3, *to yield, subdue, subject.*
subeo, īre, ii, *to undergo, sustain, carry.*
suber, ĕris, N., *cork.*
subirātus, a, um, *rather angry.*
subĭtus, a, um, *sudden.*
subjectus, a, um, *subject.*
subjĭcio, jēci, ject-, 3 (jacio), *subdue.*
sublātus (tollo), *taken away, raised.*
sublĕvo, I, *to lift.*
sublicius, a, um, *of timber.*
sublīmis, e, *high, lofty.*
subrīdeo, 2, *to smile.*
subsēdo, sēdi, sess-, 3, *to sit, squat.*
subsĭlio, ui (ii), 4, *to leap upward.*
subter, *beneath.*
succus, i, M., *juice.* sui *v.* se.
sudor, ōris, M., *sweat.*
sudus, a, um, *fair, dry.* [*of*
summus, a, um, *chief, highest, top*
sumo, mpsi, mpt-, 3, *to take.*
sumptus, ūs, M., *expense.*
suo, sui, sūt-, 3, *to sew, stitch.*
supellex, ectĭlis, F., *furniture.*
super, *over, above, on.*
‡superbiōse, *loftily, haughtily.*
superbus, a, um, *proud, haughty.*
superesse (84), *to survive.*
superfundo, fūdi, 3, *to pour over.*
superne, *above.*
supĕro, I, *to surpass, excel.*

superstes, ĭtis, C., *survivor.*
supīnus, a, um, *fallen backward.*
supplex, ĭcis, *suppliant.*
supplicium, i, N., *petition, punishment.*
supplĭco, I, *to supplicate.*
surgo, surrexi, surrect-, 3, *to rise.*
sursum, *upward.*
sus, suis, C., *hog.*
suspĭcor, I (dep.), *to suspect, suppose.*
suspirium, i, N., *sigh.*
sustĭneo, ui, tent-, 2 (teneo), *to hold up, sustain, delay.*
sustŭli (tollo), *raised.*
susurro, I, *to whisper.*
sutor, ōris, M., *cobbler.*
sutūra, æ, F., *seam.*
suus, a, um, *his* (57).

T.

tabes, tabis, F., *decay.*
taceo, tacui, 2, *to be silent.*
tacĭtus, a, um, *silent.*
tædet, tæduit, 2, *it wearies.*
talis, e, *such.*
talpa, æ, F., *mole.*
tam, *so, so much.*
tamdiu, *so long.*
tamen, *yet, nevertheless.*
tamquam (tanquam), *as if.*
tandem, *at length.*
tango, tetĭgi, tact-, 3, *to touch.*
tantum, tanto, *so much.*
tantus, a, um, *so great.*
tardus, a, um, *slow, late.*
taurus, i, M., *bull.*
tectum, i, N., *roof, shelter, house.*
tego, texi, ct-, 3, *to cover, shelter.*
telum, i, N., *weapon, spear.*
temperies, ēi, F., *weather.*
tempĕro, I, *to temper.*
tempestas, ātis, F., *tempest.*
templum, i, N., *temple;* ‡*church.*
tempto (tento), I, *to try.*
tempus, ŏris, N., *time, occasion.*
tenax, ācis, *tough, tenacious.*
tendo, tetendi, tens-, 3, *to stretch, tend.*

teneo, tenui, tent-. 2, *to hold.*
tener, era, rum, *tender.*
tento (tempto), 1, *to try.*
tenuis, e, *thin, slender.*
tenus, *up to, as far as.*
tepeo, tepui, 3, *to be warm.*
tepor, ōris, M., *warmth.*
ter. *three times, thrice.*
tergum, i, N., *back;* a tergo, *behind.*
tero, trīvi, trīt-, 3, *to wear, bruise, rub.*
terra, æ, F., *earth, ground.*
terreo, terrui, īt-, 2, *to frighten.*
terribīlis, e, *dreadful.*
terror, ōris, M., *terror, fright.*
tertius, a, um, *third.*
testa, æ, F., *shell.*
testor, 1, *to witness, testify.*
testūdo, Inis, F., *tortoise.*
texo, texui, text-, 3, *to weave.*
thalămus, i, M., *bed-chamber.*
thesaurus, i, M., *treasure.*
thoraceus, a, um, *for the breast.*
thronus, i, M., *throne.*
tibia, æ, F., *shin, pipe* or *whistle.*
tigris, Idis, C., *tiger.*
timeo, timui, 2, *to fear.*
timor, ōris, M., *fear.*
toga, æ, F., *coat, mantle.*
tolero, 1, *to endure.*
tollo, sustŭli, sublāt-, 3, *to lift, take away.*
tondeo, totondi, tons-, 2, *to clip.*
tonitrus, ūs, M., *thunder.*
tono, ui, īt-, 1, *to thunder, resound.*
tormentum, i, N., *torment.*
torpor, ōris, M., *numbness.*
torques, is, M., *chain, necklace.*
tot, *so many.*
totIdem, *just as many.*
totus, a, um (ius), *whole.*
trabs, trabis, F., *log, beam.*
trado, dīdi, dīt-, 3, *to deliver, betray.*
traho, traxi, ct-, 3, *to draw, drag.*
trajĭcio, jēci, ject-, 3 (jacio), *to throw across.*
trano, 1, *to swim across.*
tranquillus, a, um, *calm, tranquil.*
trans, *across.*

transeo, īre, īvi (ii), Xt-, *to cross.*
transvĕhor, vectus, 3, *to cross over.*
tredĕcim, *thirteen.*
tremendus, a, um, *dreadful.*
tremo, tremui, 3, *to tremble.*
tremor, ōris, M., *trembling, dread.*
trepĭdo, 1, *to tremble.*
tres, tria, *three.*
tribūnus, i, M., *tribune, legion-commander.*
tribus, ūs, F., *tribe.*
triennium, i, N., *three years.*
triginta, *thirty.*
tristis, e, *sad, gloomy.*
tritus (tero), *worn.*
triumpho, 1, *to triumph.*
trucīdo, 1, *to kill, massacre.*
truncus, i, M., *trunk.*
trux, trucis, *fierce, cruel.*
tu, tui, tibi, te, *thou.*
tuba, æ, F., *trumpet.*
tueor, tuĭtus, 2, *to look.*
tugurium, i, N., *cottage.*
tum, *then;* tum ... tum, *both ... and.*
tumultus, ūs, M., *tumult.*
tunc, *then.*
tundo, tutŭdi, tuns-, 3, *to beat, thump.*
tunIca, æ, F., *tunic, shirt.*
turba, æ, F., *crowd.*
turbĭdus, a, um, *confused.*
turbo, Inis, M., *whirlwind, top.*
turbo, 1, *to disturb.*
turgeo, tursi, 2, *to swell.*
turris, is, F., *tower.*
tussio, 4, *to cough.*
tussis, is, M., *a cough.*
tute, *you yourself.*
tute, *safely.*
tutor, 1, *to protect.*
tutŭdi (tundo), *beat, peck.*
tutus, a, um, *safe;* tutum, *safety.*
tuus, a, um, *thy, your.*

U.

uber, ubĕris, N., *breast, udder.*
uber, ubĕris, *rich, fertile.*

ubi, *where, when.*
ubīnam, *where?*
ubīque, *everywhere.*
ubīvis, *anywhere.*
ulciscor, ultus, 3, *to avenge, punish.*
ullus, a, um (ius), *any.*
ulmus, i, F., *elm.*
ulterior, us, *further, beyond.*
ultor, ōris, M., *avenger.*
ultra, *beyond.*
ultro, *voluntarily, unprovoked.*
ultus (ulciscor), *avenged.*
umbo, ōnis, M., *boss* (of shield).
umbra, æ, F., *shade, shadow.*
umquam (unquam), *ever.*
una, *together.*
unda, æ, F., *wave.*
unde, *whence.*
undecim, *eleven.*
undique, *on all sides.*
ungo, unxi, unct-, 3, *to anoint, besmear.*
unguentum, i, N., *ointment, perfume.*
unguis, is, M., *nail, claw.*
ungŭla, æ, F., *claw, talon, hoof.*
unīce, *especially.*
unīcus, a, um, *only, single.*
unigenĭtus, i, M., *only-begotten.*
universus, a, um, *whole, all, universal.*
unquam (umquam), *ever.*
unus, a, um (ius), *one.*
urbs, urbis, F., *city.*
urna, æ, F., *urn, pitcher.*
uro, ussi, ust-, 3, *to burn.*
ursus, i, M., *bear.*
usquam, *anywhere.*
usque, *as far as.*
usus, ūs, M., *use, need, service.*
ut, *that; so that, when, as.*
uter, utra, um (trīus), *which of two.*
uterque, utrăque, &c., *each, both.*
uti, *that, as.*
utīque, *surely.*
utor, usus, 3, *to use, employ.*
utro, *which way.*
utrum, *whether.*
uva, æ, F., *grape, cluster.*
uxor, ōris, F., *wife.*

V.

vacca, æ, F., *cow.*
vaco, 1, *to be at leisure.*
vacuus, a, um, *empty.*
vado, 3, *to go.*
væ, *alas.*
vagor, 1 (dep.), *stray, stroll, wander.*
valde, *very.*
vale, *farewell.*
valens, tis, *stout, vigorous.*
valeo, valui, 2, *to be well.*
valĭde, *stoutly.*
valĭdus, a, um, *stout, strong.*
vanus, a, um, *vain, void.*
varius, a, um, *various.*
vas, vasis, N., *vessel, furniture.*
vasto, 1, *to lay waste.*
vastus, a, um, *vast, desolate.*
vates, is, C., *prophet.*
vehemens, tis, *vehement.*
vehementer, *extremely.*
veho, vexi, vect-, 3, *to carry.*
vehor, vect-, 3, *to ride.*
vel, *either, or.*
velātus, a, um, *veiled.*
vellus, ĕris, N., *fleece.*
velocĭter, *swiftly.*
velox, ōcis, *swift.*
velum, i, N., *sail.*
velut, *just as, as if.*
venatĭcus, a, um, *fond of hunting.*
venatio, ōnis, F., *hunting, game.*
vendo, dĭdi, dĭt-, 3, *to sell.*
veneranter, *reverently, in awe.*
venĕror, 1, *to revere, venerate.*
venia, æ, F., *pardon, favor.*
venio, veni, vent-, 4, *to come.*
venor, 1, *to hunt.*
venter, ventris, M., *stomach, waist.*
ventūrus, a, um, *about to come.*
ventus, i, M., *wind.*
vepres, is, M., *brier, bramble.*
ver, veris, N., *spring.*
verber, verbĕris, N., *scourge.*
verbum, i, N., *word.*
vere, *truly.*
vereor, verĭtus, 2, *to fear.*
verĭtas, ātis, F., *truth.*

vernālis, e, *vernal, of spring.*
vero, *truly, but.*
verro, verri, versum, 3, *to sweep.*
versus, *towards.*
verto, verti, versum, 3, *to turn.*
verus, a, um, *true.*
vespa, æ, F., *wasp.*
vesper, ĕri, M., *evening.*
vester, tra, um, *your.*
vestio, 4, *to clothe.*
vestītus, a, um, *clad.*
vetus, ĕris, *old, ancient.*
vetustas, ātis, F., *antiquity.*
via, æ, F., *way.*
vibro, I, *to brandish, quiver.*
vice, *in the place of.*
vices (pl.), *times* or *turns.*
vicīnus, a, um, *neighboring.*
victor, ōris, M., *conqueror; victorious.*
victoria, æ, F., *victory.*
victus, ūs, M., *food, living.*
victus (vinco), *conquered.*
vicus, i, M., *village.*
videlĭcet, *plainly, clearly.*
video, vīdi, vīsum, 2, *to see.*
videor, vīsus, 2, *to appear.*
viduus, a, um, *widowed.*
vigeo, vigui, 2, *to be vigorous.*
vigil, is, C., *watchful; watchman.*
vigĭlo, I, *to watch.*
viginti, *twenty.*
vilis, e, *cheap, worthless.*
vin' (volo), *will you?*
vincio, vinxi, vinct-, 4, *to bind.*
vinco, vici, vict-, 3, *to conquer.*
vincŭlum, i, N., *bond, chain.*
vindĭco, I, *to claim, defend.*
vindicta, æ, F., *punishment, vengeance.*

vinum, i, N., *wine.*
vir, viri, M., *man.*
virāgo, viragĭnis, F., *heroine.*
vires (vis), F. pl., *strength, power, energy.*
virga, æ, F., *rod, twig.*
virgo, virgĭnis, F., *maiden.*
virĭdis, e, *green.*
viror, ōris, M., *verdure.*
virtus, ūtis, F., *virtue, manhood, valor.*
vis, vi, vim, F., *force.*
vis (volo), *you will.*
viso, 3, *to visit, frequent.*
vita, æ, F., *life.*
vitis, is, F., *vine, grape-vine.*
vito, I, *to avoid.*
vivo, vixi, vict-, 3, *to live.*
vivus, a, um, *alive, living.*
vix, *scarcely.*
vixdum, *scarce yet.*
vixi (vivo), *lived.*
voco, I (vox), *to call.*
volo, I, *to fly.*
volo, velle, volui (Tab. 15), *to wish.*
volŭcer, cris, cre, *winged; bird.*
voluntas, ātis, F., *will, choice.*
voluptas, ātis, F., *pleasure, delight.*
volūto, I, *to roll, grovel.*
vorāgo, voragĭnis, F., *gulf, chasm.*
vos, vestri, vobis, *you.*
vox, vocis, F., *voice.*
vulgus, i, N., *people, crowd.*
vulnĕro, I, *to wound.*
vulnus, ĕris, N., *wound.*
vulpes, is, F., *fox.*
vult (volo), *will, wish.*
vultus, ūs, M., *face.*

ANNOUNCEMENTS

OF

NEW BOOKS

BY

GINN AND HEATH.

Latin.

THE AGRICOLA OF TACITUS.

Edited for School and College Use by W. F. ALLEN, Professor of Latin in the University of Wisconsin. [*Ready in July.*

THE GERMANIA OF TACITUS.

Edited for School and College Use by W. F. ALLEN, Professor of Latin in the University of Wisconsin. [*In preparation.*

THE ANNALS OF TACITUS.

Edited by TRACY PECK, Professor of Latin in Cornell University. Vol. I. will contain the first six books of the Annals, covering the reign of Tiberius. [*In preparation.*

SELECTIONS FROM SOME OF THE LESS-KNOWN LATIN POETS; viz., Catullus, Lucretius, the Elegiac Writers, Lucan and Martial. With notes for colleges. By E. P. CROWELL, A.M., Professor of Latin, Amherst College. [*In preparation.*

GINN & HEATH, Publishers, Boston, New York, and Chicago.

CICERO DE NATURA DEORUM.

Translated and Edited, with the Commentary of Schoeman, by Professor Austin Stickney, formerly of Trinity College, Hartford.

[*Ready in August.*

A NEW AND COMPLETE VIRGIL.

This Edition will be printed from wholly new plates, and will be fully annotated by Professor J. B. Greenough, Harvard University. It will also have numerous illustrations from the antique.

[*Ready in June, 1881.*

ALLEN'S LATIN COMPOSITION.

Introduction to Latin Composition by Professor W. F. Allen. New Edition, revised and enlarged.

This edition has been thoroughly revised, recast, and adapted to the Revised Edition of Allen and Greenough's Grammar, with parallel references to Gildersleeve and Harkness. About twenty-five preliminary Lessons have been added on elementary constructions; also, a new and enlarged general Vocabulary. In the introductory portion, special attention has been given to oral practice, with a view to the rapid acquisition of a good Vocabulary (taken largely from Cæsar) as well as the familiar knowledge of grammatical constructions. In the revision, and in the preparation of the preliminary exercises, the Editor has been greatly aided by the advice and coöperation of Mr. John Tetlow, Principal of the Girls' Latin School, Boston.

[*Ready in July.*

In order to meet a very general demand, an edition of the

NEW LATIN METHOD

Will be published during the summer, with the "Parallel Exercises" greatly simplified, abridged, and accompanied by progressive exercises in "Reading at Sight" (interlined), taken chiefly from Cæsar. In these exercises the long vowels will be consistently marked throughout.

GINN & HEATH, Publishers, Boston, New York, and Chicago.

THE LETTERS OF THE YOUNGER PLINY.

Edited for Use in Schools and Colleges by TRACY PECK, Professor of Latin in Cornell University.

This edition will contain all the letters of Pliny, including the correspondence with the Emperor Trajan, and a commentary upon the entire series. The slight attention paid to these letters in our Latin courses has often been remarked and regretted. The light which they throw upon the public and private history of their time, the amiable and cultivated character of the writer, and their graceful style and exquisite Latinity, make them exceptionally instructive and interesting. *[In preparation.*

LATIN PRONUNCIATION.

A Brief Outline of the Roman, Continental, and English Methods, by D. B. KING, Adjunct Professor of Latin in Lafayette College.

Contains a few explanatory and historical paragraphs on the Roman, Continental, and English methods of pronouncing Latin, and a brief presentation of the main features of each, prepared for use at Lafayette College, where the character and arrangement of studies in English and Comparative Philology make it desirable that students should have a knowledge of both Roman and English methods.

The students are carefully taught in practice to use the English method, and to give the rules for the sound of the letters, this having been found a valuable aid in teaching English Pronunciation and the Philology of the English language. A knowledge of the Roman method, giving the sounds, in the main, as we believe Cicero and Virgil gave them, is required as a matter of historical information and culture, and as an important aid in determining the derivations of words and laws of phonetic change, and in illustrating the principles of Comparative Philology. Mailing price, 15 cents. *[Ready.*

LEIGHTON'S LATIN LESSONS

Will have references, in the next edition, to the Grammars of Andrews and Stoddard, Gildersleeve and Harkness.

GINN & HEATH, Publishers, Boston, New York, and Chicago.

Greek.

THE PROMETHEUS OF AESCHYLUS.

Edited, with Notes and an Introduction, by FREDERIC D. ALLEN, PH.D., Professor of Greek in Yale College.   *[In preparation.*

THE PHILIPPICS OF DEMOSTHENES.

Edited by FRANK B. TARBELL, Ph.D., Yale College, with the Zürich Edition of the Text, a Historical Introduction, and Explanatory Notes.   *[Ready in June.*

THE HELLENIC ORATIONS OF DEMOSTHENES.

Symmories, *Megalopolitans*, and *Rhodians*. With revised text and commentary by ISAAC FLAGG, Ph.D., Professor of Greek in Cornell University, Ithaca, N.Y.   *[Ready in August.*

SELECTIONS FROM PINDAR, THE BUCOLIC POETS, AND THE GREEK HYMNS.

Containing twelve Odes of Pindar, six Idylls of Theocritus, Bion's Epitaphius Adonidis, Moschus' Europa, two Homeric Hymns, a Hymn of Callimachus, and the Hymn of Cleanthes; in all, about 2,800 lines. Edited by T. D. SEYMOUR, Professor of Greek in Western Reserve College, Ohio.

    [Ready January 1, 1881.

THE FIRST THREE BOOKS OF HOMER'S ILIAD.

    [In preparation.

SIDGWICK'S FIRST GREEK WRITER.

Adapted to Goodwin's Greek Grammar by JOHN WILLIAMS WHITE, Ph.D. Intended to follow WHITE'S FIRST LESSONS IN GREEK, and to introduce SIDGWICK'S GREEK PROSE COMPOSITION.   *[In preparation.*

STEIN'S SUMMARY OF THE DIALECT OF HERODOTUS,

translated by Professor JOHN WILLIAMS WHITE, Ph.D., from the German of the fourth edition of Herodotus by Heinrich Stein. Paper, pp. 15.

GINN & HEATH, Publishers, Boston, New York, and Chicago.

This pamphlet makes a complete statement of the euphonic and inflexional peculiarities which distinguish the language of Herodotus from Attic Greek, and is suitable for use with any edition of Herodotus. Mailing price, 15 cents. *[Ready.*

WHITE'S FIRST LESSONS IN GREEK, REVISED

EDITION. With references to the revised and enlarged edition of Goodwin's Greek Grammar, and printed from entirely new plates.

The publishers beg leave to call attention to the following changes which have been made in the new edition of the First Lessons in Greek.

The number of lessons has been increased from seventy-five to eighty. The five added lessons are on the verb, the treatment of which is thus distributed over more ground. By this enlargement the difficulty of single lessons on the verb is correspondingly decreased.

After λύω has been fully presented by moods, as in the first edition, a development of the Greek verb by tense-stems has been introduced. The seven tense-stems are now fully developed.

Contract verbs are presented, in this edition, in two lessons in place of one. The lesson on liquid verbs has been brought forward. The perfect and pluperfect middle and passive of liquid and mute verbs is now fully treated. A lesson has been added to Lessons LII. and LIII. giving in full the principal parts of twenty-five additional verbs. In the Lessons on the Formation of Words and on Prepositions it has now been possible to remove the body of the text, but the exercises of Lessons LIV. and LV. remain, and a complete set of exercises has been added to Lesson LXII.

Single words and phrases have been removed from the exercises, which now consist wholly of complete sentences. In the special vocabularies the parts of the verbs are given in full and no words are repeated. In the general vocabularies the words are more fully treated, especially the prepositions, the cases required by the verbs stated, and English cognate and borrowed words distinguished by different types.

New editions of the Pamphlet of Parallel References to Hadley's Grammar, and of the Key for the use of Teachers, are to follow.

An edition of the First Lessons in Greek is to be printed and published for the use of English schools, by Macmillan & Co. in England, simultaneously with the American edition. *[Ready in July.*

GINN & HEATH, Publishers, Boston, New York, and Chicago.

AN ILLUSTRATED VOCABULARY TO THE FIRST FOUR BOOKS OF XENOPHON'S ANABASIS. By JOHN WILLIAMS WHITE, Ph.D., Assistant Professor of Greek in Harvard University.

The distinguishing features of this Vocabulary will be its illustrations, the fullness of its definitions, and its careful treatment of etymologies.

To be published both separately and bound with Goodwin and White's edition of the First Four Books of the Anabasis.

[Ready in September.

The next edition of

GOODWIN'S ANABASIS, GREEK READER, and *SELECTIONS FROM XENOPHON and HERODOTUS,* will have references to the new edition of Goodwin's Greek Grammar.

LEIGHTON'S NEW GREEK LESSONS.

With references to Hadley's Greek Grammar as well as to Goodwin's New Greek Grammar.

About seventy easy and well-graded lessons, both Greek and English, introduce the pupil to the first book of Xenophon's Anabasis, from which the Exercises and Vocabularies are mainly selected. Definite directions have been given in regard to the amount of the Grammar to be learned. The main aim has been, while introducing the simpler principles of syntax, to have the pupil *master the Inflections* and *acquire a Vocabulary*. In furtherance of this purpose, the exercises on the inflections have been increased, while those on syntax have been decreased. Vocabularies have been given under each lesson; and, in order to aid the pupil in memorizing them, some insight has been given into the derivation and into the composition of words, — how they are built up, by means of significance endings, from noun and verb stems, and from roots. The Prepositions are introduced from the first; and the pupil is taught the primary meanings, and then how these meanings are modified by the cases before which the Prepositions stand. Questions for Review and Examination as in the first edition. In rewriting these Lessons, considerable use has been made of the excellent exercises, used in most of the German gymnasiums, prepared by Dr. Wasener to accompany the Greek Grammar of Professor Curtius.

[Ready in June.

GINN & HEATH, Publishers, Boston, New York, and Chicago.

RECENT PUBLICATIONS.

Latin.

A BRIEF HISTORY OF ROMAN LITERATURE,

FOR SCHOOLS AND COLLEGES. Translated and edited, from the German edition of Bender, by Professors E. P. CROWELL and H. B. RICHARDSON of Amherst College.

This work was received with great favor in Germany, and was widely adopted by the secondary schools.

The present translation adapts it to the use of schools and colleges in America, not only by retaining all that is valuable in the German work, but by adding copious references to the best general and special English works on Roman Literature.

The table of contents has been greatly enlarged, so as to constitute a complete analysis of the whole, and the chart at the end has been put into better form; in short, the aim has been to make it a serviceable handbook for students and teachers.

The chief excellence of the work consists in its terse, suggestive, and admirable characterizations of the Roman writers and of their times. It contains just what the student ought to know, and suggests much for the teacher to enlarge upon. [*Mailing Price,* $1.05.

REMNANTS OF EARLY LATIN.

Selected and explained, for the use of students, by FREDERICK D. ALLEN, Professor in Yale College.

The object is to bring together, in small compass and convenient shape for reading, the most remarkable monuments of archaic Latin, with enough explanation to make them generally intelligible. This material has been hitherto accessible only in large and expensive books, ill suited, for the most part, to the learner's wants. Part First contains the text of about 150 inscriptions, beginning with the oldest coins and coming down to about Sulla's time. There is no intention of teaching palæography; the inscriptions are printed in small letters, without any attempt at reproducing the appearance of the originals. A single lithographed fac-simile is given as a sample. In Part

---

Second, specimens of the oldest prayers, formulæ, and laws — material which has come down to us from a high antiquity through literary channels — are collected. The remains of the Twelve Tables are included here. No literary matter has been admitted. All the selections are illustrated by a succinct commentary, and in a short introduction the leading peculiarities of the early language are enumerated. The book is meant primarily for students, but it is hoped that others may find it useful as a convenient handbook. An index has been added. [*Mailing Price*, 85 cts.

ESSENTIAL USES OF THE MOODS IN GREEK

AND LATIN. Prepared by R. P. KEEP, Ph.D., Instructor in the Classical Department of Williston Seminary, at Easthampton, Mass.

[*Mailing Price*, 40 cts.

Greek.

SELECTIONS FROM THE GREEK LYRIC POETS,

with an Historical Introduction and Explanatory Notes. By HENRY M. TYLER, Professor of Greek and Latin in Smith College, Northampton, Mass. [*Mailing Price*, $1.05.

GOODWIN'S NEW GREEK GRAMMAR.

Enlarged from 262 to 425 pages, and adapted to college use.

In this edition the following portions are entirely new : —

1. All that relates to the Inflection of the Verb, which is increased from 50 to 100 pages. 2. Part III., on the Formation of Words. 3. Part V., on Versification. 4. Greek and English Indexes, filling 30 pages.

The Catalogue of Verbs is nearly double in size, but is still confined, for the most part, to strictly classic forms. The remainder of the work has been carefully revised, and numerous changes and additions have been made.

The *London Athenæum* of October 4, 1879, says of the English Edition of the Grammar : —

"Messrs. MACMILLAN have published a new and revised edition of the ELEMENTARY GREEK GRAMMAR of that distinguished scholar, Professor GOODWIN of Harvard. It is the best Greek Grammar of its size in the English language, and ought to meet with a wide circulation on this side of the Atlantic."

[*Mailing Price*, $1.70.

GINN & HEATH, Publishers, Boston, New York, and Chicago.

ALLEN & GREENOUGH'S LATIN GRAMMAR.

The first edition was published in 1872, and was widely adopted, reaching a sale of *over 30,000 copies*. In 1877, the editors completed a revision, which has made it *virtually a new work* while *retaining all the important features of the old.* Attention is invited to the following merits of the book:

1. *The Supplementary and Marginal Notes on Etymology, Comparative Philology, and the meaning of forms.* In this department it is believed to be more full and complete than any other school text-book, and to embody the most advanced views of comparative philologists.

2. *Numerous Introductory Notes in the Syntax, giving a brief view of the theory of constructions.* These Notes are original contributions to the discussion of the topics of which they treat; they illustrate and greatly simplify syntactical construction, and are not based upon *abstract theory*, or "metaphysics of the subjunctive," but upon *linguistic science*, or upon the actual historical development of language from its simplest forms.

3. *Treatment of Special Topics of Syntax.* On these points we invite comparison with other school grammars on the score of simplicity and clearness.

4. *The extended, and often complete, lists of forms and constructions.*

5. *Tabulated examples of peculiar or idiomatic use.*

6. *The full and clear treatment of Rhythm and Versification*, corresponding with the latest and best authorities on the subject. .

7. *The unusual brevity attained without sacrifice of completeness or clearness.*

This Grammar expresses *the results of independent study of the best original sources.* It has been *strictly subordinated to the uses of the class-room* through the advice and aid of several of our most experienced teachers. The rapid adoption of this Grammar in *over three-fourths of the leading colleges and preparatory schools of the country* is believed to be a full guaranty for its adaptation to the purposes of instruction.

ALLEN & GREENOUGH'S LATIN COURSE.

Leighton's Latin Lessons (designed to accompany the Grammar).

Six Weeks' Preparation for Reading Cæsar (designed to accompany the Grammar, and also to prepare pupils for reading at sight).

Allen & Greenough's Cæsar,* Cicero,* Virgil,* Ovid,* Sallust, Cato Major, Latin Composition, Preparatory Latin Course, No. II. (with Vocabulary), containing four books of Cæsar's Gallic War, and eight Orations of Cicero.

Keep's Parallel Rules of Greek and Latin Syntax.

Allen's Latin Reader. Selections from Cæsar, Curtius, Nepos, Sallust, Ovid, Virgil, Plautus, Terence, Cicero, Pliny, and Tacitus. With Vocabulary.

Crowell & Richardson's Brief History of Roman Literature.

Crowell's Selections from the Less Known Latin Poets.

Stickney's De Natura Deorum.

Allen's (F. D.) Remnants of Early Latin.

Leighton's Critical History of Cicero's Letters.

Leighton's Elementary Treatise on Latin Orthography.

White's Junior Student's Latin-English Lexicons.

* With or without Vocabulary.

A Full Descriptive Catalogue mailed on Application.

GINN & HEATH, Publishers, Boston, New York, and Chicago.

GREEK TEXT-BOOKS.

Goodwin's Greek Grammar. Revised and Enlarged Edition for 1879.

It states general principles clearly and distinctly, with special regard to those who are preparing for college.

It excludes all detail which belongs to a book of reference, and admits whatever will aid a pupil in mastering the great principles of Greek Grammar.

The sections on the Syntax of the Verb are generally condensed from the author's larger work on the Greek Moods and Tenses. (See below.)

It contains a brief statement of the author's new classification of conditional sentences, with its application to relative and temporal sentences, which appears now for the first time in an elementary form.

It contains a catalogue of irregular verbs, constructed entirely with reference to the wants of beginners.

All forms are excluded (with a few exceptions) which are not found in the strictly classic Greek before Aristotle.

White's First Lessons in Greek. Prepared to accompany Goodwin's Greek Grammar.

A series of Greek-English and English-Greek Exercises, *taken mainly from the first four books of Xenophon's Anabasis,* with Additional Exercises on Forms, and complete Vocabularies. The Lessons are carefully graded, and do not follow the order of arrangement of the Grammar, but begin the study of the verb with the second Lesson, and then pursue it alternately with that of the remaining parts of speech. *It contains enough Greek Prose Composition for entrance into any college.*

Leighton's Greek Lessons. Prepared to accompany Goodwin's Greek Grammar.

A progressive series of exercises (both Greek and English), mainly selected from the first book of Xenophon's Anabasis. The exercises on the Moods are sufficient, it is believed, to develop the general principles as stated in the Grammar.

Goodwin & White's First Four Books of the Anabasis.

Goodwin's Greek Reader contains the first and second books of the Anabasis. Also, selections from Plato, Herodotus, and Thucydides; being the full amount of Greek Prose required for admission at Harvard University.

Goodwin's Selections from Xenophon and Herodotus contains the first four books of the Anabasis, the greater part of the second book of the Hellenica of Xenophon, and extracts from the sixth, seventh, and eighth books of Herodotus.

Anderson's First Three Books of Homer's Iliad.

Goodwin's Greek Moods and Tenses. Gives a plain statement of the principles which govern the construction of the Greek Moods and Tenses,—the most important and the most difficult part of Greek Syntax.

F. D. Allen's Prometheus of Æschylus.
Tarbell's Orations of Demosthenes.
Flagg's Public Harangues of Demosthenes.
Tyler's Selections from the Greek Lyric Poets.
Seymour's Selections from Pindar and the Bucolic Poets.
Whiton's Select Orations of Lysias.
White's Œdipus Tyrannus of Sophocles.
F. D. Allen's Medea of Euripides.
Sidgwick's Introduction to Greek Prose Composition.
White's Schmidt's Rhythmic and Metric of the Classical Languages.
Liddell & Scott's Greek-English Lexicons. Abridged and Unabridged,

A Full Descriptive Catalogue mailed on application.

GINN & HEATH, Publishers, Boston, New York, and Chicago.

Lightning Source UK Ltd.
Milton Keynes UK
UKOW05f0803051217
313899UK00006B/695/P